THE POLITICS OF ABORTION AND BIRTH CONTROL IN HISTORICAL PERSPECTIVE

Issues in Policy History
General Editor: Donald T. Critchlow

THE POLITICS OF ABORTION AND BIRTH CONTROL IN HISTORICAL PERSPECTIVE

Edited by
Donald T. Critchlow

The Pennsylvania State University Press
University Park, Pennsylvania

This work was originally published as a special issue of *Journal of Policy History* (vol. 7, no. 1, 1995). This is its first separate paperback publication.

Library of Congress Cataloging-in-Publication Data

The politics of abortion and birth control in historical perspective / edited by Donald T. Critchlow.

p. cm—(Issues in policy history : #5)
"Originally published as a special issue of Journal of policy history (vol. 7, no. 1, 1995)"—T.p. verso.
Includes bibliographical references.
ISBN 0-271-01570-5 (pbk. : alk. paper)
1. Abortion—United States—History. 2. Birth control—United States—History. 3. Pro-choice movement—United States—History. 4. Pro-life movement—United States—History. I. Critchlow, Donald T., 1948– . II. Series.
HQ767.5.U5P55 1996
363.4′6′0973—dc20 95-38897
CIP

Printed in the United States of America
Published by The Pennsylvania State University Press,
University Park, PA 16802-1003

It is the policy of The Pennsylvania State University Press to use acid-free paper for the first printing of all clothbound books. Publications on uncoated stock satisfy the minimum requirements of American National Standard for Information Sciences—Permanence of Paper for Printed Library Materials, ANSI Z39.48-1992

Contents

DONALD T. CRITCHLOW 1
Birth Control, Population Control, and Family Planning: An Overview

JAMES W. REED 22
The Birth-Control Movement Before Roe v. Wade

IAN MYLCHREEST 53
"Sound Law and Undoubtedly Good Policy": Roe v. Wade *in Comparative Perspective*

JOHN SHARPLESS 72
World Population Growth, Family Planning, and American Foreign Policy

JAMES DAVISON HUNTER and JOSEPH E. DAVIS 103
Cultural Politics at the Edge of Life

KEITH CASSIDY 128
The Right to Life Movement: Sources, Development, and Strategies

SUZANNE STAGGENBORG 160
The Survival of the Pro-Choice Movement

DONALD T. CRITCHLOW and CHRISTINA SANDERS 177
Selected Bibliography

Contributors 181

DONALD T. CRITCHLOW

Birth Control, Population Control, and Family Planning: An Overview

So great is the skill, so powerful the drug, of the abortionists, paid to murder mankind within the womb.

—Juvenal (A.D. 60? to 140), Satire VI[1]

The cultural fission created by the controversy over birth control and abortion, as Juvenal's satiric comment above indicates, has a long and bitter history. The emergence of the modern state, however, transformed cultural differences into political acrimony as reproduction rights became public policy. In the United States, reproductive rights in the post–World War II period became a matter of political controversy when the federal government began to fund family planning programs domestically and abroad in the 1960s.

The origins of the modern family planning movement in the United States emerged from three distinct, although often overlapping, forces. First, in the early twentieth century, Margaret Sanger and other feminists initiated family planning in their call for the legalization of birth control. The emergence of the black civil rights movement and the woman's movement in the 1960s gave impetus to the "rights" aspects of this cause. Second, a eugenics movement emerged in the Progressive Era to demand that the native stock of Americans be strengthened by limiting "deviant" populations and reducing the social burden of crime, prostitution, and illegitimacy—social ills often associated with "mental idiocy"—through birth control, sterilization, and immigration restric-

I would like to acknowledge Thomas Curran, Hugh Graham, James Hitchcock, Mark Neely, James Reed, and James Sharpless for reading this essay.

tion. This eugenics movement paralleled the birth-control movement and remained a presence in modern family planning circles. Finally, a population-control movement emerged following World War II that sought to address problems of social stability, war, poverty, and economic development in the United States and developing nations. Critics, often imposing their own moral and religious values on the policy debate, claimed that population control sought to solve larger social problems through a technical solution—population control—rather than confronting directly problems of social inequality, wealth and income redistribution, racism, and imperialism.

Although the birth-control movement in the United States emerged in the nineteenth century as a part of a radical feminist struggle to liberate women from the "drudgery of domesticity," birth control was transformed into a liberal civil rights issue, albeit with radical social ramifications, in the mid-twentieth century. The birth-control movement, as historian Linda Gordon has argued, passed through three distinct stages.[2] In the first stage, "voluntary motherhood" was advanced by certain feminists as part of a general struggle closely associated with women's suffrage to challenge the traditional political and social status of women in American society. In the second stage, "birth control" became a concept that found new organizational expression in separate birth-control leagues created largely by feminists involved in the revolutionary socialist movement to transform capitalist society and empower women and the working class. In the third stage, from 1920 on, the movement evolved into a liberal reform movement that gained the support of physicians, civil libertarians, and population-control advocates.[3] The transformation of the birth-control movement from a radical feminist movement in the late nineteenth and early twentieth centuries into a liberal movement for civil rights and population control in the mid-twentieth century reveals the power of liberal democracy to translate radical causes into legal issues. In each stage, birth-control advocates confronted local and state governments that had enacted anticontraceptive laws, often in response to Catholic and bluenosed Protestant constituencies.

In this long history of contending forces, Margaret Sanger (1879–1961) played a key role in the birth-control movement as it changed from a radical socialist cause into a liberal issue over legal rights.[4] Although vaginal diaphragms, cervical caps, spermatocidal compounds, condoms, and safe periods had gained widespread use among upper classes in the nineteenth century, Sanger undertook a campaign to reform sexual practices among the masses, especially the working-class poor.

Raised in the factory town of Corning, New York, Sanger grew up in a large family of eleven children headed by her father, a stonecutter who she described as "a philosopher, a rebel, and an artist." She was completing her training to become a nurse when she met William Sanger, an architect and an ardent socialist. They became active in the Socialist party and radical labor movement in New York. After her involvement with striking textile workers in Lawrence, Massachusetts, in 1912 and in Paterson, New Jersey, in 1913, she became increasingly concerned with the plight of working-class mothers and wives who bore the burden of the uncontrolled fecundity that she felt was at least partially responsible for the widespread "misery among workers."[5] After a European tour and separation from her husband, in March 1914 Sanger founded *The Woman Rebel,* a magazine devoted to birth control. The publication of a pamphlet, "Family Limitation" (1914), forced her to flee to Europe to avoid prosecution for violation of a federal law against mailing obscene literature. She returned to America in 1916 to devote her life to the birth-control movement.

During Sanger's year in exile, Mary Ware Dennett (1872–1947), a New England suffragist, formed the National Birth Control League to lobby against New York anti-birth-control laws. The National Birth Control League was disbanded in 1919, but Dennett went on to form the Voluntary Parenthood League, which conducted a campaign for the repeal of federal laws against birth control. Dennett and Sanger became lifelong rivals, which led to a schism within the birth-control movement.

In 1916 Sanger opened the first birth-control clinic in the Brownsville section of Brooklyn. Arrested in 1917 for her activities, she won her case on appeal. That same year she started the *Birth Control Review,* and in 1921 she organized the American Birth Control League. She later withdrew from the American Birth Control League in 1928 to devote herself fully to the Clinical Research Bureau and the Committee on Federal Legislation. Meanwhile, a group of physicians led by New York's leading medical advocate of contraception, Dr. Robert Latou Dickinson (1861–1950), concerned that Sanger and other reformers were giving birth control a "bad name," organized the Committee on Maternal Health in 1925 to sponsor research on fertility and sterility.

The birth-control movement remained divided until 1939, when fiscal necessity led to the merging of the American Birth Control League and Sanger's Clinical Research Bureau into the Birth Control Federation of America. Under its acting director, D. Kenneth Rose, the Birth Control League became the Planned Parenthood Federation of America in 1942.

A crucial event that led to the unifying of the birth-control movement in 1939 was Judge Augustus Hand's decision in *United States v. One*

Package (1937), which ruled that Congress, in enacting the Comstock Act (1873), had not been fully informed about the dangers of pregnancy and the usefulness of contraception. Judge Hand's decision opened the door for contraception devices and information to be sent through the mails to physicians. The case had been brought to the federal courts by Morris Ernst (1888–1976), a lawyer who had volunteered his services to Sanger's group, after U.S. Customs officials seized a shipment of Japanese pessaries sent Dr. Hannah Stone, a private physician. This qualification of the Comstock law encouraged Sanger to merge her National Committee on Federal Legislation for Birth Control with the American Birth Control League. Sanger entered into semiretirement in Tucson, Arizona, but reemerged after World War II to play a crucial role in the establishment of the International Planned Parenthood Federation and the development of the anovulant pill.[6]

In 1948 the Committee on Human Reproduction was organized to further research into reproduction. Along with the Committee on Maternal Health, headed by eugenicist Clarence Gamble, the Committee on Human Reproduction supported important research by Gregory Pincus, John Rock, and Christopher Tietze that led to the development of the birth-control pill.[7]

In this period the lower federal courts and some state courts had ruled that prescriptions of contraceptives by medical professions was legal. Still, the Supreme Court had refused to review the constitutionality of birth-control bans that remained in Connecticut and Massachusetts. In *Tileston v. Ullman* (1943) the issue was dismissed on technical grounds, while in *Gardner v. Massachusetts* (1938) the case was dismissed for want of a substantial federal question. Similarly, in *Poe v. Ullman* (1961) the Court denied review of an action challenging the Connecticut law because it believed that the statute was not being enforced.[8]

A turning point in the constitutional struggle for reproductive rights came in *Griswold v. Connecticut* (1965). In this case, the Supreme Court struck down the Connecticut law that had led to the arrest of the executive director and medical director of the Connecticut Planned Parenthood birth-control clinic for violation of a nineteenth-century state law banning the distribution of contraceptive devices or information. The Court found that married persons have a constitutionally protected right to privacy that allowed the use of contraceptives and ruled that while the right of privacy was not explicitly mentioned in the Constitution, the right itself was older than the Bill of Rights. The right to privacy was further extended to unmarried persons in *Eisenstadt v. Baird* (1972) in a decision drafted by Justice William J. Brennan.

The right to privacy laid the basis for *Roe v. Wade* (1973), which recognized the constitutional right to abortion.[9] Contrary to the Court's intentions, *Roe* polarized the pro-choice and pro-life forces. The subsequent struggle became an argument over rights—the rights of women for abortion versus the rights of the fetus for life. The battleground usually remained in the courts, occasionally spilling over into the legislative arena and sometimes into the streets, as tragically evidenced in the fire bombings and the terrorist assassinations of physicians performing abortions.

By focusing on the social history of the birth-control movement and its rich legal history in the courts, scholars have tended to obscure the importance of eugenics in the movement. Eugenics played a critical role in influencing Progressive thought in the first two decades of the twentieth century.[10] Certain feminists and birth-control advocates utilized eugenics arguments to provide coherence to their advocacy of birth control. Eugenics arguments often proved to be double-edged. While some feminists found in eugenics an argument for strengthening the place of women in a male-dominated society, the eugenics argument was also employed to show that the population pool was being weakened as deviant and the lower, uneducated, and immigrant classes were having more children than were educated, upper-class families.

The eugenics movement and the women's movement became closely associated for many. Radical feminist Victoria Woodhull argued as early as 1891 that "the best minds of today have noted the fact that if superior people are desired, they must be bred; if imbeciles, criminals, paupers, and [the] otherwise unfit are undesirable citizens they must not be bred." This type of rhetoric led Havelock Ellis, a British eugenicist and a close friend of Sanger, to claim that "the question of Eugenics is to a great extent one with the woman question."[11] While the American Eugenics Society regarded abortion as murder, unless performed on strictly medical grounds, those influenced by eugenic thought—for example, Margaret Sanger and Theodore Roosevelt—favored sterilization of the "unfit."

The relationship between the birth-control movement and the eugenics movement remains complicated and needs further exploration by scholars. Clearly many leading eugenicists refused to endorse the birth-control movement. In turn, Sanger refused to endorse eugenicists' calls for better classes to produce more children. Indeed, in 1925 Margaret Sanger was persuaded by Edward East, a Harvard biologist and member of her Clinical Research Bureau's advisory council, not to publish an editorial attacking the eugenicists for failing to support birth control. East wrote to Sanger, "Birth Control is only a part of a eugenical program. It is a secondary aspect of a larger whole, but it is the key. The mere fact that so many eugenicists have not been able to think straight does not make the abstract subject itself any less valued."[12]

The eugenics movement expressed a sincere reform sentiment that the world would improve if the race improved, if women were freed from the burdens of birth, and if social costs for institutionalized populations were reduced. Still there was a darker side to the eugenics argument. Sanger criticized philanthropists who gave free maternity care for encouraging the "healthier and more normal section of the world to shoulder the burden of unthinking and indiscriminate fecundity of the other." She added, "Instead of decreasing and aiming to eliminate the stocks that are most detrimental to the future of the race and the world, it tends to render them to a menacing degree dominant."[13] As late as 1932 Sanger called for restrictive immigration laws, sterilization of dysgenic groups, and the removal of "illiterates, paupers, the unemployable, criminals, prostitutes, [and] dope-fiends" to farms and open spaces "as long as necessary for the strengthening and development of moral conduct."[14]

Eugenics sentiments found enunciation by other birth-control advocates. In 1930 Eleanor Dwight Jones, president of the American Birth Control League, applied for funding from the Rockefeller-sponsored Bureau of Social Hygiene, stating: "We believe that the time is ripe for us to launch throughout the country a systematic campaign against the present disgenic multiplication of the unfit. The public is beginning to realize that scientific, constructive philanthropy does not merely care for the diseased, the poor and the degenerate, but takes steps to prevent the birth of babies destined to be paupers, invalids, degenerates, or all three. From every direction appeals are coming to us for help in making reliable birth control advice accessible to those women who for their own good and that of society, should not have big families." She concluded: "For the good of the race, people of poor stock, incompetent and sickly should have few or no children. In this matter, private interest is in accord with public interest."[15]

Similarly, eugenics arguments attracted the support of physicians and philanthropic foundations interested in birth control. An internal memorandum circulated in the Rockefeller Foundation in the early 1930s declared: "Birth control has the support of many of the best and most intelligent people in the world and it also has the support of some persons whose mental balance is not the best. In between these two classes, we find the people who hold debatable opinions, the most capable group being the eugenicists."[16] While the Rockefeller Foundation and family remained leery of Sanger's public efforts at birth control, they actively (and privately) supported her Clinical Research Department for biological purposes.[17]

Beginning in the early 1930s, John D. Rockefeller III also was a major sponsor of the Committee on Maternal Health for improved birth-control technology, including what the committee's founder Robert L. Dickinson described as "permanent birth control—sterilization without unsexing." In the 1930s the committee also began extensive medical research on abortion as a means of birth control. Behind this scientific research lay eugenics arguments that saw the world being overrun with populations that threatened the civilized world. Dickinson wrote to Arthur Packard of the Rockefeller Foundation in 1935: "If at this time governments were to offer this relief [birth control] to millions of families on relief, or to the swarming population of certain Oriental countries, medical science and public health would be in doubt what to advise most of these people." Most birth-control methods, whether they are mechanical or mechanico-chemical, he wrote, are impractical, for "the impoverished and for those of low intelligence, and the millions out of reach of skilled instruction."[18]

As early as the 1930s the Committee for Maternal Health and other birth-control advocates began to target developing nations, such as Puerto Rico, as a laboratory for field studies.[19] Following World War II, the Committee on Maternal Health again became actively involved in Puerto Rico. As one Rockefeller Foundation official declared in early 1947: "Puerto Ricans are coming into New York City at the rate of 15,000 a week. Many of them come by air and many are getting on the relief rolls within a month after they are here. This is simply one aspect of the problems which exist in Puerto Rico of overpopulation. There is no question about it, we ought to be much interested in the social as well as the technical point of view in any scheme which is soundly conceived to affect that problem favorably."[20]

Eugenicists played an important role in the population-control movement that appeared following World War II. For example, six out of ten men on the Population Council's demographic and medical advisory boards had been associated with the eugenics movement. In turn, the Population Reference Bureau was founded in 1929 as a eugenics organization and became a leading population-control center that received funding from Rockefeller, Ford, Mellon, duPont, and Sloan.[21] Eugenics arguments continued to find expression among population-control advocates well into the 1960s. For example, Garrett Hardin, a leading population-control advocate and early abortion proponent asked in early 1964: "And, looking at the problem [abortion] in terms of knowledge and intelligence, is it good for society that ignorant (and possibly stupid) women have more children than knowing and intelligent ones? Is the child brought up by an ignorant, or poor, or unloving mother a better bet for the next generation?"[22]

Following World War II, population-control advocates assumed a prominent place in family planning policy. While eugenicists played a significant role in the population-control movement, it is inaccurate to describe, as one historian has, population control as "the successor to eugenics in every respect—ideologically, organizationally, and in personnel."[23] The population-control movement expressed a range of opinions concerning eugenics and the need for population control. Population-control advocates generally accepted a neo-Malthusian perspective that the advancement of modern medicine had thrown into imbalance "natural" population growth and available food supplies and natural resources. Nevertheless, proponents of population control differed among themselves over strategies for addressing this global problem.

For example, John D. Rockefeller III, a key figure in the postwar population-control movement, called for a dual strategy of increasing the food supply in developing nations through the so-called Green Revolution—a program designed to improve agricultural production through high-yield crops—as well as containing population growth through advanced birth-control technology and birth-control programs in developing countries.[24] He criticized what he perceived as extreme and hysterical proponents of population control, such as General William Draper, Hugh Moore, and other "zero population" advocates.

As early as the 1930s, John D. Rockefeller III had decided to make birth control his cause. His travels to Asia and Africa before the war convinced him of the need for population control. Following the war, he tried to convince the Rockefeller Foundation to initiate a program in this field. When the foundation decided against expanding its involvement in population beyond the medical field, Rockefeller decided to establish his own organization—the Population Council.

Founded in November 1952, the Population Council grew out of the Conference on Population Problems held in Williamsburg, Virginia, that summer. Sponsored by the National Academy of Sciences, the conference brought together scientists, demographers, social scientists, and birth-control leaders for an intensive two-day meeting.[25] The purpose of the Population Council was to support medical research in reproduction and to train demographers and population experts who could be employed in developing nations in Asia and Africa. Rockefeller's commitment to this area was only reinforced when he learned that the Ford Foundation had decided to enter the population field as well. At the same time, he also founded the Council on Economic and Cultural Affairs to promote farm management in the developing world.

Rockefeller saw the Population Council as a way of providing leadership to a movement that was dominated by "alarmists." The Population Council deliberately dissociated itself from men such as Hugh Moore, founder of Dixie Cup. Two years after the founding of the Population Council, the Hugh Moore Fund published a pamphlet, "The Population Explosion" (1954), that Rockefeller and his associates found sensationalist. The "Population Explosion" warned of a population crisis that could only play into the hands of the communists. Moore privately wrote to Rockefeller that "we are not primarily interested in the sociological or humanitarian aspects of birth control. We are interested in the use which the Communists make of hungry people in their drive to conquer the earth."[26] Although the pamphlet gained wide circulation in elite policy circles, Rockefeller wanted to place population control on a scientific and humanitarian basis.

Under the leadership of its first chairman, Frederick Osborn, a longtime activist in eugenics circles, the council sponsored demographic and medical research into the population problem. In its activities, it cultivated elite connections and avoided public controversy by identifying itself as a neutral, scientific organization.[27] From the outset, however, the council was policy oriented. Through an extensive fellowship and grant program, it reshaped the field of demography into a social science and a policy science.

Joined by the Ford Foundation, the Population Council played a principal role in establishing an international network of population experts who shared a set of assumptions about population dynamics and a consensus as to population intervention.[28] In the course of the next decade, the council's staff and field officers became increasingly involved in technical-assistance programs to implement population control in developing countries and the United States. At the same time, the council remained involved in the medical research side of family planning. In 1957 it established a biomedical research laboratory at Rockefeller University to pursue contraceptive research and became actively involved in the development, testing, and distribution of an intrauterine device.

As the 1950s drew to a close, John D. Rockefeller III increasingly lobbied American policymakers to pursue more activist public policies. The Population Council, along with Planned Parenthood, the Population Crisis Committee, the Rockefeller Foundation, and the Ford Foundation, proved instrumental in changing American population policy in the 1960s. This shift in population policy in the 1960s marked a sharp break from the past. For example, in the 1950s, as the population lobby was organizing, American policymakers carefully avoided involvement in population policy for fear of the political consequences.

Only late in Eisenhower's administration did the issue even arise, when a presidential commission headed by General William Draper, a former member of Eisenhower's staff during World War II and a Wall Street financier, recommended that population-control programs in developing countries be funded through the military-assistance program. The Draper Committee reported that "no realistic discussion of economic development can fail to note that development efforts in many areas of the world are being offset by increasingly rapid population growth." The committee also recommended that the federal government should support expanded medical research relating to the physiology of human reproduction.

When the National Conference of Catholic Bishops issued a statement in November 1959 that opposed "any public assistance, whether at home or abroad to promote artificial birth control, abortion, or sterilization," Eisenhower backed down and declared that the population problems of other countries were their own and not the problem of the United States government.[29] Eisenhower's personal feelings about population control proved considerably more ambivalent than his rejection of the Draper report indicated.

After leaving office, Eisenhower and Draper began a lengthy correspondence concerning the burgeoning population of poor people abroad and at home. Draper sent Eisenhower a steady stream of pamphlets on the problem and progress reports on the population-control movement. In 1964 Eisenhower, after some hesitation, agreed to become honorary co-chair with former president Harry S Truman of the Planned Parenthood Federation.[30] Eisenhower's alarm over the population explosion—"one of the most critical world problems of our times and daily grows more serious"—led him to call for population control abroad and at home. He wrote privately to H. J. Porter of Planned Parenthood that the "alarming increase in illegitimate children" in this country by mothers seeking to increase their welfare benefits called for legislation to "take cognizance of this practice sooner or later. I agree with you that some day we might have to propose practical limitations through political channels."[31]

Yet if Eisenhower skirted the population question while in office, the Democrats were equally worried about becoming too quickly immersed in a potentially explosive political issue. John F. Kennedy, a Roman Catholic, quietly pursued a subtle shift in American population policy. He endorsed increased federally sponsored research into reproduction, and in late December 1962 he authorized Assistant Secretary of State Richard

Gardner to issue the first broad statement of the United States on population policy before the United Nations. In the spring of 1963 Secretary of State Dean Rusk issued a memorandum to AID missions stating that the United States would assist family planning programs.

The Johnson administration completed this quiet revolution begun under Kennedy. Still, the Johnson administration moved slowly into expanding population programs. Concerned with the potential of a Catholic and black backlash, Johnson pursued a gradualist approach. When Rockefeller III tried to arrange a meeting with Johnson to get him to sign a "World Leader's Declaration on Population," Johnson initially refused to meet with him. He told his staff: "I want to encourage Rockefeller, but that doesn't mean that Rockefeller encourages me. There's a difference."[32] Eventually he signed the declaration late in his administration, but only after Rockefeller had enlisted the support of other key leaders in the world.

Similarly, even as late as 1967, Johnson refused to meet with U.S. Senator Ernest Gruening of Alaska, who had proposed legislation establishing an Office of Population Problems in both the State Department and the Department of Health, Education, and Welfare and a White House Conference on Population. The White House believed that specific legislative action proposed by Gruening might "actually set us back in the administrative efforts at family planning." The White House was especially concerned that Gruening's call for a White House conference on population might "polarize public opinion, particularly at any time prior to the Pope's final decision on birth control."[33] Throughout his administration, Johnson kept in close contact with key bishops on the Catholic Welfare Council.

The decision to proceed slowly on family planning came early in the administration. In the fall of 1965, White House aide Harry C. McPherson called a high-level meeting in his office of key agency officials to discuss the liberalization of federal efforts in family planning. While officials at the meeting believed that the United States was facing a global and national population crisis, they expressed deep anxiety about the volatility of the issue. It was agreed that "with or without fanfare, development should be carefully thought out to avoid misunderstanding by civil rights, religious and other groups." Fearful of public opposition, the meeting became known as the "Never-Never Committee."[34] While LBJ's War on Poverty became closely linked with family planning efforts, the administration consciously decided to pursue a strategy that downplayed public fanfare for an incremental approach to family planning.

Tensions over the issue of family planning became evident nevertheless when Sargent Shriver, head of the Office for Economic Opportunity, proposed to issue new regulations that would allow the OEO to provide grants for family planning. HEW Secretary Anthony Celebrezze warned that the publication of the regulations would "arouse widespread controversy." He argued that OEO should follow general HEW policy that allowed the department to avoid potential political problems by offering grants to state agencies that allotted the funds for family planning programs. The White House refused to become involved in the dispute, even though presidential aide Bill Moyers felt that "there is every evidence that even the Pope realizes the times are changing."[35]

When the regulations were finally issued in 1967, the Catholic bishops protested. The regulations allowed for family planning clinics to be established through the Community Action Program. The regulations explicitly stated that participation in family planning programs was to remain voluntary and that program funds were not to be used to "promote a particular philosophy of family planning." Furthermore, OEO grants excluded unmarried women or women not living with their husbands.[36] In the end, when church officials appeared to back down, the administration felt that it had won a victory. As Wilbur Cohen of HEW observed, when pressured, the church proved to be conciliatory. "There's a moral in that."[37]

Throughout most of his administration, Johnson tried to "assuage" the Catholic church by assigning Shriver and other Catholics in his administration to cooperate with liberal bishops in the National Catholic Welfare Conference and with liberal Catholic academics at Georgetown University and the University of Notre Dame.

By 1967 the administration was ready to press the population issue further. The administration's public commitment to family planning found expression in Johnson's State of the Union Address in 1967. Johnson boldly declared: "Next to the pursuit of peace, the really great challenge of the human family is the race between food supply and population increase. That race tonight is being lost. . . . The time for concerned action is here, and we must get on with the job." In the summer of 1967, HEW decided that family planning was not moving as rapidly as it should. A review of departmental programs by Frederick Jaffe (Planned Parenthood), Oscar Harkavy (Ford Foundation), and Samuel Wishik (Columbia University) led to the creation of the new position of Deputy Assistant Secretary for Population and Family Planning, to be headed by Katherine Brownell Oettinger, former head of the Children's Bureau, who had worked closely with Planned Parenthood in her post.

Meanwhile, Congress enacted legislative changes that marked a critical turning point in family planning policy. Although executive agencies often resisted legislative changes as unnecessary and unmanageable, Congress aggressively pursued an agenda that intended to increase funding and activities for family planning programs. The Foreign Assistance Act (1967), under Title X, earmarked $35 million for family planning. On the domestic front, Congress specifically earmarked OEO funding for family planning.[38] A second piece of domestic legislation proved even more important: the Social Security Amendments of 1967. Proposed by Congressmen George Bush (R-Tex.) and Herman Schneebeli (R-Pa.), not less than 6 percent of appropriated funds for Maternal and Child Health Services and for Material and Infant Care projects were to be made available for family planning services. Under the law, states were required to make family planning available to adult recipients. Moreover, the amendment allowed the federal and state governments to grant family planning funds to private organizations such as Planned Parenthood. The bill's requirement that welfare recipients, including mothers with young children, work attracted widespread opposition, especially among liberals in the Senate, led by Senator Robert Kennedy (D-NY). As a result, the workfare requirement was dropped from the final bill, but the issue distracted opponents from the significant changes in family planning policy proposed by act. Still, what is noteworthy about the shift in federal policy that occurred in 1967 was that it received widespread bipartisan support.[39]

By 1968 OEO was funding more than 120 family planning clinics in the country. Abroad, AID projects now totaled $11 million. By 1969 U.S. government appropriations for family planning and contraceptive service had risen to an unprecedented level of $50 million.

The election of Richard M. Nixon to the presidency in 1968 initially marked a continuation of efforts to expand federal involvement in family planning. In the summer of 1969, Nixon requested from Congress that family planning services be made available within the next five years to all that wanted them but could not afford them. Responding to Nixon's initiative, Congress enacted the Family Planning Service and Population Research Act of 1970. The law established an Office of Population Affairs and a National Center for Family Planning Services in HEW. In the following three years, Congress authorized $382 million for family planning services, research, personnel training, and educational activities. Congress also authorized the establishment of the Commission on Population Growth and the American Future, a commission long sought by the population lobby, to be headed by John D. Rockefeller III.[40]

The Rockefeller Commission report, when issued in May 1972, marked a turning point within the Nixon administration. The report's endorsement of abortion elicited bitter opposition from the Catholic Conference, which claimed that the Commission on Population Growth and the American Future had entered into an "ideological valley of death." Nixon quickly distanced himself from the report by reaffirming his opposition to "unrestricted abortion." He also criticized the commission's proposal to remove legal restrictions for minors seeking birth control.

The Johnson administration, as well as Rockefeller, had sought to keep the family planning issue free from partisan politics. Pope Paul VI's *Humanae Vitae,* issued in July 1968, indicated the divisiveness of family planning both within the general electorate and the Roman Catholic Church.

Nixon saw a political opportunity to lure Catholic voters away from the Democratic party. Pursuing what the White House called the "Catholic Strategy," Nixon denounced his Democratic opponent, George McGovern, in 1972 as an advocate of the three A's, acid (LSD), amnesty (for Vietnam draft dodgers), and abortion. Even before the election, Nixon had begun to pursue a strategy of "Creative Federalism," which called for the turning over of federal dollars to states in the form of block grants. One consequence of this policy was to lump family planning funds into welfare and health-care funds. At the same time, state governments would set eligibility requirements for birth-control services. Although a House Republican research task force on population policy, under Representative George Bush of Texas, urged that states not be given control over family planning grants in the immediate future, Nixon remained committed to his new strategy. Nixon ordered no further increases in family planning grants and then impounded remaining funds. He also ordered the disbanding of the separate Center for Family Planning Services in the HEW.[41]

The Supreme Court's decision in *Roe v. Wade* (1973), which recognized the constitutional right of abortion, only intensified, although unintentionally, growing polarization over the issue. Whatever the benefits of *Roe,* as legal scholars Elizabeth Mensch and Alan Freeman observe, it lifted a divisive moral problem deeply affecting women's lives out of the legislative arena into what became an irreconcilable rights issue. Absolutism, they observe, easily took on the character of moral high ground at no political costs to either side in an environment of an ever-deepening political and cultural divide. Serious moral dialogue and political compromise became increasingly difficult, even though surveys consistently showed that those who consider themselves "anti-abortion" (placing strict restrictions on abortion even in the first trimester) probably numbered no more than one-fourth of the population, while those who consider themselves "pro-abortion" (abortion on demand) probably are equal in number. In between remains a confused and ambivalent middle.

Evidence of increasing polarization became evident in the United Nations–sponsored World Population Conference, held in Bucharest, Romania, in August 1974. The Bucharest conference turned acrimonous when developing nations attacked the Western nations for imperiously imposing population-control programs on Third World nations instead of addressing the issue of the redistribution of wealth. Ali Oubouzar of Algeria expressed the general resentment of the developing nations when he declared that "the underdeveloped countries want to restore the paramountcy of development over the matter of negatively influencing fertility rates."[42] John D. Rockefeller III had suspected that the conference would divide on the issue of population control, so in his keynote address he declared that he had come to Bucharest "with an urgent call for a deep and probing reappraisal of all that had been done in the population field, all that has been learned."[43] Nevertheless, many Western population experts left the conference stunned and uncertain about their efforts at family planning in the developing world.

Following the Bucharest Conference, the Population Council was left in disarray. The general feeling within the council was that Bucharest would have a "net depressant effect on donors, both public and private."[44] The council's leadership came under attack for pressing for population control to the exclusion of economic development. Joan Dunlop, special assistant to Rockefeller on population policy, led the attack on the older leadership within the family planning movement and the Population Council. In a series of private memorandums sent to Rockefeller in 1974, she declared that "[William] Draper and [Remiert] Ravenholt, et al are hurting the U.S. abroad in profound and long term ways. They have hurt your reputation by including you implicitly and explicitly in their articulation of the problem. . . . For myself, I do not want to identify my career and reputation with their policies unless I can be clearly seen as opposing them."[45] She maintained that "we need to prove that the United States is indeed a pluralistic society and that there are other voices to be heard and other ways of looking at the problem." "Population planning," she emphasized, "must be placed within a context of economic and social development." In emphasizing economic development, she came to her central concern: the role and status of women in developing nations needed to be given a paramount place in economic development and population control. If the economic status of women in developing nations was improved, she argued, it would lead to a decline in family size.[46]

Dunlop did not oppose population control per se, but she insisted that it needed to be placed within a context of economic development and should espouse the cause of women's rights globally. Her call for the appointment of more women to the Population Council's board helped precipitate the final split. In late 1974 Bernard Bereleson resigned as president of the council. He was followed by resignations from other longtime council associates, including Frank Notestein. After considering Sarah Weddington to replace Bereleson, the council appointed George Zeidenstein, a former Ford Foundation field officer, to shake up the council. Zeidenstein saw himself as a "development man," not a "population man," even though he considered abortion as "one form of contraception."[47] Under Zeidenstein, the Population Council shifted its focus to issues of economic development, women's rights, and family planning.

The shake-up in the Population Council reflected the growing partisan nature the debate. Within the family planning movement, divisions had become apparent over issues of abortion, women's rights, economic development, and population control. At the same time, opponents of family planning and population control had extended beyond the Catholic Church into the radical left, the black power movement, developing nations, and the communist countries, including China, the Soviet Union, and Cuba. Within the United States, the contentious issue of family planning polarized the electorate into pervicacious opposition. As a consequence, each presidential administration since Nixon's confronted an intractable issue that left all sides dissatisfied.

The emergence of an organized pro-life movement in the mid-1970s spilled inevitably into partisan politics. The *Roe v. Wade* decision had activated pro-life opposition. In 1975 the National Conference of Catholic Bishops adopted a thirteen-page "Pastoral Plan for Pro-Life Activities." Four years later, in 1979, the National Right to Life Committee was formed with more than eighteen thousand affiliates and 11 million members. Courted by the New Right in the Republican party, the pro-life movement became a major political force in the presidential election of 1980, which put Ronald Reagan in the White House. While Reagan denounced abortion, he avoided efforts in Congress to enact pro-life legislation. Instead, Reagan appointees carried the fight to the federal bureaucracy, especially within the Department of Health and Human Services, the Centers for Disease Control, and the United Nations.[48]

Although Congress thwarted many pro-life efforts to undermine the federal government's commitment to family planning, it was evident that Americans were engaged in what sociologist James Hunter called a "culture war," which spilled into the public policy arena. Bill Clinton experienced the brunt of this war over values when the Vatican, joined by

Muslim militants, attacked his administration's support and involvement in the Cairo Conference on Population, held in August 1994.

While there is an extensive literature on the social history, politics, and legal aspects of birth control and abortion in the United States, family planning as a policy history remains to be fully recorded. This volume is intended to contribute to this history by examining birth control and abortion within a larger cultural, policy, and comparative framework. The essays contained in this volume represent a variety of perspectives and scholarly interests. In many instances the authors—as well as the editor of this volume—differ on fundamental points of historical interpretation. The authors, however, share a commitment to frame the politics of population within a scholarly framework that emphasizes the importance of policy history for understanding past and contemporary problems.

In the first essay, James Reed examines the history of the birth-control movement in the United States in the nineteenth century. He follows the history of the movement through the polarization of the birth-control issue in the mid-1970s. John Sharpless examines the growth of the population-control movement from its origins in the social sciences to its policy consequences in American foreign policy in the 1990s. Ian Mylchreest offers a comparison of abortion policy in the United States, Britain, and Australia in the late 1960s and early 1970s. The cultural politics of the abortion debate in contemporary America are explored by James Davison Hunter and Joseph E. Davis. Hunter and Davis's essay sets thc backdrop for Keith Cassidy's exploration of the Right to Life Movement and Suzanne Staggenborg's analysis of the pro-choice movement in the 1990s. Cassidy and Staggenborg find that the issue of population policy will remain a profoundly divisive issue in American politics.

Saint Louis University

Notes

1. Tantum artes huius, tantum medicamina possunt, que steriles atque homines in ventre necandos conducit. Guade, infelix et vexare uterum pueris salientibus, esses Aethipiic fortasse pater, mox decolor here imperet tabulas numquam tibi mane videndus. Trans. G. G. Ramsay, *Juvenal and Persius* (Cambridge, Mass., 1918), 31.

2. Linda Gordon, *Woman's Body, Woman's Right: Birth Control in America* (New York, 1976).

3. Linda Gordon offers a nuanced, dialectical feminist/Marxist analysis of the transformation of the birth-control movement from a radical feminist movement into a liberal political movement. Her analysis, however, often becomes too categorical in its description. As a consequence, conservative tendencies in the voluntary motherhood movement

and the "social purity" movement, intended to abolish prostitution and other sexually deviant behavior, are downplayed in order to emphasize the radical feminist thrust of the movement. Both the voluntary motherhood movement and the social purity movement evidenced strong nativist, elitist, and racist prejudices that coexisted with sincere feminist motivations. Recognition of these less than savory aspects of the birth-control movement or the early feminist movements is not to suggest that these movements should be dismissed, but it does indicate that often social movements need to be seen historically as multidimensional.

4. Literature about Sanger is extensive. See Gloria Moore and Ronald Moore, *Margaret Sanger and the Birth Control Movement: A Bibliography, 1911–1884* (Metuchen, N.J., 1986); Ellen Chesler, *Woman of Valor: Margaret Sanger and the Birth Control Movement in America* (New York, 1992); Linda Gordon, *Woman's Body, Woman's Right: Birth Control in America* (New York, 1976); Madeline Gray, *Margaret Sanger* (New York, 1979); Lawrence Lader, *The Margaret Sanger Story* (Garden City, N.Y., 1955); David M. Kennedy, *Birth Control in America: The Career of Margaret Sanger* (New Haven, 1970); and James Reed, *The Birth Control Movement and American Society: From Private Vice to Public Virtue* (Princeton, 1983).

5. Margaret Sanger, *Pivot of Civilization* (New York, 1922), 6–8. See also Margaret Sanger, *An Autobiography* (New York, 1938), and Reed, *The Birth Control Movement and American Society*, 67–89.

6. For a discussion of the *One Package* decision and its importance for the birth-control movement, see Reed, *The Birth Control Movement and American Society*, 120–23 and 265.

7. For the development of the birth-control pill, see Albert Q. Maisel, *The Hormone Quest* (New York, 1965); Gregory Pincus, *The Control of Fertility* (New York, 1965); and Loretta McLaughlin, *The Pill, John Rock, and the Church: The Biography of a Revolution* (Boston, 1982). James Reed provides a detailed discussion of the pill in *the Birth Control Movement and Modern Society*, 311–83.

8. For a succinct discussion of these cases, see Mary L. Duziak, "Contraception," *The Oxford Companion to the Supreme Court of the United States*, ed. Kermit L. Hall (New York, 1992), 193–94.

9. A detailed account of the constitutional struggle for reproductive rights is found in David Garrow's rich *Liberty and Sexuality: The Right to Privacy and the Making of "Roe v. Wade"* (New York, 1994).

10. For example, Ellen Chesler, in her excellent biography of Margaret Sanger, generally downplays the importance of eugenics in the birth-control movement by suggesting the Sanger "courted the power of eugenically inclined academics and scientists to blunt the attacks of religious conservatives against her." In addition, Chesler suggests that eugenicists did not play a significant role in the birth control movement by accurately pointing out that many leading eugenicists such as Charles Davenport remained vocal opponents of birth control. Furthermore, Chesler notes that few eugenicists were willing to associate with Sanger publicly. Nevertheless, she fails to note Sanger's close relationship with leading English eugenicists. Furthermore, while many American eugenicists did not publicly endorse Sanger—as scientists and physicians, many considered her too flamboyant—they supported birth control and sterilization well before the 1930s, when Chesler argues that eugenicists switched to a pro-birth-control position. Ellen Chesler, *Margaret Sanger*, 216–17, 343–45. For a critical appraisal of Sanger and eugenics, see Kennedy, *Birth Control in America: The Career of Margaret Sanger*.

Linda Gordon offers subtle argument concerning the progressive impetus behind the eugenics argument as it was employed by certain feminists. My discussion of eugenics draws from Gordon's insights, although I disagree with her that eugenics became predominantly anti-feminist and anti-birth control. This difference, I suspect, follows from my own reading of the recently opened Population Council papers at the Rockefeller Family Archive (RFA) in Tarrytown, New York, and the Frederick Osborn papers at the American

Philosophical Society in Philadelphia. These papers were not available to the early students of the birth-control movement and have not been utilized by more recent scholars such as Ellen Chesler. Linda Gordon, *Woman's Body, Woman's Right,* 125–35. For a more general discussion of eugenics in reform thought, see Daniel J. Kevles, *In the Name of Eugenics* (New York, 1990); Mark Heller, *Eugenics: Hereditarian Attitudes in American Thought* (New Brunswick, 1963); and Donald K. Pickens, *Eugenics and the Progressives* (Nashville, 1968).

11. Quoted in Kevles, *In the Name of Eugenics,* 84, 86.

12. Quoted in Reed, *The Birth Control Movement and American Society,* 135.

13. Margaret Sanger, *Pivot of Civilization,* 177.

14. Margaret Sanger, "Plan for Peace," *Birth Control Review* 16 (April 1932): 107.

15. Eleanor Dwight Jones to Lawrence B. Dunham, 3 November 1930, RG2 Medical Interests, Box 1, RFA.

16. Lawrence B. Dunham to Thomas M. Deboise, 5 March 1931, RG 2, Box 1, RFA.

17. Raymond Fosdick to John D. Rockefeller Jr., 7 February 1931 and 21 January 1932, RG2, Box 1, RFA.

18. Robert L. Dickinson to Arthur Packard, 3 March 1925, RG 2, Box I, RFA. John D. Rockefeller III also contributed financially to the Eugenics Society. See Arthur W. Packard to John D. Rockefeller, 9 June 1937, RG 2, Box 1, RFA.

Daniel Kevles has argued that eugenicists in the 1930s shifted from a hereditarian position to a progressive eugenic position that sought economic and social change. While more research needs to be done in this area, the story appears to be more complicated than Kevles suggests. Eugenicists such Clarence J. Gamble and his Pathfinder Fund continued to remain concerned about race and dysgenic qualities found in the population. In most respects, Gamble remained out of the mainstream (although he was actively involved in the birth-control movement), but eugenicists such as Frederick Osborn and others involved in the population-control movement continued to use hereditarian language. See Gordon, *Woman's Body, Woman's Right,* 395–98.

19. An extensive correspondence dating back to the 1930s on using Puerto Rico as a laboratory for birth-control techniques and programs is found in the Rockefeller Family Archives.

20. Arthur W. Packard, Internal Memorandum, 24 January 1947, RG 2, Box 1, RFA.

21. Gordon, *Woman's Body, Woman's Right,* 396.

22. Hardin, a professor of biology at the University of California, Santa Barbara, later apologized for the remark, which he claimed was only intended to challenge taboos in our society. See Garrett James Hardin, *Stalking the Wild Taboo* (Los Altos, Calif., 1979), 10–11; see also Garrett Hardin, *Population, Evolution, and Birth Control* (San Francisco, 1964).

23. Gordon, *Woman's Body, Woman's Right,* 395. Interestingly this same position has been taken up by some Catholic conservatives in their attack against birth control and abortion. See Elasah Drogin, *Margaret Sanger: Father of Modern Society* (New Hope, Ky., 1979).

24. These perspectives found early expression in an internal Rockefeller Foundation memorandum circulated in 1952 that declared: "We need to see birth control in expansive terms." Birth control should be interrelated to increasing food supply, improving health, and developing education. This entailed the development of a "cheap and effective pill, as well as increasing food from the sea, solar power, and developing genetic mechanisms that affect the yield of crop plants." Warren Weaver, Memorandum, 1 January 1952, RG 2, Box 1, RFA.

25. A detailed record of the meeting is found in the John D. Rockefeller III papers, RG 2, Box 47, and the Rockefeller Foundation papers, RG 3.2, Box 57, RFA.

26. Hugh Moore Fund, *The Population Bomb* (New York, 1954), and Will L. Clayton, Hugh Moore, and Ellsworth Bunker to John D. Rockefeller III, 26 November 1954, RG 2, Box 45, RFA.

27. Suzanne A. Onotaro, "The Population Council and the Development of Contraceptive Technologies," *Research Reports from the Rockefeller Archive Center,* Spring 1991, 1–2.

28. John B. Sharpless, "The Rockefeller Foundation, the Population Council, and the Groundwork for New Population Policies," *Rockefeller Archive Center Newsletter*, Fall 1993, 1–4.

29. "Eisenhower Bars Birth Control Help," *New York Times*, 31 December 1959, 20.

30. Dwight D. Eisenhower to William H. Draper, 30 December 1963, and William H. Draper to General Dwight D. Eisenhower, 18 November 1964, Office of Dwight D. Eisenhower Files, Box 33, Dwight D. Eisenhower Library (DDE), Albilene, Kansas.

31. William H. Draper to General Dwight D. Eisenhower, 18 November 1964, and Dwight D. Eisenhower to William H. Draper, 30 December 1963, Office of Dwight D. Eisenhower, Box 33; and Dwight D. Eisenhower to H. J. Porter, 20 November 1964, Office of Dwight D. Eisenhower, Box 49, DDE.

32. Lyndon Baines Johnson to Douglass Cater, 5 December 1966, Douglass Cater File, Lyndon Baines Johnson Library (LBJ).

33. Philip S. Hughes to Harry C. McPherson, 1 February 1967, Legislative Files, Box 164, LBJ.

34. Joseph A. Kershaw to Harry C. McPherson, 19 October 1965, Office of Economic Opportunity Files (Microfilm), National Archives.

35. Douglass Cater to the President, 30 March 1965, Cater File, Box 66, LBJ.

36. The regulations drew criticism in the press. Columnists Rowland Evans and Robert Novak attacked the exclusion of unmarried women from OEO-funded family planning programs. "Yet the precise heart of the problem is unmarried women and married women not living with their husbands. The American problem of exploding population is centered in illegitimate Negro births in the slums of the great Northern cities." Rowland Evans and Robert Novak, "Birth De-Control," unidentified column, 10 April 1965, Douglass Cater File, Box 66, LBJ.

37. Harry C. McPherson Jr. to Bill Moyers, 28 January 1966, Douglass Cater File, Box 66, LBJ.

38. Wilbur J. Cohen, "Statement by Wilbur J. Cohen before President's Committee on Population and Family Planning," 24 October 1968, Wilbur J. Cohen File, LBJ. Also, Katherine Brownell Oettinger, Children's Bureau Chief: A Pioneer in the Twentieth Century, Oral History (1985), Women in the Federal Government Project, Schlesinger Library, Radcliffe College. Oettinger's relations with Planned Parenthood are found in an extensive correspondence in Records of the Children's Bureau, Central File, Box 1141, National Archives.

39. Phyllis Tilson Piotrow, *World Population Crisis: The United States Response* (New York, 1974).

40. John D. Rockefeller III to Daniel Moynihan, 26 March 1969, Population Commission Files (unprocessed files), RFA.

41. Nixon's successor, Gerald Ford, continued to oppose efforts to expand federal planning programs. In 1974 and 1975 he vetoed authorization and appropriation bills for HEW that included family planning funds. Only a concerted effort by Congress in 1975 overrode Ford's veto. Thomas B. Littlewood, *The Politics of Population Control* (South Bend, Ind., 1977), 107–33.

42. One of the best accounts of the conference is found in Charles Yost, "An Ominous Failure at Population Conference," *Des Moines Register*, 8 September 1974, 1, 10.

43. John D. Rockefeller, "Population Growth: The Role of the Developed World" (1974), RG3, Box 493, RFA.

44. Robert C. Bates to Rockefeller Brothers Foundation Files, 2 October 1974, Rockefeller Brothers Fund papers, Box 210, RFA.

45. John Dunlap to John D. Rockefeller III, 2 May 1974, FG3, Box 494, RFA.

46. Joan M. Dunlop to John D. Rockefeller III, 2 May 1974; Joan M. Dunlop to William Ruder, 29 May 1974; and Joan M. Dunlop to John D. Rockefeller III, 19 April 1974, RG 3, Box 494, RFA.

Dunlop's argument was supported by others within the Population Council. As one Rockefeller Foundation officer wrote: "It is now also clear that the solution to the population problem involves more than contraceptive technology and family planning service. The social, cultural, and economic determinants of desired family size and contraceptive motivation will be critically important to the solution. . . . To achieve this kind of relevance, the population field must go beyond lip service to a full integration of population policy and social planning." Gerald O. Barney to Robert C. Bates, 1 April 1975, RG 3.2, Box 88, RFA.

47. Gerald O. Barney to Rockefeller Brothers Fund Files, 9 March 1976, Rockefeller Brother Fund Files, Box 88, RFA.

48. Michele McKeegan, *Abortion Politics: Mutiny in the Ranks of the Right* (New York, 1992).

JAMES W. REED

The Birth Control Movement Before *Roe v. Wade*

I

Beginning in the 1970s, historians and social scientists published a great deal on the birth-control movement in the United States, a subject that had been neglected. They were seeking perspective on the issues raised by profound changes in society that rendered problematic the gender system and family values of previous generations. It is no fluke that these scholars began to write the history of the effort to promote the separation of sex from procreation during the same decade that Congress removed contraception from the practices and information prohibited by the national obscenity laws (1971), and the Supreme Court ruled that married couples had a constitutionally protected right to practice contraception (1965), that the unmarried had a similar right of "privacy" (1972), and that pregnant women had the right to induced abortions performed by physicians during the first trimester of their pregnancies (1973). The Court's affirmation of a limited right to "abortion on demand" in *Roe v. Wade* followed a decade of intense political struggle and judicial action at the state level, and Justice Harry A. Blackmun, who wrote the majority opinion, was self-consciously attempting to forge a consensus in areas of human behavior and public policy where conflicts were literally lethal and threatened the social order.[1] In turn, much of the vitality of the scholarship on reproductive history that coincides with changes in the law sprang from the self-consciousness of women. Feminist scholars raised the consciousness of their disciplines by insisting that "the personal is political," and that gender, no less than class or race, ought to be recognized as a potent social fact.[2]

Since the 1980s more American historians have been interested in sexual politics than in the history of political parties. Historians discovered that public policies on prostitution, smut, contraception, induced abortion, and sterilization were shaped by elites as part of larger struggles between the sexes, between classes, and between ethnic groups. This new scholarship demonstrated the extent to which government had always been involved in reproductive decisions, despite the self-serving myth of male politicians and opinion leaders that the family was a private zone into which government ought not intrude. This essay is a brief synthetic narrative of the birth-control movement in the United States that will place the changes in public policy concerning human reproduction in historical context. This history draws upon the rich scholarship that was inspired by social change and the new feminist movement, but the emphasis is on description of changes in sexual behavior, social values, and public policy rather than on the delineation of feminist ideas as such or critical analysis of the leaders or opponents of the birth-control movement. Criticism of the ethics and wisdom of the historical actors in this story are abundant in the scholarship cited, but I attempt to minimize them in this account.[3]

II

While efforts to separate sex from procreation are ancient and widespread, there were no social movements to justify or promote contraception or abortion before the nineteenth century.[4] Individuals pursued their self-interests through such practices as coitus interruptus, periodic abstinence, by placing objects in the vagina to create a barrier between sperm and uterus, or by inducing abortion through drugs or mechanical means, but they did so in flagrant violation of official standards of sexual conduct. Systematic cooperative efforts on the part of married couples to limit fertility seem to account for dramatic declines in birthrates among particular ethnic groups such as Pennsylvania Quakers during the late eighteenth century, but these groups were singular in their respect for the sexual rights of women and their emphasis on the control of carnal desire. Beginning in the 1820s in England and the 1830s in the United States, however, a small number of freethinkers argued that family limitation would help the poor by limiting the labor supply, or that it would strengthen the family by easing the burdens of overtaxed parents.[5]

In the United States, marriage-manual writers representing all ideological persuasions soon joined the public debate begun by a few iconoclasts.

The family was undergoing rapid change as home and workplace were separated, new white-collar classes emerged, and the quest for economic opportunity led increasing numbers of young adults away from their families or "communities of origin." The new marriage manuals found a market among those who were no longer willing or able to depend on kin for personal advice, and who were attempting to cope with the contradictory demands of a new kind of family. Whereas men once married to gain a working junior partner in the family business, marriage began to be understood less as an economic alliance between kinship groups and more as a fulfillment of passion between two individuals. The expected result of heterosexual cohabitation inspired by sexual excitement (romantic love) might be ten to fifteen children, but that number of dependents represented an intolerable burden on the socially ambitious in an economy in which children were no longer economic assets and required large investments in the forms of Christian nurture and lengthy educations.[6]

Nineteenth-century Americans responded to the new social environment of a developing capitalist economy and the companionate family ideal by dramatically lowering their fertility. Whereas in the late eighteenth century the average native-born white woman bore seven or eight children, by the middle of the nineteenth century she was the mother of five, by the early twentieth century the mother of three, and by the Great Depression she was no longer replacing herself. One of the remarkable features of the American demographic transition is that there were no large declines in infant mortality before the end of the nineteenth century. Several generations of American women had fewer children than their mothers, despite a murderous infant mortality and the wails of social leaders that women were shirking from their patriotic duty and sinning against nature.[7]

The discovery by social leaders of the declining fertility of native-born white women inspired the first self-conscious attempts to influence fertility through legislation. Long before the term "Manifest Destiny" was coined in 1845, patriots used rapid population growth as proof of the superiority of American institutions. Benjamin Franklin provided Thomas Malthus with his generalization that humans can double their numbers every twenty-five years in a 1751 pamphlet intended to show that the vigorous growth of the North American population would lead to a crisis in colonial relations with England. After the first United States census in 1790, Secretary of State Jefferson was disappointed that fewer than four million had been counted and feared that this figure would provide ammunition for European critics of the United States. By the 1850s, when Samuel Morton and Josiah Nott, the leaders of the "American School of Ethnographers," provided a scientific rationale for racial caste systems and the extinction of non-Anglo-Saxons who stood in the way of United States expansion, the alleged cultural superiority of the republic was increasingly attributed to the biological origins of dominant Caucasian groups. Social facts were soon discovered that mocked this racial interpretation of American destiny.[8]

By the 1850s the pioneers of American social statistics had defined the "population problem," which would be an ever-present consideration in discussion of birth control, feminism, and the family until the 1960s. Francis A. Walker, economist and director of the 1870 U.S. Census, was a leader in the effort to raise public awareness of the phenomenon of differential fertility among ethnic groups and classes. Walker, a proud Yankee, was appalled while standing in a voter registration line because illiterate Irishmen were extended the same privilege. The social tensions associated with mass migration were especially frightening because of the declining fertility among the native-born. Walker argued that the native-born were being "shocked" into barrenness by exposure to and competition with the foreign-born, and he became both an exponent of "Muscular Christianity" and of immigration restriction. Among social leaders such as Walker no voices were raised in favor of a stable or declining population. Rather, population growth was viewed as an important index of national well-being.[9]

Walker did not explain whether the "shock principle" worked through biological or psychological changes. Historians now attribute the fertility decline to a combination of practices—contraception, abortion, and abstention from coitus—rather than biological changes in fecundity or shifts in the percentage of individuals who married or their age at marriage. As might be expected, physicians were prominent in the nineteenth-century debate about the causes and consequences of this vital trend. They wrote many of the marriage manuals, which provided counsel on the question of family limitation; they received requests for relief from women who were "irregular"; and they could not avoid questions of morality in a culture that increasingly looked to science for answers. Doctors, rather than ministers, lawyers, or businessmen, took the lead in campaigns to criminalize abortion.[10]

Prior to 1840, the law on abortion in the United States was generally permissive before quickening. This casual attitude reflected the fact that there were no means of determining whether a woman was pregnant or amenorrheic before the fetus began to move in the womb. Those seeking abortions were usually unmarried women, generally viewed as victims of male lust. Between 1840 and 1870 apparent changes in the social status of women seeking relief from pregnancy alarmed many physicians and led them into successful campaigns to outlaw induced abortion at any stage of pregnancy. As historian James Mohr has demonstrated, the medical leaders of anti-abortion campaigns believed that many married Protestant women had begun to seek abortions, and they seem "to have been deeply afraid of being betrayed by their own women."[11] They reacted with denunciations of feminists and successful lobbying campaigns in state legislatures. By 1880 induced abortion was illegal, many streetwise women and irregular practitioners had been driven out of business, and physicians had gained new status as moral arbiters.

The culmination of the campaigns against abortion in state legislatures coincided with the passage of the Comstock Act (1873), a strengthened national obscenity law, in which no distinctions were made between smut, abortafacients, or contraceptives—all were prohibited. As a result, explicit discussion of contraception was omitted from post-1873 editions of books in which the subject had been given space.[12]

Anthony Comstock was a lobbyist for the New York Society for the Suppression of Vice. Popular accounts of his activities have trivialized his concerns by portraying him as an idiosyncratic fanatic whose success depended on congressional desire to divert attention away from the Crĕdit Mobilier scandal. Comstock's concerns were shared, however, by the prominent New York businessmen who paid his salary, the eminent physicians who campaigned for the criminalization of abortion, and political leaders at all levels of government. The declining birthrate, the broadly acknowledged dissatisfaction among women, the new visibility of urban vice, the hedonism of popular culture, and streets teeming with the foreign-born—all seemed to threaten the hegemony of Protestant values and the stability of the middle-class family.[13]

Despite the criminalization of "vice," birthrates continued to decline among the socially ambitious groups of occupationally skilled and property-owning individuals who made up the ever-rising middle class. Both as individuals and as couples, husbands and wives had complex and compelling motives for restrictive behavior. An adequate analysis of them requires separate monographs, but the declining birthrate is in itself strong evidence of the success of men and women in gaining some measure of control over aspects of their lives that had often been resigned to fate. The birthrate also testifies to the limited capacity of the state to control reproductive decisions.[14]

The conflict between public and individual interests, between eros and civilization, was mediated at great cost, however, for the generation that came of age in the last decades of the nineteenth century. The inability of many young adults to cope with the demands of "civilized sexual morality" provided the first American specialists in psychosomatic disease with many cases of neurosis.[15] While the new ideal of companionate marriage based on romantic love, first popularized for a mass audience in nineteenth-century marriage manuals, might in retrospect seem to require recognition of erotic bonding and nonprocreative marital sex, most Victorians remained preoccupied with the need to sublimate eroticism to higher ends. For example, historian Linda Gordon has identified a group of progressive Victorian idealists who advocated "voluntary motherhood." Gordon argues that these progressive thinkers represent the nineteenth-century origins of a feminist birth-control movement. The advocates of "voluntary motherhood" shunned abortion and artificial contraception, however, in favor of abstinence when fertility control was needed. They recognized female sexuality and celebrated erotic bonding between husband and wife but feared that the separation of sex from parenthood would diminish the power that women gained through the ideal of cooperative self-denial.[16] An amazing array of mechanical birth-control methods were described in nineteenth-century marriage manuals and medical literature, but physicians failed to conduct systematic investigations into the relative efficacy or safety of competing methods, in large part because they shared the strong pronatalist values of their culture and feared the declining birthrates among their paying customers.[17]

The suppression of contraceptive information did not change the pattern of declining birthrates. In 1901 the populist sociologist E. A. Ross coined the term "race suicide," and President Theodore Roosevelt declared that America's future as a world power was being undermined by the pursuit of the soft life, exemplified by barren marriages. Between 1905 and 1909 more than thirty-five articles appeared in popular magazines discussing the infertility of native Americans.[18] The widespread idea that there was a crisis in the family was paralleled by the discovery of adolescence as a "problem" and the invitation of Sigmund Freud to visit Clark University, where he explained in 1909 how the tension between eros and civilization could lead to madness.[19]

One of the best contemporary explanations of the crisis in the social relations of reproduction was provided by the University of Pennsylvania economist Simon Patten. In 1905 Patten announced the arrival of a new era of abundance with a series of lectures that was published under the title *The New Basis of Civilization.* Patten argued that the Protestant values of hard work and dedicated abstinence had been an important resource in American economic development, but the success of Protestant asceticism in promoting capital accumulation had led to an economic revolution symbolized by the giant corporation and mass production. In the new world of mass consumption and economic bureaucracy, Americans needed to learn how to consume. The heroic entrepreneur whose iron "character" was appropriate to a society of scarcity was being replaced by the organization man, whose other-directed "personality" was expressed in the arts of leisure and consumption.[20]

Patten's call for new sexual attitudes appropriate to an affluent society was not heeded by most social arbiters, who continued to fret over "race suicide" and the equally threatening phenomenon of "clandestine prostitution," or the appearance in public of large numbers of unchaperoned women.[21] As the dynamic service sector of the economy drew ever-larger numbers of women into jobs outside the home, relations between the sexes began to reflect a new social reality. Married companionship seemed the best that the nineteenth-century economy could support for its young middle classes. Young men and women in the early twentieth century sought the pleasure of companionship before marriage in the world outside the home. The generous figure of the "Gibson girl" was replaced in the popular imagination by a creature with slim hips and short hair, who played tennis or swam, danced the fox-trot, smoked cigarettes, and necked with men she might not marry. The "flapper" was a comrade in arms with male friends against the sexually segregated adolescence and rigid gender roles of their parents.

As youth heard the appeals of the newly prominent advertising industry to relax, consume, and enjoy, the traditional values of austerity and sacrifice that supported nineteenth-century sexual ideals eroded. Among the predominantly upper-middle-class women interviewed by Alfred Kinsey in the 1940s, those born between 1900 and 1909 set a pattern of premarital sexual behavior that remained essentially unchanged until after World War II. These women made necking America's favorite pastime, and 36 percent of them engaged in premarital intercourse. Premarital coitus among men born between 1900 and 1909 did not increase, and coitus with prostitutes decreased by over 50 percent; the slack was taken up by friends, two-thirds of whom were fiancées.[22]

The new courting pattern—prolonged heavy petting, sometimes leading to coitus, and usually followed by marriage—did not signal the collapse of monogamy, marriage, or the family. Rather, it reflected the emergence of a single standard of permissiveness with affection. As the sociologist Ira Reiss shrewdly observed, the new standard did not mean frivolous sexuality or acceptance of "body-centered" coitus. Sex as self-centered pleasure was the standard of men who avoided coitus with their fiancées because they were "good girls" and sought relief with prostitutes.[23] Young people simply expanded the limits of the nineteenth-century ideal of companionate marriage and "person-centered" coitus developed by their parents. Petting provided the opportunity for the sexes to learn to know one another. It was a necessary prelude to mature sexual relationships and an appropriate form of sexual expression for adolescence, the prolonged period of social dependency necessary for the middle classes in an industrial society. Kinsey's study showed a correlation between heavy petting and the ability of women to achieve orgasm in marriage. Sexual compatibility in marriage in turn was associated with a low divorce rate.[24]

III

Both the nineteenth-century ideal of companionate marriage and the twentieth-century standard of permissiveness with affection were relationships based on mutuality and justified by affection. In the twentieth-century version of ideal love between man and woman, sex and procreation could be separated, but sex was still justified by the investment of much psychological capital in a stable relationship. Permissiveness with affection rested even more narrowly on intimate and personal values than on companionate marriage, and thus was more dependent on sexual attraction and fulfillment.

In retrospect, the emergence around 1915 of a movement to legitimate and spread contraceptive practice might be viewed as a logical, if not inevitable, response to one source of tension in the sex lives of socially ambitious Americans. The essential cultural prerequisite for public acceptance of the separation of sex from procreation was secularization of society or the celebration of material well-being and pleasure exemplified by the growth of the advertising industry. Many Americans were not ready to believe, however, that affection alone justified sex. A great majority of the more than 24 million immigrants to the United States between 1880 and 1920 had traditional attitudes toward sexuality. Their presence gave a tremendous boost to nativist anxieties over the future composition of the American population. The foreign- and native-born united in suspicion of those who wanted to change contraception from a furtive and illegal private practice into a legal and socially accepted right. For nativist and immigrant, Protestant, Catholic, and Jew, the population problem was not too many people but a dearth of people of the "right kind," although the definition of "right kind" varied.

At the turn of the twentieth century, those who publicly questioned suppression of contraception may be divided into two groups: civil libertarians, who were most concerned with the right of individuals to manage their sexuality according to personal preference; and quality controllers, those who wanted to redefine "the population problem" from a need for more people to a need for more people of the right kind.[25]

The civil libertarians were a relatively small group that included some advanced feminists, the anarchist Emma Goldman, and the medical journalist William Robinson. Margaret Sanger, the charismatic leader of the American birth-control movement during its heroic phase (1915–37), began as a protégé of Goldman.[26] Sanger's chief competitor for leadership of the birth-control movement, Mary Ware Dennett, was also a civil libertarian. Most of the civil libertarians were strong public proponents of the liberating potential of erotic fulfillment, and in this respect they differed from the majority of the professional women, who led the feminist civil rights movement of the era.[27]

The quality controllers were a much larger and socially distinguished group. They included the social housekeepers, academics, and patrician nativists who enlisted in the eugenics movement. Although many eugenicists were rigid hereditarians, whose zealous pursuit of Mendelian explanations for crime, prostitution, juvenile delinquency, and poverty alienated geneticists and hurt the effort to redefine the population problem, the most influential of the quality controllers—Raymond Pearl, Frederick Osborn, and Frank Notestein, for example—explicitly dissociated themselves from naive hereditarianism and were as concerned over the effects of poor environment as poor heredity. A number of prominent physicians—for example, Robert Dickinson, Haven Emerson, Adolphus Knopf, Howard Taylor Jr., and Alan Guttmacher—were influenced by eugenics but seem to have been drawn into the effort to influence reproductive behavior by their discovery of the threats posed to stable family life by sexual incompatibility and such diseases as syphilis and tuberculosis.[28]

Quality controllers enjoyed some early legislative victories. In 1907 Indiana was the first of sixteen states that passed eugenic sterilization laws in the decade before World War I. By 1940 eugenic sterilization acts had been on the books in some thirty states, but the advocates of this practice were never able to mobilize a consensus among key medical groups. More than 36,000 individuals had been sterilized under the authority of these laws, but this number was insignificant in terms of a scientific program of negative eugenics.[29]

Eugenicists enthusiastically lobbied Congress for the immigration restriction bills passed between 1921 and 1927. These acts mark the end of the open door to mass migration and were intended to discriminate against eastern and southern Europe. Recent scholarship has questioned the influence exerted by eugenicists as such upon Congress during a period of strong popular nativist sentiment.[30] By the time the door was shut, the nativists had already lost the war because a century of mass migration guaranteed that the United States would no longer be either a Protestant or a Nordic nation.

Even these hollow victories for negative eugenics were impossible to match on the positive side of the quality-control agenda. The birthrate among the middle classes continued to decline. As it became apparent that the "fit" would not breed more, some quality controllers began considering means for "democratizing" birth-control practice. A vigorous movement to legitimate contraception had already been organized, however, by civil libertarian feminists, whose calls for birth strikes and autonomy for women were not congenial to quality controllers.

By 1925 Margaret Sanger had solidified her position as leader of the birth-control movement. Her success depended on a pragmatic resourcefulness that infuriated competitors and baffled opponents. Sanger first gained notoriety in 1912–14 as an organizer for the Industrial Workers of the World and radical journalist with a special interest in the plight of working-class mothers. After some frustrating experiences with male radicals, whose attitudes toward women seemed little different from those of other men, Sanger decided to concentrate on women's issues. Her background as a nurse working in the tenements of Manhattan provided vivid stories of poor women whose lives were destroyed by unwanted pregnancies and septic abortions. As a first step toward liberating women, Sanger set out to remove the stigma of obscenity from contraception through a strategy of flamboyant defiance of the law. Faced with an indictment for publishing obscenity (specifically a defense of political assassination), she fled to England in October 1914. When she returned a year later, she barnstormed the country urging women to take matters into their own hands by establishing contraceptive advice centers, and she opened her own center in October 1916.[31]

The "clinic" in the Brownsville section of Brooklyn was staffed by Sanger and her sister, also a nurse, who for a fee of ten cents showed how to use pessaries and apparently fitted some women with devices. The police closed the Brownsville center after ten days and 488 clients. The "birth-control sisters" went to jail after highly publicized trials, but, on appeal of her case, Sanger got a judicial decision that she used as a mandate for a shift in strategy.

While upholding the constitutionality of the New York Comstock law, the appellate court judge ruled in 1918 that the law would not prevent licensed physicians from prescribing contraceptives when medically necessary. Thus Sanger's claim that the law was unconstitutional because it compelled women to risk death through unwanted pregnancy was rejected. Characteristically, she turned this apparent defeat into a victory by recruiting physicians to direct the birth-control clinics organized under the auspices of her American Birth Control League (founded 1921). The first clinic opened in New York in 1923, and, although there was a police raid in New York as late as 1929, the medical community rallied behind the clinic's medical director (Hannah Stone), and the charges against her were dismissed.[32]

Historians who have criticized Sanger's decision to "medicalize" contraception have taken their cue from Mary Ware Dennett, the leader of a series of competing birth-control organizations.[33] The differences between Sanger and Dennett began in 1916, when Dennett criticized Sanger's strategy of flamboyant lawbreaking and argued that a more effective and ethically defensible tactic would be to lobby for amendment of state and national Comstock laws.

In 1917 and 1918 Dennett's group lobbied without success in Albany and in 1919 began work in Washington, D.C. A federal bill was introduced in 1923 and 1924 but never got out of committee. Meanwhile, Sanger's American Birth Control League began pushing a "doctors only" bill, which simply recognized the right of physicians to give contraceptive advice, in contrast to Dennett's bills, which called for a clean repeal of all prohibitions on contraception. Dennett could not understand how a "radical" like Sanger could campaign for "class and special-privilege legislation" establishing a "medical monopoly" on contraceptive information.[34]

Sanger was willing to compromise on the kind of legislation that she supported, despite the fact that she was mailing her own *Family Limitation* to anyone who asked for it.[35] She needed support from at least some medical groups in order to recruit clinicians and to publish case studies from her clinics in medical journals.[36] "Doctor's only" bills aroused less opposition from organized medicine at a time when the profession was gaining status and jealously defending its hard-won prerogatives. The "doctors only" approach also mitigated the damaging claim that birth controllers were encouraging immorality and undermining national vitality.

There was another important reason for Sanger's opportunism. In contrast to Dennett, she was pessimistic about the prospects for legislative success. As a detailed diary of lobbying efforts in Washington revealed, most politicians regarded women lobbyists with contempt. The ideal of reproductive autonomy for women was literally a joke among them.[37] Sanger was aware of these attitudes but believed that lobbying campaigns were good publicity and provided a chance to educate the public.

She continued to break the law when necessary to operate a clinic, import diaphragms, or to embarrass the opposition. Breaking the law provided access to the courts, another public forum, but more important, a forum in which the political power of Roman Catholics would be minimized and one could appeal to a relatively well-educated arbiter. It was in the federal courts, in the *One Package* decision of 1936, that Sanger finally won a clarification of the federal obscenity laws and established the right of physicians to receive contraceptive supplies through the mail.[38] The *One Package* decision set the stage in turn for a successful lobbying effort in the American Medical Association by Robert L. Dickinson, the most prominent medical activist in the birth-control movement. In 1937 Dickinson secured a resolution endorsing contraception as a legitimate medical service that ought to be included in the medical school curriculum.[39] Chagrined over Sanger's mounting popularity among women financial backers of the movement, Dennett left the fight for birth control in 1925. Since no bill to amend New York's birth-control laws got out of committee until 1965, and contraception was not removed from the federal Comstock Act's prohibitions until 1971, in retrospect Sanger's strategy of combining opportunistic lobbying with selective litigation was the more effective.

Sanger regarded her most important achievement to be the national chain of birth-control clinics that she successfully promoted. These clinics provided case histories that disproved irresponsible claims by some medical leaders that contraceptive practice did not work and caused disease. The clinics also served as teaching centers, where the great majority of physicians who offered contraceptive services in their private practice received training that was not a part of regular medical education. Finally, the clinics made more reliable contraceptive practice possible for thousands of women, a behavioral change documented by the sexual histories gathered by Alfred Kinsey and his colleagues.[40] Organized by middle- and upper-class women, who gained new confidence and social skills, as well as access to better birth control, staffed by sympathetic women physicians, and eagerly patronized by working-class women who thus "participated" in the movement and demonstrated their desire to gain greater control over their lives, these clinics represented a remarkable effort by women to act on behalf of their gender.[41]

Some quality controllers criticized the birth-control clinics because they were not reversing "dysgenic" birthrates. In their view too many able mothers and not enough incompetent women were influenced. The popular appeal of the birth-control movement was based, of course, on the desire of a majority of married couples to manage their fertility in the interest of a higher standard of living. The birth-control movement was not responsible for this restrictive behavior but simply made it easier than it might have been.

During the late 1920s Sanger developed an increasingly conservative rhetoric, in part because her major sources of support—including society women who worked in her campaigns, the industrialist J. Noah Slee, whom she married in 1920, intellectual mentors such as Havelock Ellis, and silent financial backers such as John D. Rockefeller Jr.—urged her to cultivate a new image as a married mother lobbying among legislators and professional elites. In building a coalition for birth control, she learned that the ideal of reproductive autonomy for women commanded little respect among the great majority of American male influentials. Often treated with condescension by higher-born and better-educated women competitors such as Dennett, Sanger lost control of the American Birth Control League in the late 1920s and chafed when, in 1937, a male public relations expert was brought in to serve as president and removed "birth control" from the organization's title in favor of "planned parenthood" in an effort to soft-pedal the movement's feminist past and "face the fact that most pivotal groups upon which advancement of birth control is dependent are controlled by men, such as, Federal and State legislatures, hospital boards, public health boards, etc."[42] For several decades the "reformed" national organization would pursue the modest goal of securing a place in the voluntary health organization establishment—with emphatic emphasis upon contraceptive services for married mothers, to be delivered in a physician-directed clinic.

IV

During the Great Depression few policymakers were interested in either feminist or quality-control issues. For them "the population problem" remained a declining birthrate. Efforts by birth controllers to obtain public funds were sometimes frustrated by Roman Catholic opposition, but the greatest barrier was a widely shared fear of the economic and political results of demographic change. For example, the Harvard economist Alvin H. Hansen, one of the most influential exponents of the ideas of Alfred Keynes, devoted his 1938 presidential address before the American Economic Association to what became known as the doctrine of "secular stagnation." Hansen argued that the low birthrate was a principal cause of the inadequate demand and the low rate of capital investment associated with the Great Depression. In 1938 Harvard took advantage of the Swedish sociologist Gunnar Myrdal's visit to the United States by inviting him to give the prestigious Godkin Lectures. Myrdal had come under the auspices of the Carnegie Corporation of New York to study the race problem and published his classic study of the conflict between American ideals and its racial caste system in 1944. In 1938, however, he drew attention to *Population: A Problem for Democracy*. Myrdal argued that the Western liberal states would have to develop a state-supported system of family services if they wanted to avoid disastrous declines in population and to compete with Germany and other fascist states. Although the birthrate began to rise in the late 1930s, scholarly opinion remained bearish on population until there was overwhelming evidence that Americans had regained the will to reproduce themselves. As late as 1950 sociologist David Riesman based his analysis of the country's "character structure" on a presumed "incipient decline" in its population.[43]

While social scientists and politicians blamed the Great Depression on the low birthrate, ordinary people struggled to manage their own afffairs, and in 1937 spent $38 million on condoms and more than $200 million on "feminine hygiene," the commercial euphemism for contraceptive vaginal douching. According to the law, contraceptives could be sold only with a medical prescription. Thus condoms were "for the prevention of disease," and tons of douche powder passed over the counter in the name of internal cleanliness, despite agreement among medical authorities that the genital tract was self-cleansing and douching might cause disease. The clandestine nature of the contraceptive industry allowed manufacturers and retailers to charge exorbitant prices. A gross of condoms that cost the manufacturer $4.80 and the druggist $6 retailed for $24, a markup of 400 percent. Because testing condoms almost doubled the cost of manufacture, many defective articles were sold. Advertisements claiming that a product was "sure, safe, and dependable" for feminine hygiene were interpreted by the public to mean "sure, safe, and dependable" for contraception. The result was an enormous amount of money spent on marginally effective or harmful products. A *Ladies Home Journal* poll showed 79 percent of American women "believe in birth control," but they also considered four children the ideal. The most important reason why the two-child family was the behavioral norm was "family income." Thus, in the midst of the Depression, the public desire to maintain a decent standard of living was used to cheat consumers out of millions of dollars.[44]

During these dog days of the birth-control movement, initiative passed to a small group of physicians associated with the National Committee on Maternal Health, which had been founded by the gynecologist Robert Latou Dickinson in 1923 to promote medical sex research. Dickinson's original plan to conduct clinical investigations of contraceptive regimens was co-opted by Sanger's Birth Control Clinical Research Bureau, but under Dickinson's energetic leadership the committee published a series of authoritative monographs that convinced reluctant colleagues to accept contraception and marriage counseling as essential medical services. During the 1930s Dickinson's protégé, Clarence J. Gamble, an heir to the Ivory Soap fortune, organized an effort to publicize the scandalous practices in the birth-control business, with the result that the Food and Drug Administration began to test condoms and to confiscate defective articles; the AMA's Council on Pharmacy and Chemistry began to issue reports that defined standards for contraceptive products, and efforts were made to suppress the least effective douching products.

In contrast to Margaret Sanger, whose mission as a birth controller was to liberate women from unwanted pregnancies, or the majority of pro-birth-control physicians, who hoped to strengthen family life through better marital sex, Dr. Gamble's principal concern was differential fertility among classes and the high cost of social programs for the poor. While Sanger and Dickinson saw the birth-control clinic as a way of bringing a new sense of self to women, Gamble chafed over the high cost of medical attention for everyone. During the 1930s he initiated a series of remarkable experiments in the mass delivery of contraceptives and achieved some surprising successes. In Logan County, West Virginia, for example, door-to-door distribution of free lactic-acid jelly between 1936 and 1939 led to a 40 percent decline in birthrates among the poor women who were willing to try the method. In Logan, as elsewhere, Gamble's efforts ran into problems of cost and the reluctance of public officials to devote scarce resources to contraception. The annual cost per patient for distribution of contraceptive jelly by a nurse was less than $6, but in 1938 West Virginia spent $1.25 on public health per rural family.[45] Birth-control services seemed an extravagance beyond the means of private philanthropy or government. Gamble initiated other programs, distributing condoms in North Carolina, experimenting with foam-powder-on-a-sponge in Florida, and paying missionary doctors to show Indian peasants how to make a cheap vaginal barrier by dipping a rag in brine solution. He remained a quixotic outsider, but only slightly less influential than Sanger and Dickinson, until the redefinition of "the population problem" provided a powerful new rationale for experiments in population control and innovations in contraceptive technology.

V

During the 1950s the social and political climate changed in ways that began to strengthen the hand of birth-control advocates. First, married women with children were drawn in ever larger numbers into paid work outside the home. The great majority of American families could not attain the American dream of affluence with a single income. This underlying economic and behavioral reality was reflected in a 1955 national survey of representative married women. By the end of their fertile years, "substantially all" married couples had tried to regulate conception if they were not subfecund. Half began contraceptive practice before the first pregnancy, an additional 32 percent before the second, and 11 percent more before the third. Their reasons were overwhelmingly economic, although Catholics were more likely than Protestants to mention health as a rationale. The researchers concluded that the major determinant of family size in the United States is the number of children that couples want to have." Even more important for the future of public policy on reproduction: "All classes of the American population are coming to share a common set of values about family size." More couples wanted five or more children than none at all, but most wanted between two and four and actually had two or three.[46]

Despite the almost universal determination of married couples to limit their families, and their successful contraceptive practice, birth control remained a controversial political issue because of the opposition of the Roman Catholic hierarchy and the feeling on the part of most non-Catholics that higher birthrates were good for the economy. In June 1958, the cover of *Life* magazine showed several dozen infants modeling expensive walkers, rockers, and other "kiddie-care" paraphernalia under the headline "Kids: Built-in Recession Cure," but in July a controversy broke out in Brooklyn that marked the point at which even the Catholic Church tacitly began accepting the consensus on family planning.

Dr. Louis M. Hellman (later first director of population affairs in the U.S. Department of Health, Education, and Welfare during the Nixon administration), a gynecologist at King's County Hospital, a tax-supported municipal institution, decided to defy the de facto regulation against birth-control services in public institutions. His well-chosen martyr was a diabetic Protestant, two of whose three children had been delivered by caesarean section. The city commissioner of hospitals honored the traditional understanding among Catholic, Protestant, and Jewish politicians by ordering Hellman not to fit his patient with a diaphragm, but during the ensuing controversy, skillfully orchestrated by the Planned Parenthood Federation of America, important divisions emerged in the Catholic community. *Commonweal*, the lay Catholic magazine, editorialized: "Where consensus once existed, it no longer does. . . . There are many sound and compelling reasons why Catholics should not strive for legislation which clashes with the beliefs of a large portion of society." Eventually the New York City Board of Hospitals voted 8-to-2 to lift the ban on contraception, and the emergence of John F. Kennedy as a serious contender for the 1960 Democratic presidential nomination provided both Catholic bishops and laity with powerful incentives for avoiding controversy over issues of Catholic power in shaping public policy.[47]

As Catholic opposition to contraception softened, an influential group of social scientists redefined "the population problem" from how to encourage growth, or the right kind of growth, to how to bring zero population growth with a minimum of social disruption. This remarkable reversal of informed opinion helped set the stage for dramatic changes in public policy regarding human reproduction.

Around the turn of the century, the United States emerged not only as one of the dominant economic and political powers in the world but also as a center of scientific research. The private foundation rather than the state provided the resources for such institutions as the Rockefeller Institute for Medical Research and a National Research Council with numerous grant-making committees, including a Committee for Research in Problems of Sex (Sex Committee). The Sex Committee provides a direct link to the crisis in "civilized morality" because it was funded by the Bureau of Social Hygiene, an organization that quite literally sprang from John D. Rockefeller Jr.'s concern over the ties between political corruption and commercial vice. In an age that increasingly looked to science for models of social efficiency, the younger Rockefeller believed that effective responses to such disturbing phenomena as prostitution, venereal disease, drug abuse, and juvenile delinquency required scientific knowledge. This faith had some unexpected consequences as Sex Committee–sponsored research led to the development of the hormone concept, the identification and clinical use of the sex hormones, and eventually to the birth-control pill, marketed in 1960. The Sex Committee also sponsored the research of Alfred Kinsey, who in effect documented the decline of "civilized sexual morality" through sexual histories of several statistical generations of Americans.[48]

Concern over possibly dysgenic population trends also led American philanthropists to sponsor institutions for the study of vital trends, including the Scripps Foundation for Research in Population (founded in 1922), the Research Division of the Milbank Memorial Fund (1928), the Population Association of America (1931), and the Office of Population Research at Princeton (1936).[49]

When Frank Notestein, influential in population studies, began work at Milbank in 1928, his first assignment was to analyze unused data from the 1910 census on the relationship of social class to fertility. His study, published in 1930, was the first extensive empirical investigation of differential fertility, one of a series of distinguished Milbank monographs that provided an empirical basis for analysis of vital trends.[50] Frederick Osborn, the leader of the American eugenics movement, believed that Notestein's work deserved a secure academic setting, and he persuaded Albert Milbank, a fellow trustee of Princeton, to establish an office of population research at Princeton with Notestein at its head. Notestein went on to develop the now-conventional theory of demographic transition, which showed how fertility was shaped by socioeconomic determinants rather than by changes in fecundity.[51]

After World War II, demographers associated with the Office of Population Research and the Milbank Memorial Fund were the prime movers in an effort to focus the attention of world leaders on "the population explosion" and its detrimental impact on Third World economies. Just as differential fertility between classes and regions exacerbated social problems in the United States, they argued that the rapid expansion of population threatened the possibility of engineering rapid economic development in the Third World.

Engineering dramatic decreases in mortality had proved relatively easy because inexpensive mass procedures could be introduced by small numbers of technicians with little more than passive support from the general public. As Notestein explained in 1947 to a Milbank Round Table on International Approaches to Problems of Underdeveloped Areas:

> Human fertility . . . responds scarcely at all in the initial, and often super-imposed, stages of such changes [in mortality]—changes that too often leave the opportunities, hopes, fears, beliefs, customs, and social organization of the masses of the people relatively untouched. These latter are the factors that control fertility, and since they are unmodified, fertility remains high while mortality declines. . . . If gains in production only match those in population growth, "improvement" may result principally in ever larger masses of humanity living close to the margins of existence and vulnerable to every shock in the world economic and political structure. Such "progress" may amount to setting the stage for calamity.[52]

Public-health campaigns provided examples of the dangers inherent in the failure to develop comprehensive strategies for social change that took into account the effects of population growth. Nations newly liberated from colonial status wanted to share the prosperity of the West. Failure to develop their economies would lead to bitter internal divisions and to the rejection of Western alliances in favor of communist models of development. Thus, political stability depended on rapid economic development and, in Notestein's view, that development could succeed only if the rate of population growth did not eat up the necessary capital.

John D. Rockefeller III became the principal sponsor of Notestein's efforts to do something about the world population problem. As the eldest of John D. Rockefeller Jr.'s five sons, Rockefeller was expected to assume his father's role as a hard-working philanthropist, but the specific focus of his career, Asian-American relations and population control, was only partly dictated by established family interests. While attending Princeton University, where he majored in economics and wrote a senior thesis on industrial relations, Rockefeller took an independent reading course on Malthus and was exposed to several academic eugenicists. In 1928 his father had him appointed to the board of directors of the Bureau of Social Hygiene, the means through which the elder Rockefeller invested in social science research and action programs in such areas as criminology, sex education, and birth control. Rockefeller became especially interested in birth control and population issues. When the bureau was terminated in 1934, Rockefeller wrote to his father that he intended to maintain a strong interest in birth control. The elder Rockefeller also drew his son into his work with the League of Nations. He spent the summer of 1928 as an intern in the Information Section of the league's Geneva, Switzerland, office, and he began a lifelong engagement with international relations, which included a deep attachment to Japanese culture. After World War II, Rockefeller experienced great frustration in his efforts to interest the Rockefeller Foundation in population control, but through John Foster Dulles, a trustee of the Rockefeller Foundation since 1935 and chairman of its board in 1950, he was encouraged to regard international cultural relations as an important public service, and he would become the most influential U.S. citizen promoting economic and cultural exchanges with Asia. Rockefeller-supported experts would be mobilized in a comprehensive effort to promote capitalist development in the Third World, with special emphasis on improved food production and population control.[53]

After failing to gain a commitment to population control from the cautious professionals who dominated the Rockefeller Foundation, Rockefeller decided that there was a need for a small private organization "able to work closely with foreign governments without the publicity about Americans which so often arouses nationalistic feelings."[54] In 1952, after convening a conference of experts to discuss the world population situation, he founded the Population Council with his own funds. The governing body included Rockefeller, Frank Notestein, Frank Boudreau of the Milbank Memorial Fund, and Frederick Osborn as chief executive officer.

The council began spending half a million dollars a year on population research. Conscious of the need to avoid ideological conflicts, Osborn was "anxious to keep the work . . . in the hands of competent scientists, believing that accurate determination of the facts must precede propaganda rather than the other way around, and that when verifiable information was available it would inevitably be used in the guidance of policy."[55] Throughout the 1950s the "verifiable information" poured in, its collection spurred by Population Council grants that brought students from around the world to the United States to study and subsidized the establishment of demographic studies in foreign universities. The "intolerable pessimism" of demographers that had aroused the contempt of agricultural scientists in the early 1950s became acceptable as study after study showed per capita food production declining, largely, Rockefeller-backed social scientists argued, because of the acceleration of population growth. Fear of famine gained a growing audience for those who insisted that population control was the only alternative to social catastrophe. In 1954 India requested help from the Council in organizing its family planning program, and Pakistan followed in 1959.[56]

The council's growing influence might lead to frustration for both demographers and foreign governments, however, because the available technology and delivery systems, a diaphragm or condom from a physician or drugstore, assumed a developed Western-style economy. Notestein, who succeeded Osborn as president of the council in 1959, remembered his frustration in believing that something had to be done to control rapid population growth but lacking the contraceptive means that would enable the council to take decisive action. This sense of urgency led the council to investigate the possibilities of an old and discredited method, the intrauterine device (IUD), in a world where antibiotics had made the risks of infection seem acceptable.[57]

The council invested more than $2.5 million in the clinical testing, improvement, and statistical evaluation of the IUD, which worked well enough. Armed at last with a method that was relatively inexpensive to deliver and required little motivation from the user, family planning programs began to have an effect on birthrates in South Korea, Taiwan, and Pakistan. In 1967 a review article in *Demography* criticized the overoptimism of the Population Council technocrats about the prospects for controlling world population growth. Other observers argued that population control was getting too much of the development dollar and pointed out that it was no substitute for social justice. Notestein was acutely aware, however, that technology alone could not solve the problems of economic development. Basic social reforms were necessary in many developing countries, but private American agencies could not force those reforms on others. "What can a white capitalist do in a very sensitive world?"[58] Notestein's answer was that he could provide high-quality technical assistance when asked.

The second major advance in contraceptive technology in the 1960s was the "anovulant" pill, based on synthetic analogues of the steroid hormones progesterone and estrogen. When Gregory Pincus, the biologist who is generally credited as the "father of the Pill," reviewed the factors that drew him into the search for a better contraceptive, he cited "(a) a visit from Mrs. Margaret Sanger in 1951, and (b) the emergence of the appreciation of the importance of the 'population explosion.' "[59] Notestein began with a social concern and sought a solution through technological innovation that had previously seemed unnecessary, if not unethical. In the same way, Pincus began his search for a new contraceptive, in part because feminists urged him to do so and promised to pay him well for his efforts, and in part because population control was becoming a legitimate, and even glamorous, field of research. The realization of Sanger's dream of a female-controlled method that would be completely divorced from coitus could be achieved only when her feminist motives were bolstered by new economic and political sanctions for birth control.

Pincus was a scientific entrepreneur par excellence. Carl Djerassi and his team of chemists at Syntex provided Pincus with the key drug he needed when they synthesized the first orally active progestin from relatively inexpensive vegetable sources in 1951. The rationale for Djerassi's new molecule was cancer therapy, however, and there was no guarantee that this wonder drug would be translated into a marketable contraceptive. Pincus had to overcome much resistance and skepticism on his way to winning acceptance for oral contraception. He had to win over critics within J. D. Searle and Company, his commercial sponsor, which argued that one could never justify interfering with basic reproductive mechanisms simply for the sake of easier contraception. Pincus had to enlist clinicians and their patients to test powerful drugs that had many side effects, and finally to overcome resistance in the Food and Drug Administration (FDA) to licensing the massive dosing of healthy women with synthetic hormones. He was able to do these things because of major changes in attitudes toward sexuality and population growth. It is possible that oral contraceptives never would have gotten onto the market if the FDA had not approved them in 1960, because of the Thalidomide scandal and other events which soon changed the regulatory atmosphere in the FDA and made the public anxious about the side effects of steroids.[60]

The claim is often made that the new and "scientific" pill and IUD had a "revolutionary" impact on sexual behavior and values, but these innovations should be understood as responses to a changing cultural environment rather than as major causes of change. Americans were successful contraceptors before 1960. After 1960 doctors in birth-control clinics often encountered "hurting diaphragm syndrome" among women who believed their well-being required a pill, but their parents had controlled their fertility with condoms, diaphragms, and douches. Ironically, the "use effectiveness" of the Pill was not higher among many groups than that of conventional methods. The motivation of the contraceptor remained the key factor in the effectiveness of even a magic bullet.

By 1965 the Population Council's skillful lobbying among professional elites and the availability of apparently potent new contraceptive technologies had led to the acceptance of population control as a relatively noncontroversial part of economic wisdom.[61] The United States, rather than India or China, was the "backward" nation in terms of public policy. Osborn and Notestein were appalled by the growing hysteria over the prospects of ecocatastrophe fanned by such zealots as the Dixie-cup tycoon, Hugh Moore, whose Cold War rhetoric and ticking bomb advertisements in *Time* seemed to be parodies of the council's positions.[62]

Ironically, from 1966 onward the birthrate in the United States was below any recorded for the 1930s, but, instead of a revived pronatalism, the public heard shrill demands for yet fewer children from Zero Population Growth, Inc. According to surveys, the organization's membership was predominantly highly educated white males with a median age under thirty. These were the boom babies, a generation that from primary grades on had been squeezed into crowded classrooms and was now competing for scarce jobs. From their point of view, the United States was desperately overcrowded.[63]

Women of the baby boom generation experienced many of the frustrations of their brothers, but they shared grievances with their mothers as well. In the 1960s the voices of women were added to the criticism of population growth and the social values that supported it. The publication of Betty Friedan's *The Feminine Mystique* in 1963 helped to explain the malaise and the rage that found expression in the revival of the feminist movement. Apparently the stage had been set for a mass rebellion among women by structural changes in the economy. With the postwar expansion of the service sector, married women with children were drawn in ever-larger numbers into permanent work outside the home. The great majority of American families felt the need for two incomes. The existential reality of the working mother was ignored, however, as women workers continued to be regarded as transients who should be paid less and promoted with discretion because they were in theory working to supplement someone else's income. The growth of the "universal marketplace," or a society in which ever-more human relationships were commodities, generated immense desires and immense frustration that provided the basis for a renewed feminist movement. Young women activists in the civil rights movement for blacks and the opposition to the Vietnam War experienced frustrations with male radicals that were in some ways analogous to Margaret Sanger's experience fifty years earlier. They became conscious of the need for a movement specifically to address the needs of women. They began to repeat Margaret Sanger's half-forgotten demands that they be allowed to control their lives in their interests, and they found a mass audience among women who had not been activists but had been prepared for their message by discrimination at work, the condescension of male-dominated service professionals, and the insensitivity of husbands and lovers who thought contraception was a woman's problem, as well as child care and housework. Perhaps the fundamental insight of the new women's liberation movement was the intimate relationship between private and public: women could not achieve equality in the workplace without a rethinking of gender roles and a new division of labor within the home.[64]

The redefinition of the population problem meant that for the first time in American history the desire of the majority of married persons to limit the burdens of parenthood was not in conflict with the "public interest." A private vice had become a public virtue. This convergence of private and public need paralleled two other events that helped to shape a revolution in public policy concerning human reproduction: the rapid expansion of the welfare state and of judicially dictated "entitlements" or rights to public services.

In the United States the distinctive role of the judiciary in interpreting a written constitution that has proven extraordinarily flexible and the absence of an effective alternative to the middle-of-the-road two-party system led the dissatisfied to organize outside the political system and to present their demands as claims under the Bill of Rights. As Margaret Sanger's attorney explained after the *One Package* decision, the process of social reform "is a simple one, it is a matter of educating judges to the mores of the day."[65] By the mid-1960s the concerns that had previously inhibited judges from denying police powers to the state had eroded. In 1965 the U.S. Supreme Court, in *Griswold v. Connecticut,* struck down an "uncommonly silly law" that prohibited contraceptive practice. The Court continued to expand the rights of individuals to defy outdated restrictions in *Eisenstadt v. Baird* (1972), which established that the unmarried had the same right to contraceptives as the married. In 1973 the Court decided that women and their physicians, rather than legislatures, should decide whether or not to abort a fetus during the first three months of pregnancy.[66]

Removing positive barriers to reproductive choice of course did not guarantee that all persons would have equal opportunity to control their fertility in an age when the state was expected to assume a paternalistic role on behalf of the "medically indigent." As Lyndon Johnson's War on Poverty emerged from Congress in 1964, a number of planned parenthood groups successfully applied to the Office of Economic Opportunity for funds under the "local option" policy that allowed community groups to initiate welfare programs. Pro-population controllers such as Senator Ernest Gruening (D-Alaska) orchestrated public hearings that emphasized "freedom of choice" and the "right to equal access" as rationales for including budgets for family planning services in domestic social welfare legislation. Whereas birth controllers had for years been stopped by the problem of justifying use of taxpayers' money for a purpose that many citizens considered immoral, in the context of Lyndon Johnson's War on Hunger abroad and War on Poverty at home, the question became, How can we justify withholding from the poor birth-control services that the middle classes already enjoy? With the population problem redefined in such a way that population growth was no longer a national necessity, there was indeed no secular rationale for denying anyone access to contraceptives.[67]

The Social Security Amendments of 1967 specified that at least six percent of maternal and child health-care funds be spent on family planning, and contraceptives were removed from the list of materials that could not be purchased with Agency for International Development funds. These changes mark the point at which the federal government clearly adopted a pro-family-planning policy for the first time.[68]

VI

By 1970 it seemed that a politically potent population-control coalition had emerged, based upon perceived demographic imperatives and Great

Society entitlements. In July 1969 President Richard Nixon announced the creation of the Commission on Population Growth and the American Future and appointed John D. Rockefeller III its chairman. Nixon declared, "One of the most serious challenges to human destiny in the last third of this century will be the growth of the population. . . . When future generations evaluate the record of our time, one of the most important factors in their judgment will be the way in which we responded to population growth."[69] Rockefeller's commission was given a mandate to recommend ways in which existing birth-control programs at home and abroad might be strengthened. Impressive studies were commissioned on a broad range of domestic trends and policies relating to population growth and distribution, employment and economic growth, resources and the environment, immigration and internal migration, education and research, and the status of children and women. The commission's 1972 report made a strong case for an aggressive national policy to promote family planning, but Nixon disappointed Rockefeller by publicly dissociating himself from the report's recommendations on sex education and abortion and by ignoring the rest of the commission's recommendations.[70]

Rockefeller's population coalition of experts and professionals backed by foundations, university think tanks, and government agencies had come under withering attack from both the Right and the Left. In 1973, the same year that the Supreme Court found a constitutionally protected right to abortion, Congress passed the Helms Amendment to the Foreign Assistance Act of 1961, which prohibited the direct use of U.S. foreign-aid funds for abortion services. Within six months of the *Roe v. Wade* decision, 188 anti-abortion bills were introduced in 41 states. The 1970s would witness continuing regression from the goals envisioned by birth-control advocates as the Roman Catholic hierarchy in the United States found common cause with Protestant fundamentalists and conservative critics of the welfare state in a "Right-to-Life" and "Family Values" movement, which fed upon the insecurities generated by a declining standard of living for American workers and by the broad changes in the economy that led a majority of married women into wage labor outside the home.[71]

The population-control coalition also faced major challenges from liberals and progressives, who found fault with both the biomedical research establishment and the quality of health care for the poor. In 1971, under grants from the Office of Economic Opportunity, about one hundred thousand sterilizations a year were performed upon medically indigent women, but adequate guidelines to ensure the rights of these women to informed consent had not been implemented, in part because President

Nixon did not want to draw attention to his administration's association with federally funded sterilization services. The Committee to End Sterilization Abuse was founded in 1974 by a group of New York health-care professionals who became alarmed at the way some of their colleagues were using excessive zeal to recruit Hispanic and black women for sterilization. Convincing evidence of coercion supported complaints by such organizations as the National Women's Health Movement and the International Women's Health Coalition that the American health-care establishment had gone radically wrong in its high-tech, top-down, paternalistic approach to reproductive health issues. In 1973 a self-help book by the Boston Women's Health Book Collective, *Our Bodies, Ourselves,* sold 250,000 copies, mostly to members of the twelve hundred local groups that considered themselves part of the feminist women's health movement. After negotiating an agreement with a national commercial publisher, the Boston women's collective used all of its substantial profits from book sales of more than two million to support the women's health movement. As historian Linda Gordon observed, the Boston group's success "might indeed appear magical if one disregarded the intense material needs that the group met."[72]

By 1973 the birth-control movement's history had in some respects come full circle. The vision of the civil libertarians and feminists who fought Comstockery had been in part realized by the development of a body of constitutional law that legitimated individual birth-control practices under the umbrella of a "right to privacy." Yet that right was contested, as always, by those who claimed that the country needed women in the home nurturing children. The imperatives of a mature capitalist economy seemed to preclude full-time domesticity for the great majority of women, but it was still not clear how high a price women would have to pay for reproductive autonomy or if the "right to privacy" would survive another redefinition of the "population problem." Most mothers with school-age children worked for wages outside the home because of felt necessity, but the question of whether their burdens should be socialized remained a source of deep dispute. Despite the vigorous efforts of civil libertarians and feminists, politicians and social scientists most often discussed reproductive policy issues from the perspective of demographic imperatives and economic efficiency. Metaphors of ticking "population bombs," "epidemics" of premarital pregnancies, and threats to "family values" had more effect than observations that women deserved reproductive autonomy as a matter of justice.[73]

Rutgers University

Notes

1. Twelve states reformed their abortion laws between 1967 and 1975, with four permitting abortion virtually on request. In response, a nascent right-to-life movement mobilized coalitions of political fundamentalists opposed to reform or repeal of abortion laws, and a bitter struggle was launched between contending interests. Blackmun seems to have been personally moved by the agonies of women who had late trimester saline abortions performed by unskilled or callous practitioners.

For the social history that informed the emergence of an aggressive women's rights movement for legal abortion, see Leslie Jean Reagan, "When Abortion Was a Crime: The Legal and Medical Regulation of Abortion, Chicago, 1880–1973" (Ph.D. diss., University of Wisconsin, 1991). For the legal history that led to the "right to privacy" doctrine and the decisions affirming the rights of individuals to control their fertility, see David J. Garrow, *Liberty and Sexuality: The Right to Privacy and the Making of Roe v. Wade* (New York, 1994). Arlene Skolnick, *Embattled Paradise: The American Family in an Age of Uncertainty* (New York, 1991), provides an analysis of the changes in social structure and the family that proved profoundly unsettling to many Americans.

2. Linda Gordon's *Woman's Body, Woman's Right: Birth Control in America* (New York, 1976; rev. ed., 1990) is an influential example of the new feminist history. For review essays on the emerging scholarship by feminist historians, see Mary P. Ryan, "The Explosion of Family History," *Reviews in American History* 10 (December 1982): 181–85; Estelle B. Freedman, "Sexuality in Nineteenth-Century America: Behavior, Ideology, and Politics," ibid., 196–215; Elaine Tyler May, "Expanding the Past: Recent Scholarship on Women in Politics and Work," ibid., 216–33; Elizabeth Fox-Genovese, "Comment on the Reviews of *Woman's Body, Woman's Right,*" *Signs* 4 (Summer 1979): 804–9.

3. This account draws heavily on James Reed, *From Private Vice to Public Virtue: The Birth Control Movement and American Society Since 1830* (New York, 1978), hereafter cited as *Private Vice.* For a defense of this approach to the history of the struggle for reproductive rights, see "Preface to the Princeton Edition" of *Private Vice,* published under the title *The Birth Control Movement and American Society: From Private Vice to Public Virtue* (Princeton, 1984), and "Public Policy on Human Reproduction and the Historian," *Journal of Social History* 18 (March 1985): 383–98.

4. Norman Himes, *Medical History of Contraception* (Baltimore, 1936); Angus McLaren, *A History of Contraception: From Antiquity to the Present Day* (Oxford, 1990).

5. Reed, *Private Vice,* 6–7; Angus McLaren, *Birth Control in Nineteenth-Century England* (New York, 1978); Robert V. Wells, "Family Size and Fertility Control in Eighteenth-Century America: A Study of Quaker Families," *Population Studies* 25:1 (1971): 73–82.

6. Reed, *Private Vice,* 19–33.

7. Robert Wells, "Family History and Demographic Transition," *Journal of Social History* 9 (1975): 1–19; Edward Meeker, "The Improving Health of the United States: 1850–1915," *Explorations in Economic History* 9 (1972): 353–73.

8. Robert Wells, *Revolutions in Americans' Lives* (Westport, Conn., 1982), 75–76; James H. Cassedy, *Demography in Early America: Beginnings of the Statistical Mind, 1600–1800* (Cambridge, Mass., 1969), 216–20; William Stanton, *The Leopard's Spots: Scientific Attitudes Toward Race in America, 1815–1859* (Pittsburgh, 1960); Reginald Horsman, *Race and Manifest Destiny: The Origins of American Racial Anglo-Saxonism* (Cambridge, Mass., 1981).

9. Reed, *Private Vice,* 198–201.

10. James Mohr, *Abortion in America: The Origins and Evolutions of National Policy* (New York, 1978); Carol Smith-Rosenberg, "The Abortion Movement and the AMA, 1850–1880," in *Disorderly Conduct: Visions of Gender in Victorian America* (Oxford, 1985), 217–44.

11. Mohr, *Abortion in America,* 168.

12. Reed, *Private Vice,* 34–35.

13. Heywood Broun and Margaret Leech, *Anthony Comstock: Roundsman of the Lord* (New York, 1927); R. Christian Johnson, "Anthony Comstock: Reform, Vice, and the American Way" (Ph.D. diss., University of Wisconsin, 1973); David Pivar, *Purity Crusade: Sexual Morality and Social Control, 1868–1900* (Westport, Conn., 1973).

14. Daniel Scott Smith, "Family Limitation, Sexual Control, and Domestic Feminism in Victorian America," *Feminist Studies* 1 (1973): 40–57; Janet F. Brodie, *Contraception and Abortion in 19th-Century America,* (Ithaca, N.Y., 1994).

15. Nathan Hale, *Freud and the Americans: The Beginnings of Psychoanalysis in the United States, 1876–1917* (New York, 1971), 116–50; F. G. Gosling, *Neurasthenia and the American Medical Community, 1870–1910* (Urbana, 1987).

16. Gordon, *Woman's Body,* 95–115. See also John Spurlock, *Free Love: Marriage and Middle-Class Radicalism in America, 1825–1860* (New York, 1988). Karen Lystra demonstrates that the celebration of erotic mutuality was characteristic of many nineteenth-century Americans in *Searching the Heart: Women, Men, and Romantic Love in Nineteenth-Century America* (New York, 1989).

17. Reed, *Private Vice,* 3–18, 39–45, and "Doctors, Birth Control, and Social Values: 1830–1970," in Morris Vogel and Charles Rosenberg, eds., *The Therapeutic Revolution: Essays in the Social History of American Medicine* (Philadelphia, 1979), 109–34.

18. Reed, *Private Vice,* 201–2.

19. Hale, *Freud and the Americans,* Joseph Kett, *Rites of Passage: Adolescence in America* (New York, 1977).

20. Simon Patten, in *The New Basis of Civilization,* ed. Daniel M. Fox (Cambridge, Mass., 1968; 1st ed., 1907).

21. Mark Connelly, *The Response to Prostitution in the Progressive Era* (Chapel Hill, 1980).

22. Alfred Kinsey et al., *Sexual Behavior in the Human Female* (Philadelphia, 1953), 267–69, 300, 330–32.

23. Ira L. Reiss, *Premarital Sexual Standards in America* (Glencoe, Ill., 1960), 126–45, 183–92.

24. Reed, *Private Vice,* 54–63. For a critique of the new expressiveness, with emphasis upon the dangers that women faced with the decline of Victorian standards of self-denial, see Kevin White, *The First Sexual Revolution: The Emergence of Male Heterosexuality in Modern America* (New York, 1993).

25. At this time only the most radical proponents of reproductive autonomy for women publicly defended induced abortion as a civil right. During the first half of the twentieth century, birth-control advocates often cited the high mortality and morbidity rates associated with illegal aboriton as justification for contraception. One of the most dramatic changes in the birth-control movement came in the 1960s, when tentative efforts to reform prohibitive abortion laws were suddenly replaced by strong demands that they be abolished, and the great majority of birth-control advocates aggressively defended abortion as a woman's right. Although the birth-control clinics of the 1930s sometimes provided aid to pregnant women who sought abortions, usually in the form of referral to sympathetic physicians, this assistance was offered at great risk of criminal prosecution. See Reed, *Private Vice,* 118–19.

26. The term "birth control" was coined by Otto Bobsein, a friend of Margaret Sanger, and printed for the first time in the fourth issue of Sanger's radical journal, *The Woman Rebel* (June 1914). See Ellen Chesler, *Woman of Valor: Margaret Sanger and the Birth Control Movement in America* (New York, 1992), 97. Sanger has had numerous biographers, and both Reed and Gordon devote considerable attention to her in their histories of the birth-control movement, but Chesler's work is the most complete interpretation of Sanger's career.

27. Reed, *Private Vice,* 130–34.

28. Mark H. Haller, *Eugenics: Hereditarian Attitudes in American Thought* (New Brunswick, 1963); Kenneth M. Ludmerer, *Genetics and American Society* (Baltimore, 1972); Frank Lorimer and Frederick Osborn, *Dynamics of Population: Social and Biological Significance of the Changing Birth Rate in the United States* (New York, 1934); Frederick Osborn, *Preface to Eugenics*, rev. ed. (New York, 1951); Frank W. Notestein, "Demography in the United States: A Partial Account of the Development of the Field," *Population and Development Review* 8:4 (1982): 651–87; John C. Burnham, "Medical Specialists and the Movement Toward Social Control in the Progressive Era: Three Examples," in Jerry Israel, ed., *Building the Organizational Society* (New York, 1971); Reed, *Private Vice*, part 3, "Robert L. Dickinson and the Committee on Maternal Health," 143–93; Interview with Howard Taylor Jr., 27 April 1971, New York City; Alan F. Guttmacher, "Memoirs," autobiographical manuscript, Allan F. Guttmacher Papers, Countway Library of Medicine, Boston.

29. Gerald N. Grob, *Mental Illness and American Society, 1875–1940* (Princeton, 1983), 166–78; Julius Paul, "Population 'Quality' and 'Fitness for Parenthood' in the Light of State Eugenic Sterilization Experience, 1907–1966," *Population Studies* 21 (1967): 295–99; Philip R. Reilly, *The Surgical Solution: A History of Involuntary Sterilization in the United States* (Baltimore, 1991); James Reed, "Misguided Scientism," *Science* 252 (28 June 1991): 1863.

I do not mean to imply that eugenic sterilizations were ethically insignificant. They are a tragic fact of American medical and social history. The point is that the eugenics program would have required millions of sterilizations in order to have any statistically significant impact upon the gene pool of fertile citizens of the United States.

30. Franz Samelson, "On the Science and Politics of IQ," *Social Research* 42 (1975): 467–88; "World War I Intelligence Testing and the Development of Psychology," *Journal of the History of the Behavioral Sciences* 13 (1977): 274–82.

31. Chesler, *Woman of Valor*, 74–242.

32. The Birth Control Clinical Research Bureau was opened with funds that Sanger solicited from Clinton Chance, a British manufacturer, and it was not legally affiliated with the American Birth Control League because, as a membership corporation, the league could not operate a medical dispensary, and, as usual, Sanger's plans seemed too bold to other leaders of the ABCL. Once Sanger demonstrated that a birth-control clinic could stay open, this form of service became one of the principal activities of the ABCL and its successors. Reed, *Private Vice*, 112–20.

33. Mary Ware Dennett, *Birth Control Laws* (New York, 1926). For example, see Gordon, *Woman's Body*, 370–90, and Sheila M. Rothman, *Woman's Proper Place: A History of Changing Ideals and Practices, 1870 to the Present* (New York, 1978), 200–209.

Probably the fundamental influence on Sanger's feminist critics of the 1970s was the women's health movement. As the sociologist and feminist Ruth Dixon-Mueller observed in *Population Policy and Women's Rights* (Westport, Conn., 1993), "The feminist critique of the 'medicalization' of birth control focused on two related issues: the health risks and neglect of women's interests in the development of new birth control technology, and the appropriation of technology and service delivery by physicians" (47). I think that Gordon's and Rothman's treatments of Sanger's relationship with the medical profession provide an example of how presentist concerns sometimes lead to distorted interpretations of the past. See Reed, "Public Policy on Human Reproduction and the Historian," *Journal of Social History* 18 (March 1985): 383–98.

34. Reed, *Private Vice*, 98–105.

35. This opportunism, pragmatism, or plain dishonesty was characteristic of Sanger and accounts for the considerable confusion that exists concerning her positions on many issues, and especially her relationship to the eugenics movement, other feminists, and the medical establishment. See Joan M. Jensen, "The Evolution of Margaret Sanger's *Family Limitation* Pamphlet, 1914–1921," *Signs* 6 (1981): 548–55; Reed, *Private Vice*, 129–39, and Chesler, *Woman of Valor*, passim.

36. Probably the most important single medical publication in the history of contracep-

tion was Hannah Stone's 1928 monograph demonstrating the effectiveness of the diaphragm-with-spermicidal-jelly regimen. It proved amazingly difficult to collect this data and to get it published. This accomplishment owed much to Hannah Stone and Robert L. Dickinson, but Sanger also deserved a great deal of credit, and this kind of achievement depended upon her opportunism in comparison to Dennett's hard-line civil liberties strategy. See Reed, *Private Vice,* 115–16, 167–80, and Hannah Stone, "Therapeutic Contraception," *Medical Journal and Record* (21 May 1928): 8–17.

37. "Congressional Report: January 1 to May 1, 1926," American Birth Control League papers, Houghton Library, Cambridge, Mass.; Reed, *Private Vice,* 100–104.

38. C. Thomas Dienes, *Law, Politics, and Birth Control* (Urbana, 1972), 82–83, 89–91, 104–15, 195–96; Chesler, *Woman of Valor,* 373–76.

39. Reed, *Private Vice,* 187–90.

40. Kinsey gathered data on contraceptive practice but did not publish it. It is available in Reed, *Private Vice,* 124–26.

41. Ibid., 114–28.

42. D. Kenneth Rose, quoted in ibid., 265.

43. Alfred Hansen, "Economic Progress and Declining Population Growth," *American Economic Review* 29 (March 1939): 1–15; Gunnar Myrdal, *Population: A Problem for Democracy* (Cambridge, Mass., 1940), 18–19, 22, 24, 57–58, 102–3, 105; David Riesman, *The Lonely Crowd: A Study in the Changing American Character* (New Haven, 1950), 7–31.

44. Reed, *Private Vice,* 239–56.

45. Gilbert Beebe, *Contraception and Fertility in the Southern Appalachians* (Baltimore, 1942); Reed, *Private Vice,* 247–56.

46. Ronald Freedman et al., *Family Planning, Sterility, and Population Growth* (New York, 1959), 62, 168, 257, 402.

47. *Commonweal,* 12 September 1958, 583. Quoted in Thomas Littlewood, *The Politics of Population Control* (Notre Dame, Ind.), 22–24. For the biography of one influential Roman Catholic birth-control advocate, see Loretta McLaughlin, *The Pill, John Rock, and the Church* (Boston, 1982).

48. James F. Gardner Jr., "Microbes and Morality: The Social Hygiene Crusade in New York City, 1892–1917" (Ph.D. diss., Indiana University, 1973); Sophie Aberle and George W. Corner, *Twenty-Five Years of Sex Research: History of the National Research Council Committee for Research in Problems of Sex, 1922–1947* (Philadelphia, 1953); Diana Long Hall, "Biology, Sex Hormones, and Sexism in the 1920s," *Philosophical Forum* 5 (1973–74): 81–96.

49. Reed, *Private Vice,* 202–8; Dennis Hodgson, "The Ideological Origins of the Population Association of America," *Population and Development Review* 17 (March 1991): 1–34.

50. Frank Notestein, "Differential Fertility According to Social Class," *Journal of the American Statistical Association* 25 (March 1930): 9–32.

51. Dennis G. Hodgson, "Demographic Transition Theory and the Family Planning Perspective: The Evolution of Theory Within American Demography" (Ph.D. diss., Cornell University, 1976); idem, "Demography as Social Science and Policy Science," *Population and Development Review* 9 (March 1983): 1–34.

52. Frank W. Notestein, "Summary of the Demographic Background of Problems of Underdeveloped Areas," *Milbank Memorial Fund Quarterly* 26 (July 1948): 250, 252. Quoted in Reed, *Private Vice,* 282.

53. For Rockefeller's biography, see John E. Harr and Peter J. Johnson, *The Rockefeller Century* (New York, 1988), and *The Rockefeller Conscience: An American Family in Public and in Private* (New York, 1991).

54. Frederick Osborn to James Reed, 2 May 1973; quoted in Reed, *Private Vice,* 287.

55. Ibid.

56. Ibid., 286–88.

57. Ibid., 303–8.

58. James Reed interview with Frank Notestein, 12 August 1974, Princeton. Quoted in Reed, *Private Vice,* 307.

59. Gregory Pincus, *The Control of Fertility* (New York, 1965), 5–6.

60. Reed, *Private Vice,* 309–66; Carl Djerassi, "The Chemical History of the Pill," in *The Politics of Contraception* (New York, 1979), 227–55; R. McFayden, "Thalidomide in America: A Brush with Tragedy," *Clio Medica* 11 (1976): 79–93.

61. Kurt W. Back provides a substantial discussion of the multiple demographic studies and population-control pilot projects that were the empirical basis for the acceptance of birth control in public health and economic development plans in *Family Planning and Population Control: The Challenges of a Successful Movement* (Boston, 1989), 77–110. See also John B. Sharpless, "The Rockefeller Foundation, the Population Council, and the Groundwork for New Population Policies," *Rockefeller Archive Center Newsletter* (Fall 1993): 1–4.

62. Reed, *Private Vice,* 303–4.

63. Larry D. Barnett, "Zero Population Growth, Inc.," *Bioscience* 21 (1971): 759–65; "Zero Population Growth, Inc.: A Second Study," *Journal of Biosocial Science* 6 (1974): 1–24.

64. Peter Filene, *Himself/Herself: Sex Roles in Modern America* (New York, 1974), 177–232; Harry Braverman, *Labor and Monopoly Capitalism* (New York, 1974), 271–83; Sara Evans, *Personal Politics: The Roots of Women's Liberation in the Civil Rights Movement and the New Left* (New York, 1979). On Sanger's alienation from Alexander Berkman and Big Bill Haywood, see Reed, *Private Vice,* 76–78.

65. Morris Ernst, quoted in Dienes, *Law Politics and Birth Control,* 114 n. 29.

66. Garrow, *Liberty and Sexuality,* 233–69, 457, 473–599.

67. Phyllis T. Piotrow, *World Population Crisis: The United States Response* (New York, 1973), 129, 153, 154, 103–11.

68. The high tide of public support for family planning programs was reached in the early 1970s, when Louisiana, a poor state with a particularly reactionary social order, witnessed the growth of a comprehensive effort to provide reproductive health services to poor women under the auspices of federal and foundation grants. By 1974 the Louisiana Family Health Foundation had begun to collapse and its leader, pediatrician and Tulane Medical School professor Joseph Beasley, went to jail for misuse of grant funds. This tragic story illustrates the barriers to social justice for women, which would become higher in the 1980s. See Martha Ward, *Poor Women, Powerful Men: America's Great Experiment in Family Planning* (Boulder, Colo., 1986).

69. "Message from The President of the United States Relative to Population Growth," House of Representatives, 91st Cong., 1st sess., Document No. 91–139 (Washington, D.C., 1979), 9.

70. U.S. Commission on Population Growth and the American Future, *Population and the American Future* (New York, 1972), Harr and Johnson, *The Rockefeller Conscience,* 395–420.

71. Dixon-Mueller, *Population Policy and Women's Rights,* 66–78.

72. Thomas M. Shapiro, *Population Control Politics: Women, Sterilization, and Reproductive Choice* (Philadelphia, 1985); James Reed, "Misconstruing Social Change," *Family Planning Perspectives* 19 (March–April 1987): 89–90; Gordon, *Woman's Body* (rev. ed., 1990), 436.

73. Maris A. Vinovskis, *An "Epidemic" of Adolescent Pregnancy? Some Historical and Policy Considerations* (New York, 1988); Rickie Solinger, *Wake Up Little Susie: Single Pregnancy and Race Before Roe v. Wade* (New York, 1992), 205–31; Gordon, *Woman's Body* (rev. ed., 1990), 386–488; Dixon-Mueller, *Population Policy and Women's Rights,* passim.

IAN MYLCHREEST

"Sound Law and Undoubtedly Good Policy": *Roe v. Wade* in Comparative Perspective

I

The Supreme Court changed abortion laws across the United States on 22 January 1973. Abortion had been illegal in many states, and in others a closely regulated medical procedure. In only four states did the law provide a broad right to terminate a pregnancy in the early months. *Roe v. Wade* declared that this right in the context of the doctor-patient relationship was protected by the Constitution's "right to privacy."[1] In practice, abortion became a matter of personal choice.

Policies akin to *Roe v. Wade* came to govern abortion in Britain and Australia between 1967 and 1973. By comparing these reforms, this essay offers a perspective beyond the constitutional argument over the right to privacy. Doctrine is important, but it confines discussion to the idiom of rights. In the English-speaking world, however, medical practice, the common-law background, and changed social attitudes underwrote abortion law reform. A comparison will draw out those common threads.

Critics of *Roe* have been legion. Justice Byron White's bitter dissent called it "an exercise of raw judicial power."[2] Alluding to the 1905 case that struck down minimum-wage laws, John Hart Ely denounced the decision as "Lochneresque" for enshrining the Court's policy values in constitutional law.[3] Robert Bork called the decision "a serious and wholly unjustifiable usurpation of state legislative authority."[4] In either form or substance, the critics argued, *Roe* amounted to judicial legislation.

Advocates of the right to privacy have consistently rejected this critique. They argue that *Roe* only gave substance to an unenumerated

This article was written with the support of a faculty development leave from the University of Nevada, Las Vegas.

constitutional right. Justice Harry Blackmun, the author of the Court's 1973 opinion, wrote in 1989 that constitutional benchmarks are "judge-made methods for evaluating and measuring the strength and scope of constitutional rights or for balancing the constitutional rights of individuals against the competing interests of government."[5] In other words, the text of the Constitution implied the right to privacy, and the right to abortion was one specific example of the right in action.[6] Rhetoric about judicial hubris or defending rights has obscured the common ground *Roe* shared with reform in other industrial societies.

The comparative approach is well established in the literature on abortion. Mary Ann Glendon argued that the federal judiciary disrupted the legislative process. Elsewhere legalization resulted from democratic compromise that offered women protective social support. State legislatures would have found politically legitimate solutions had they not been overridden by the Supreme Court.[7] Laurence Tribe, on the other hand, saw *Roe* as the only acceptable American solution. Given our cultural and legal emphasis on rights, he could imagine no other result. By 1973 the debate was stalemated, and *Roe* broke the political impasse.[8] These counterfactual speculations exaggerate the exceptional nature of the decision.[9] It does not look so extraordinary in the light of abortion reform elsewhere.

Preemptive judicial rulings played a crucial role in Britain and Australia. Policymakers, whether judges or legislators, adopted similar rationales to reform criminal abortion statutes. In Britain, Parliament legalized medically supervised abortion on social grounds. No political consensus emerged in Australia, but legal rulings gave doctors broad professional discretion to perform abortions. British courts cannot review the constitutionality of legislation, and judicial review under the Australian Constitution generally turns on the allocation of powers in the federal system. This only meant that the formal path to reform in the parliamentary systems differed from the constitutional right articulated in *Roe*. The Australian process in that formalist sense diverged from the British despite their common parliamentary systems. Tracing the three reform processes shows that, in much of the English-speaking world, similar rhetoric and policy rationales supported abortion reform.

II

In Victorian Britain and the Australian colonies abortion had been made a criminal offense under a variety of statutes. In its final version, sections

58 and 59 of the Offences Against The Person Act of 1861 outlawed supplying abortifacients or "using an instrument with intent to procure miscarriage." The Australian states wrote the same language into their law. In 1857 Texas made abortion illegal except to save the life of the mother. British law allowed no exceptions until 1929, when increased diagnostic knowledge made therapeutic abortion common enough to persuade Parliament to set twenty-eight weeks as the upper limit for legal abortions. The Infant Life (Preservation) Act then made it unlawful to destroy the life of a child capable of being born alive except to save the life of the mother.[10] Thus viability became a benchmark in the practice of abortion.

Medical practice and judicial interpretation modified the criminal laws in all jurisdictions. Middle-class women arranged abortions privately with their doctors. Even in Texas, an informal regime of therapeutic abortion operated in major teaching hospitals.[11] Throughout the first half of the twentieth century, British and Australian authorities enforced the laws against those running abortion mills or those who were not licensed doctors. On the other hand, they informally tolerated private medical practitioners offering discreet services and medically sanctioned therapeutic abortion.

A British test case in 1938 formalized the limits of professional discretion.[12] Aleck Bourne, obstetrical surgeon at St. Mary's Hospital, had been charged with procuring a miscarriage. But this was no ordinary prosecution. Bourne himself wrote to the attorney general informing him of the procedure. The patient was a fourteen-year-old rape victim. Bourne assured himself that the girl did not have what he called "a prostitute-mind." In his defense, he claimed that the abortion was lawful because bearing a child conceived in rape would have made the girl a "mental wreck."

Summing up the case, Justice Macnaghten underlined how different Bourne's case was from the typical abortion trial. Usually untrained women stood in the dock. They performed the service for money (a fee of £2.5s was mentioned), and the case came to trial because the patient died. Bourne, Macnaghten said, was "a man of the highest skill" operating "in one of our great hospitals" as "an act of charity." The judge took great pains to limit abortion to conscientious doctors helping gravely distressed patients.

Macnaghten hoped to sway the jury to acquit Bourne, but the section under which the obstetrician was charged provided no exceptions. The judge nonetheless carved a loophole out of the verbiage "unlawfully."

From this word Macnaghten inferred that the statute preserved the old common-law exception to save the mother's life. He also instructed the jury that the prosecution had to prove that the abortion was unlawful.

Even this might not have been sufficient to secure Bourne's acquittal, because the girl would physically have survived the birth. Bourne relied on a broad definition of preserving life. Under cross-examination he had asserted that there was no clear line between preserving life and preserving health. The judge instructed the jury that a doctor could perform an abortion if the pregnancy would "make the woman a physical or mental wreck." Pregnancy for one so young would produce "great mental anguish." In these exceptional circumstances Bourne was acquitted.

As a matter of law this opened an exception that had very little basis in the statute. Macnaghten argued that the law neither prohibited abortion absolutely nor permitted unrestricted medical discretion. He mentioned the two extreme views "merely to show that the law lies between them." Courts everywhere continued to invoke this solomonic approach.

Bourne's case was much more dramatic in form than in substance. British and Australian courts enforced the distinction between narrow medical grounds and the much more common practice of abortion for "social" reasons. "Back-alley abortionists," even medical practitioners, had to meet a very different burden of proof. A doctor running a boardinghouse near Sydney was convicted of manslaughter in 1911 when he inadvertently killed a patient. Her boyfriend testified that they had gone to the boardinghouse to have her pregnancy aborted. That was sufficient for the jury to convict the doctor, despite his assertion that he had only been removing a dead fetus from the woman's womb.[13] In 1943 a Melbourne nurse was convicted in similar circumstances; she too claimed that she had only been removing the dead fetus.[14]

These standards still obtained in the late 1950s. Prosecutors charged even Harley Street specialists working in a discreet circle trying to operate within the "mental wreck" exception carved out in Bourne's case. An unmarried but pregnant nurse consulted a psychiatrist who was known to be a conduit to abortion. The woman made threats to injure herself and expected to be found suicidal. This ritual provided the necessary pretext to the procedure.

The psychiatrist referred her to an obstetrician, who quickly agreed to perform a surgical abortion. The nurse unfortunately insisted on a simpler office procedure. The obstetrician referred the nurse to a second psychiatrist, Dr. Stungo. He too declared her suicidal and referred her to an endocrinologist, Dr. Newton, who agreed to perform the nonsurgical abortion. Soon afterward infection set in and the nurse died of renal failure nine days later. Newton was convicted of procuring an abortion and of manslaughter, for which he was given a five-year sentence.

This case starkly illustrated the psychiatric subterfuges that provided abortions to middle-class patients before the 1960s. Newton based his defense on Bourne's case, arguing that he had made a *bona fide* medical judgment that an abortion should be performed because the patient was suicidal. The judge instructed the jury that the mental condition of the patient was relevant, and that the prosecution had to prove that the abortion was not performed in good faith.

The evidence damaged Newton's credibility. He had made only a perfunctory effort to establish the patient's mental health and demanded a large cash fee before the consultation. Worst of all, Newton had lied about the abortion when the nurse was admitted to the hospital.[15] Despite the justice meted out to the doctor, this case illustrated the contradictions of therapeutic abortion. Extreme cases such as rape made abortion therapeutic, but if a doctor performed the procedure too often or without scrupulous respect for medical procedures, he raised suspicions that he was a professional abortionist, who should be subjected to the rigors of the law.

Cases involving rape, incest, and fetal damage formed the leading edge of the reform campaign. In 1936 the British Medical Association (BMA) had recommended this reform, and the Birkett Committee made similar recommendations in the wake of Bourne's case. Nothing was done, however, until the Abortion Law Reform Association was revived in the 1950s. Cambridge law professor Glanville Williams was the association's president, and he publicized the contradictions between the law and medical practice.

The distinction between "good" and "bad" abortionists proved unstable. Medical advances had made therapeutic abortion in its original sense very uncommon because pregnancy rarely threatened life directly. Yet most safe abortions had to be obtained under this legalistic regime. Medical supervision of abortion produced widely differing results. In Los Angeles County Hospital, for example, the abortion rate fell from 1 in 106 live births in 1931 to 1 in 8,000 live births in 1950. During the same period the ratio did not change at the Chicago Lying-in Hospital.[16] Gynecologist and reform leader Alan F. Guttmacher believed that the discrepancies between committees made the policy incoherent in New York.[17] Doctors making these judgments did not share a common definition of "therapeutic."

Doctors performing abortions in Britain relied on the nebulous definition of preserving the life of the mother and their professional standards to shield themselves from prosecution. Rape and incest were not sufficient grounds for a therapeutic abortion unless the mother's health was threatened. Neither was fetal deformity an exception, but by the early 1960s obstetricians routinely aborted pregnancies of women exposed to rubella or X-rays. Their only legal justification was that the anguish of bearing the damaged child met the legal standard of threatening maternal health.[18] The fear of a handicapped or retarded child likewise provided psychiatric grounds for 7 percent of all abortions at the Chicago Lying-in Hospital.[19] By the 1960s mental health routinely justified eugenic abortions. On both sides of the Atlantic, the letter of the law was ignored.

Activists in all three countries propounded similar arguments to change the law. Inconsistencies and injustices were the core of the reform campaign. The hypocrisy of forcing poor women to use back-alley abortionists while middle-class women had access to medical abortions offered an obvious target.[20] The brief on behalf of Jane Roe pointed out this kind of inequality; New York legalized abortion in 1970, but only women of means traveled for safe abortions.[21]

The determination of women to secure an abortion became an article of the reform faith. As Glanville Williams wrote in 1958: "When a woman is faced with the prospect of having a child that will tend to impoverish her existing family, or that will disgrace her in the eyes of others, she does not generally regard an early termination of pregnancy as wrongful." He backed this assertion with estimates that one hundred thousand women a year sought illegal abortions. The American College of Obstetricians and Gynecologists and the American Psychiatric Association made this argument in support of Jane Roe. As many as one million illegal abortions, they claimed, were performed annually in America and resulted in approximately five thousand deaths.[22]

The professional literature often emphasized the proportion of older married women seeking abortions. They could not afford more children, and this led reformers to articulate the view that economic or other family circumstances often justified abortion. They understood the procedure as integral to solving social problems. Judges also accepted this necessity. In 1949 a man accidentally killed his wife while trying to abort her pregnancy. His sentence was reduced to time served because of their desperate situation. Said Chief Justice Goddard:

> . . . the appellant, who certainly deserves the description of a devoted husband, was living with his wife and two children in circumstances which were truly deplorable. They were all living in one small room, and the prospect of another child being added to their

> number was such as might have moved anyone to the greatest pity. . . . The circumstances were that this man and his wife were trying to prevent another little life from being brought into the conditions in which they were living.[23]

The death of the mother made it tragic, and proponents of abortions often focused on such pathetic cases.

Reformers consistently argued that abortion would reduce poverty. The poor were especially cursed with unwanted children—an unconsciously Malthusian view. Glanville Williams argued that reform should include social grounds because "imbeciles" came under no other classification:

> Eugenic abortion is resisted on the ground that this work should be done not by abortion but by contraception. Yet contraception is useless for people, such as mental defectives, who are unable or unwilling to practise it. There are many defectives who are not thought to require institutional treatment, who yet are prone to sexual irresponsibility; for these, abortion accompanied by sterilization is a social [*sic*] desirable operation.[24]

In 1972 the Commission on Population and the American Future recommended legalization on similar grounds.[25] Roe's brief appealed to these ideas. Citing the 1965 National Fertility Study, it argued that one-fifth (nearly five million) of births were unwanted, and "two million of these births occurred among the poor and the near-poor and half of these among Negro poor and near-poor." These women particularly needed access to abortion.[26]

Thurgood Marshall angrily dissented when the Court allowed states to refuse to pay for Medicaid abortions. The same concern can be glimpsed in his discussion of the plight of the poor woman denied such funding:

> . . . she may well give up all chance of escaping the cycle of poverty. Absent day-care facilities, she will be forced into full-time child care for years to come; she will be unable to work so that her family can break out of the welfare system or the lowest income brackets. If she already has children, another infant to feed and clothe may well stretch the budget past the breaking point. All chance to control the direction of her own life will have been lost.

He pointed out that minority women depended disproportionately on Medicaid, which made the measure even more discriminatory. Incensed at seeing the Court curtail abortion rights, he declared that *Roe* was still "sound law and undoubtedly good policy."[27] This mixture of progressive eugenics and social reform disappeared from the pro-choice argument when pro-life rhetoric likened legalized abortion to the death toll of chattel slavery and the Nazi Holocaust.

Arguing that access to abortion would help poor women escape poverty implied a clear judgment of the status of the fetus. Before viability, it was much less significant than the woman and her family. Glanville Williams spoke of the "medical sense" of abortion meaning before viability. Justice Clark made exactly the same point: "The phenomenon of life takes time to develop, and until it is actually present, it cannot be destroyed. Its interruption prior to formation would hardly be homicide, and as we have seen, society does not regard it as such." In the early days of legislative reform, Clark expected that striking the balance between the fetal and maternal interests would lead states to set viability as the dividing line.[28] The American Law Institute (ALI) published its Model Penal Code in 1961, which included broad exceptions, for medical abortion. The logic of the code, which included social and mental health grounds as well as rape and incest, obviously made fetal life a far from absolute value.

Williams also defined the reform campaign's sense of history. Abortion, he argued, had been widely practiced in all historical periods, but rarely had it been considered a serious crime. Traditionally penalties had been imposed only for abortion after quickening, and they were rarely enforced. Nineteenth-century moralists had criminalized the time-honored practice of women procuring their own early abortions. The modern reform would only restore the ancient law.

These ideas routinely informed the American debate. Lawrence Lader set them out in his 1966 polemic, *Abortion.*[29] They prefaced Justice Blackmun's opinion in *Roe v. Wade.*[30] They were also deployed unsuccessfully to defend Sydney doctors from criminal prosecution. While they did not help legal interpretation very much, they performed a similar function everywhere. This history was designed to minimize the sense that legalizing abortion departed radically from traditional values. It provided a usable past.[31]

III

The new consensus on abortion had been building for more than a decade in all three countries before abortion was fully legalized. The increasingly casual reliance on the rubric of therapeutic abortion blurred the line between medical and social need.[32] Abortion became more acceptable because it furthered social justice. The medical profession in Britain, Australia, and the United States now provided the varnish of respectability for the once-dubious practice of abortion.[33]

The discovery in Australia that exposure to rubella damaged the fetus greatly increased the number of therapeutic abortions in the late 1950s and early 1960s. The thalidomide scandal in Britain further dramatized the need for reform. Public opinion overwhelmingly approved abortion for fetal deformity.[34] Therapeutic abortion depended on maintaining a discreet silence. In 1962 Sherri Finkbine, the star of a children's television show in Phoenix, Arizona, sought an abortion because she had inadvertently taken thalidomide. The child would in all likelihood be deformed. In the glare of the publicity she attracted, the hospital reversed its decision to perform the abortion. With only fetal damage to justify the procedure, the district attorney refused to promise that he would not prosecute. In the end, Finkbine flew to Sweden, where the pregnancy was aborted.[35]

The rubella epidemic in San Francisco created another crisis for hospital committees. They had routinely processed the numerous requests, but one member of the California State Board of Medical Examiners, Dr. James McNulty, demanded an investigation. Disciplinary charges were brought against two doctors. The San Francisco Medical Society immediately voted by a margin of 10 to 1 to support reform. The California Medical Association had been considering its abortion policy, but the prosecutions goaded it into action. A reform bill providing a range of medical grounds for therapeutic abortion finally became law in 1967.[36]

If the law was to meet the new demands, to adjust to changed attitudes, and to account for the more open availability of abortions, reform had to be legislated or the courts had to make new law. In Britain, a progressive coalition finally succeeded in pushing a major reform bill through Parliament. In Australia, the politicians took the line of least resistance. They generally refused to endorse reform but made only token efforts to reverse legal rulings that shielded doctors from the criminal law.

The reform movement in the United States had pushed some states to adopt more liberal abortion laws, usually modeled on the broad therapeutic exceptions of ALI's Model Penal Code. American politicians also tried to avoid identifying with either side, but abortion eventually became entangled in partisan politics. After 1973 *Roe v. Wade* provided the most visible target for opponents of reform. By the 1980s the Republican party was committed to reversing the decision; Democrats responded by promising to defend, judicially and legislatively, a woman's right to choose.

Between 1953 and 1966 four attempts to liberalize British abortion laws had petered out. In 1966 a bill introduced by Liberal member David Steel formed the basis for reform as the Abortion Act of 1967. The bill was designed to deal with widespread illegal abortion and the farcical use of the therapeutic exception. Proponents of the bill vehemently denied that it would result in abortion on demand. The BMA opposed the rape clause, fearing it would become the loophole for any women seeking an abortion. The BMA and the Royal College of Obstetricians and Gynaecologists opposed any kind of social clause because they saw it as another invitation to abortion on demand. Steel, however, insisted on the social clause to end the hypocritical reliance on mental health grounds.

The central issue then became how to define the social grounds. The legislative formula emerged in the Lords' debate when Lord Parker suggested that the law should allow abortion if, considering the total environment, the procedure was less dangerous than allowing the pregnancy to continue.[37] Parker thought this amendment would limit abortion to the most serious cases. In fact, early abortion *was* safe, and this social clause quickly became the *pro forma* grounds for wide access to abortion.

Opponents of reform such as Norman St. John-Stevas predicted that the social clause would translate into abortion on demand, and they were proved correct. Medical organizations had finally supported the reform because they believed it protected their professional discretion and gave them a controlling role. Many general practitioners, however, soon provided abortion services on request. Specialists acted more conservatively. By 1969 doctors were admitting that they had not expected the Abortion Act to operate as it did in practice.[38]

Australian politicians of most ideological persuasions shunned abortion reform. Only South Australia modeled its law on the British Abortion Act, and it legislated reform with bipartisan support in a conscience vote.[39] Abortion was legalized in New South Wales and Victoria even though the conservative (Liberal–Country Party coalition) administrations in those states set themselves against any reform.

Formal government opposition to reform owed as much to political convenience as to moral conviction. The conservative parties needed the continued support of the Democratic Labor Party (DLP), a splinter group that had broken from the Labor Party (ALP) in the 1950s over Communist influence in the trade unions. Socially conservative Catholic voters dominated the DLP; they steadfastly opposed abortion reform. Some reform leaders belonged to the ALP, but the party also had a significant constituency of working-class Catholics. In the interests of unity, that party consistently refused to take any position on abortion.

The lobbying activities of the Abortion Law Reform Society and the increased use of therapeutic abortion in Sydney and Melbourne demanded some response if the state governments were to prove their good faith in enforcing the abortion laws. Police began prosecuting doctors known to offer abortion services. Paradoxically, these trials unraveled the criminal abortion statutes. They legalized abortion, like the *Roe* decision, as a matter of medical discretion.

Judicial "reform" came in Victoria in 1969. Justice Menhennitt dramatically reinterpreted the criminal statute to the advantage of an accused doctor.[40] Expanding on Bourne's case, the judge relied on the word "unlawfully" to surmise that some abortions had to be lawful. He then read the statute in the light of the doctrine of necessity. That was to say, some criminal actions might be lawful if legally necessary. This usually meant self-defense. Menhennitt extended it to include the honest belief of the doctor that the abortion was "necessary" to prevent a greater mischief, such as damage to the patient's mental health. With these instructions, the jury acquitted the doctor on all counts.

This creative use of the necessity doctrine opened a very broad loophole. In effect, it legalized the burgeoning underground of "therapeutic" abortion for social reasons. Doctors relied on their professional status to support abortion as medically necessary. The Victorian government made no attempt to appeal Menhennitt's ruling, because it suited their immediate political ends to claim that the ruling was much narrower than in fact it was. So long as this remained a lower court ruling, they could leave the criminal law on the books and pretend that it was being enforced. They could argue that the ruling did not amount to abortion on demand, even though it plainly gave doctors complete discretion over the decision.

A racketeering scandal in 1969 paralyzed the Victorian government's will to enforce the abortion statutes. Some Melbourne doctors alleged that they had been bribing police for fifteen years. When the abortionists refused to cooperate with the police investigation, the government was forced to appoint a special board to investigate.[41] The inquiry resulted in months of revelations about the corrupt abortion trade. Headlines such as "Ex-policeman 'ran crime syndicate' " and "Inspector tells of lunch with abortionist" appeared regularly.[42] Police had warned doctors of pending raids, advised them to prepare bogus medical records, and coached them on diverting police suspicion. The inquiry provided a catalog of information dramatically illustrating the claims of abortion reformers: doctors did perform illegal abortions for large fees, the law was unenforceable, and abortion had become a thriving but sordid business.

A similar, if less dramatic, turn of legal events nullified the New South

Wales abortion laws. The conservative government would have happily left the issue alone, but it too had to pay lip service to enforcing the law. A squad of thirty police was maintained to investigate abortionists. Few prosecutions resulted, but in September 1971 three doctors were tried for procuring abortions.[43] Police rarely became involved unless patients died or suffered injury, and this was the first trial for an abortion to which the patient consented. The prosecution was designed to rein in medical abortions.[44] Again the trial judge ambushed the prosecutors.

The defense used two strategies. Jim Staples, representing the owners of the clinic, argued that at common law abortion was not a crime unless the woman was harmed. He asked the court to overrule Bourne's and Davidson's cases and read the statute as an addendum to the ancient common law, articulated by Sir William Blackstone, which treated abortion very leniently until "quickening."[45] Judge Andrew Levine replied that would not "indulge in any judicial legislation" but would simply construe the statute. Such a ruling would have dramatically reinterpreted and effectively overturned the criminal laws.

Sir Jack Cassidy, representing Dr. Wald, employed a different strategy. He relied on the modern cases to assert that abortion was lawful if performed skillfully by a qualified practitioner, with the woman's consent and on reasonable grounds. Echoing the litany of social causes, he argued that

> [the women] had exhibited the social, economic and domestic factors that contributed to mental and physical health—uncertainty as to the future, financial hardship, trouble with past pregnancies, disgrace attending an illegitimate child and fear of an unwanted pregnancy. The doctors stood well within the law for they honestly believed beyond a reasonable doubt that in each particular case a termination of pregnancy was necessary for the health of the woman.[46]

The defense emphasized the clinic's scrupulously high standards. Patients testified about their distressed circumstances and personal anguish. Cassidy reminded the jury that the Crown had to prove that the abortion was unlawful.

Judge Levine construed the law very favorably for the defendants. Society, he asserted, had an interest in "the preservation of the human species," and the word "unlawfully" in the statute might "well afford a safeguard to implement the society interest." He fully accepted the reading of the statute offered by the doctors' lawyers: "In my view it would be for the jury to decide whether there existed in the case of each woman any economic, social or medical ground or reason which in their view could constitute reasonable grounds upon which an accused could honestly and reasonably believe there would result a serious danger to her physical or mental health."[47]

The judge still sent the case to the jury because prosecution evidence suggested that the clinic's business was abortion, not general practice. Fees were paid in cash without receipts and the account books contained irregularities. One defendant referred a constant stream of patients to the clinic, and they invariably received abortions. The doctors were acquitted. Like the Melbourne case, this verdict left abortion to the discretion of the medical profession.

Again the state government acted as if the law were unchanged. One acquittal did not threaten the prohibition on abortion. The premier, Robert Askin, immediately announced that his administration would not amend the abortion laws to accommodate more liberal attitudes. He announced that the cabinet was "against legalised abortion" and would "not alter the present law." The police, Askin told Parliament, would investigate all abortionists.[48] But "the present law" was a duplicitous phrase because Judge Levine had given that law a very liberal interpretation, which led the jury to acquit the doctors.

The police tried to make the law enforceable by prosecuting a specialist gynecologist. They targeted Dr. George Smart, who was known to offer abortion services. Twenty-three separate charges were filed that suggested Smart was a professional abortionist. Again Sir Jack Cassidy led the defense; again he worked the themes of abortion reform into his argument.

Cassidy wanted to persuade the jurors that his client was more than a mercenary, exploitative abortionist. The legal test, he told the court, was the "belief of the medical practitioner." Smart's academic credentials were impeccable. Cassidy reminded the jury that the patients, whatever their present demeanor, had all been troubled when Smart first saw them. Performing an abortion had been an integral part of their recovery. He even excused Smart's abortion practice by telling the jury that the doctor had treated many women whose illegal abortions had been botched. In Cassidy's telling, Smart became a hero who never stopped helping patients.[49]

The prosecution case followed the usual routine to discredit the doctor. Smart had no interest in the women's health. He had told police "cold-blooded, deliberate lies" about his appointments schedule and about checks in his possession. The Crown alleged that Smart charged three to five times the standard fee for a therapeutic abortion.[50] Such rates automatically cast doubt on the doctor's good faith.

The jury reported after six hours' deliberation that it could not reach a unanimous verdict. Judge Alf Goran blamed the mistrial on the long and complicated case. "The issues were such," he commented, "that it affected different people with different opinions."[51] In reality, the jury was hung because its members could not agree to convict a specialist gynecologist who was operating on consenting women. Smart had performed the acts with which he was charged, but the jury refused to convict. It had nullified the abortion laws. With two such strikes, the attorney general decided to drop all charges.[52] For partisan purposes, the government continued to pay lip service to the law, but those sections of the Crimes Act had become a dead letter.

IV

This comparative perspective suggests that *Roe v. Wade* brought American law into line with developments elsewhere in the English-speaking world. The ideas underpinning that decision had been used in Britain and Australia to effect reform. The doctrine of privacy derived from *Griswold v. Connecticut* made abortion a constitutional issue,[53] but the other elements of the decision reflected medical experience and legal values like those of Britain and Australia.

Most obviously, *Roe* relied on the doctor-patient relationship to regulate abortion on demand. Justice Blackmun discussed professional attitudes toward abortion at some length. He recounted the American Medical Association's policies on abortion; in 1967 it finally endorsed therapeutic reform. After much divisive debate, the AMA amended its code of ethics in 1970 to leave the decision to "the best medical judgment." The Court took this medical route to repeal the ban on early abortion.[54]

The Court discounted the idea that abortion statutes would either discourage illicit sex or protect women from a dangerous procedure. The Court then endorsed the third possible rationale—the state's limited right to protect the potential life of the fetus. The opinion explicitly rejected both the view that life began at conception and the idea that only the woman's interest could legally be protected. There were different interests, and the Court had to decide how to weigh each one. The Court would not extend Fourteenth Amendment protection to the fetus; irrespective of constitutional doctrine, that lack of personhood embodied the reformer's thinking about the fetus before viability. It also followed the common-law tradition that full legal rights depended on live birth.

The right of privacy covered the abortion decision, Blackmun wrote, but "the right . . . is not absolute and is subject to some limitations; . . . at some point, the state interests as to protection of health, medical standards, and prenatal life become dominant." This inadvertently echoed Macnaghten's dictum in Bourne's case that the law neither prohibited abortion entirely nor left it unrestricted.[55]

Both the medical literature and professional experience set the balance of interests where Blackmun's opinion did.[56] Both state and federal courts had struck down abortion statutes under the rubric of privacy.[57] Privacy was held to be a fundamental right that could be abridged only for a compelling state interest. Viability provided that compelling state interest. The Court rejected claims that fetal rights constituted an all (Texas) or nothing (*Roe*) proposition. In form, it endorsed a middle path in the trimester framework.

The Court left first-trimester abortion to private medical decision because it was safer than childbirth. Abortion in the second trimester could be regulated to protect women's health. The Court declared: "Up to those points the abortion decision in all its aspects is inherently, and primarily, a medical decision, and basic responsibility for it must rest with the physician. If an individual practitioner abuses the privilege of exercising proper medical judgment, the usual remedies, judicial and intra-professional, are available."[58] Only after viability did the traditional restrictions meet constitutional standards. Like the *Roe* decision, the British legislation had made abortion readily available before viability. This issue was not well articulated in Australia. The prosecutors in Sydney and Melbourne assumed, however, that the doctors had performed the procedures in accordance with sound medical practice. That meant early termination.[59]

The *Roe* majority relied on varied reasoning.[60] William O. Douglas wrote a libertarian treatise on constitutional privacy.[61] The medical framework in the Court's opinion included suggestions from William Brennan and Thurgood Marshall. Potter Stewart's concurrence insisted that *Roe* would not bring back the bad old days of substantive due process, because criminal abortion laws were "a broad abridgment of personal liberty."[62] Chief Justice Burger expounded his naive view that the medical profession would not countenance abortion on demand.[63] None of this strengthened the doctrinal claims of *Roe v. Wade,* but it did reflect the diversity of opinion supporting reform.

However legalization came about, it centered on the professional competence of the practitioner. This remained constant whether the Supreme Court of the United States,[64] the British Parliament, or the Australian criminal courts with the tacit consent of state government reformed the law. The 1967 British law embraced the medical policy openly, but the same thinking underpinned judicial legalization in Australia and the United States.

Designating abortion a medical decision was sufficiently ambiguous to create majority coalitions irrespective of the institutional context. It attracted seven justices of the Supreme Court, who did not think unanimously on the issue. Subsequent decisions have illustrated the instability of the *Roe* coalition. Access to abortion generally commanded a majority on the Court, but the *Roe* majority soon disagreed on that case's significance for issues such as parental consent and medical regulation.[65] The funding cases tore the original majority asunder.[66]

Legalized abortion in Britain and Australia shared that ambivalence. Opponents of abortion regularly decried the advent of abortion on demand under the Abortion Act but were never able to muster sufficient support to restore the *status quo ante.* Elected officials in Australia consistently refused to repeal abortion laws but paid only lip service to enforcing them.[67]

Similar values produced similar policies to legalize abortion. *Roe v. Wade* was one of three routes to reform. Whatever the institutional differences, a generation of campaigning to make abortion a personal choice resulted in the medical "compromise." Judges and politicians always rejected an absolute personal right to choose, but they achieved almost the same thing when they sanctioned the modern doctor-patient relationship.

Monash University

Notes

1. *Roe v. Wade,* 93 S.Ct. 705 (1973). *Roe* invalidated old criminal statutes. Its companion case, *Doe v. Bolton,* 93 S.Ct. 739 (1973), invalidated laws creating a narrow therapeutic exception; both infringed the right to privacy. Here the common rubric "*Roe*" includes both decisions.

2. *Roe v. Wade,* 763.

3. John Hart Ely, "The Wages of Crying Wolf: A Comment on *Roe v. Wade,*" *Yale Law Journal* 82 (April 1973): 937.

4. Testimony on S. 158, Human Life Bill, May 1981, in J. Douglas Butler and David F. Walbert, *Abortion, Medicine, and the Law,* 3d ed. (New York, 1986), 542.

5. *Webster v. Reproductive Health Services,* 109 S.Ct. 3040 (1989), 3073–74.

6. Unenumerated rights are not in the text of the Bill of Rights, but they are said to be implicit in the enumerated rights or in the structure of government. *Roe*'s constitutional basis is debated in Ronald Dworkin, "Unenumerated Rights: Whether and How *Roe* Should Be Overruled," and Richard A. Posner, "Legal Reasoning from the Top Down and from the Bottom Up: The Question of Unenumerated Constitutional Rights," in Geoffrey

R. Stone, Richard A. Epstein, and Cass R. Sunstein, eds., *The Bill of Rights in the Modern State* (Chicago, 1992), 381–450.

7. Mary Ann Glendon, *Abortion and Divorce in Western Law* (Cambridge, Mass., 1987), 2–20, 52–58.

8. Laurence H. Tribe, *Abortion: The Clash of Absolutes* (New York, 1990), 51–52, 73–112. The gulf between the two sides is irreconcilable, but public opinion supports choice and privacy while rejecting "abortion on demand." On the divisive nature of the issue, see Kristin Luker, *Abortion and the Politics of Motherhood* (Berkeley and Los Angeles, 1984); Faye Ginsburg, *Contested Lives: The Abortion Debate in an American Community* (Berkeley and Los Angeles, 1989); and James Davison Hunter, *Culture Wars: The Struggle to Define America* (New York, 1991), 33–34, 42–51, 96–158. On public opinion, see Rosalind Pollack Petchesky, *Abortion and Woman's Choice: The State, Sexuality, and Reproductive Freedom*, rev. ed. (Boston, 1990), xxv, and E. J. Dionne Jr., "Poll Finds Ambivalence Persists on Abortion in U.S.," *New York Times*, 3 August 1989.

9. Before reform, the moral debate was very bitter in Australia and England. Political and legal structure has sustained the controversy in the United States, but not in the parliamentary systems. See my forthcoming essay, "A Slightly Old-Fashioned Analysis of the Legalized Abortion Controversy."

10. Offences Against the Person Act, 1861, 24 and 25 Vic., c. 100; Crimes Act, 1900, ss. 82–84 (N.S.W.); Crimes Act, 1958, ss. 65–66 (Victoria); Texas Penal Code, Arts. 1191 and 1196; Infant Life (Preservation) Act, 1929, 19 and 20 Geo. 5, c. 34.

11. Marian Faux, *Roe v. Wade: The Untold Story of the Landmark Supreme Court Decision That Made Abortion Legal* (New York, 1989), 33–38. In 1968 a Texas Medical Association study appeared that recommended reform to clarify the legal situation. The report included a survey of hospitals which reported that 81 abortions had been performed for fetal indications and one each for rape and incest, although all were, strictly speaking, illegal. See Appellants' Brief, *Roe v. Wade* (1973), in *Landmark Briefs and Arguments of the Supreme Court of the United States: Constitutional Law* 75, Philip B. Kurland and Gerhard Casper, eds. (Arlington, Va., 1975), 122.

12. *R. v. Bourne* [1939] 1 K.B. 687.

13. *Peacock v. King* (1911) 13 CLR, 619.

14. *R. v. Trim* (1943) Argus Law Reports, 236. The appeals court ruled that the claim was not credible enough even to be presented to the jury.

15. *R. v. Newton, Criminal Law Review* (1958), 469, and J. D. J. Havard, "Therapeutic Abortion," *Criminal Law Review* (1958): 600–613. The patient had requested an interuterine injection of utus paste, which led to the infection that killed her.

16. Glanville Williams, *The Sanctity of Life and the Criminal Law* (London, 1958), 155–60.

17. Alan F. Guttmacher, "The Genesis of Liberalized Abortion in New York: A Personal Insight," in Butler and Walbert, *Abortion, Medicine, and the Law*, 230–32.

18. Glanville Williams, "Legal and Illegal Abortion," *British Journal of Criminology* 4 (October 1964): 562–63. These practices were openly discussed in the *British Medical Journal*, which led Williams to conclude that the police had stopped prosecuting doctors who performed abortions for medical reasons. Lord Denning, Master of the Rolls (chief judge of the Court of Appeal), had told doctors in 1956 that abortion for fetal deformity was permissible, but he gave no legal reason. See *British Medical Journal* 2 (1956): 811.

19. Cited in Williams, *Sanctity of Life*, 162.

20. Tom C. Clark, "Religion, Morality and Abortion: A Constitutional Appraisal," *Loyola University Law Review* 2 (1969): 6.

21. Appellants' Brief, *Roe v. Wade*, 102. Roe's poverty obviated the state's claiming that she might have traveled interstate for her abortion.

22. Amicus Brief, *Roe v. Wade*, in *Landmark Briefs and Arguments of the Supreme Court of the United States*, 344.

23. Williams, "Legal and Illegal Abortion," 557.
24. Williams, *Sanctity of Life*, 212.
25. Jack Rosenthal, "Population Panel Warns Growth Must Be Slowed," *New York Times*, 12 March 1972.
26. Appellants' Brief, *Roe v. Wade*, 123–26.
27. *Poelker v. Doe* 97 S.Ct. 2391 (1977), 2395 and 2398.
28. Clark, "Religion, Morality and Abortion," 9–11.
29. Lawrence Lader, *Abortion* (Indianapolis, 1966), 75–77.
30. *Roe v. Wade*, 715–21. Scholars and activists have debated the historical significance of abortion. James Mohr's *Abortion in America: The Origins and Evolution of National Policy, 1800–1900* (New York, 1978) argued that abortion was only criminalized in the nineteenth century when doctors wanted to protect morals and enhance their status. Joseph Dellapenna argued that abortion has always attracted serious legal penalties, in Dellapenna, "The History of Abortion: Technology, Morality, and Law," *University of Pittsburgh Law Review* 40 (Spring 1979): 359–428. Whichever history is "correct," it is surely significant that Williams set out these ideas fifteen years before Blackmun incorporated them into the Court's opinion in *Roe v. Wade*.
31. Williams in 1958 and Blackmun in 1973 discounted Jane Roe's argument (Appellants' Brief, *Roe v. Wade*, 103–23) that the criminal statutes were designed to protect the mother. New knowledge about the fetus encouraged laws to protect it.
32. In England the National Health Service performed 2,300 abortions in 1961 but 9,700 abortions in 1967. The number of private clinic abortions rose even more dramatically. See Victoria Greenwood and Jock Young, *Abortion in Demand* (London, 1976), 20–21.
33. Although it eventually became an ideological mainstay of "choice," feminism played a small role in legalizing abortion. Betty Friedan, *The Feminine Mystique* (London, 1963) criticized conventional views of women's role, but abortion was not explicitly on her agenda. Kate Millett alluded to the criminalization of abortion as a symptom of patriarchy. See Millett, *Feminist Politics* (London: 1972), 44, 54. Germaine Greer ignored the issue. Family limitation was for her an unhealthy sign of modern capitalist values that had destroyed authentic sexuality in favor of consumption. See Greer, *The Female Eunuch* (London, 1970), 232–38.
34. Keith Hindell and Madeleine Simms, "How the Abortion Lobby Worked," *Political Quarterly* 39 (July 1968): 273.
35. The doctor and hospital sought a declaratory judgment to protect themselves, but the court found no justiciable issue. See Faux, *Roe v. Wade*, 45–54, and Luker, *Politics of Motherhood*, 62–65.
36. Faux, *Roe v. Wade*, 59–65. The California statute did not, however, authorize abortion for fetal deformity.
37. Greenwood and Young, *Abortion*, 23–30.
38. T. L. T. Lewis, "The Abortion Act," *British Medical Journal* 25 (1969): 241–42.
39. Section 82A, Criminal Code Consolidation Act (S.A.).
40. *R. v. Davidson* [1969] V.R. 667.
41. *Report of the Board of Inquiry into Allegations of Corruption in the Police Force in Connection with Illegal Abortion Practices in the State of Victoria*, 31 August 1970.
42. *The Australian*, 7 March 1970 and 14 March 1970.
43. *R. v. Wald* [1971] 3 NSWDCR 25.
44. Frances McLean, "NSW Courts and the law on abortion," *Sydney Morning Herald*, 30 October 1971.
45. Ibid.
46. "Word 'unlawful' is Vital—Defence," *Sydney Morning Herald*, 21 October 1971.
47. *R. v. Wald*, 29.
48. "Doctors, Govt Will Study Abortion Hearing Verdict," *Sydney Morning Herald*, 30

October 1971, and "Askin: No 'Open Go' on Abortion," *Sydney Morning Herald,* 3 November 1971.

49. "QC Outlines Legal Test of Abortion," *Sydney Morning Herald,* 10 October 1972.

50. "Abortion Doctor's Job—QC," *Sydney Morning Herald,* 11 October 1972.

51. "Abortion Jury Can't Decide," (Sydney) *Daily Telegraph,* 13 October 1972.

52. *It's Nobody's Baby: Documented Facts About Abortion* (Sydney, 1973), 25.

53. 85 S.Ct. 1678 (1965). In *Griswold* the Court struck down Connecticut's Comstock-era law prohibiting the use of contraceptives. It infringed constitutionally protected privacy.

54. *Roe v. Wade,* 721–24. The American Public Health Association and the American Bar Association had both endorsed a similar policy.

55. *Roe v. Wade,* 726 and 728; *R. v. Bourne,* 693.

56. Blackmun read the medical literature before he wrote the decision. See Faux, *Roe v. Wade,* 276–88. Law journal articles had canvased extending the right of privacy to abortion. One author, Roy Lucas, had been active in litigating the abortion issue. See Lucas, "Federal Constitutional Limitations on the Enforcement and Administration of State Abortion Laws," *North Carolina Law Review* 46 (June 1968): 730–78, and Clark, "Religion, Morality and Abortion," 7–9.

57. When *Roe* was decided, federal courts had struck down abortion laws in Connecticut, Georgia, Illinois, Kansas, New Jersey, and Wisconsin. The Connecticut legislature reenacted the statute, and the federal court again struck it down. Federal courts in Kentucky, Louisiana, North Carolina, Ohio, and Utah had upheld those states' statutes. State courts had also ruled both ways on claims of privacy invoked to invalidate criminal abortion laws.

58. *Roe v. Wade,* 733. Blackmun's opinion explained at length the traditional view that live birth was required for legal personhood. He addressed the issue because Texas had argued that the fetus enjoyed Fourteenth Amendment protection from conception. Lower courts upholding state statutes had accepted this argument. In rejecting that view, the Court's opinion stood on the common law that underpinned British and Australian decisions.

59. The only conviction of a licensed medical practitioner in New South Wales since 1971 occurred in 1981, when Dr. Smart, suffering from Parkinson's disease and near bankruptcy, botched a late-term abortion. "Doctor Put on Bond for Abortion Conviction," *The Australian,* March 31 1981.

60. The best accounts of the convoluted process by which the decision was finally made are Bob Woodward and Scott Armstrong, *The Brethren: Inside the Supreme Court* (New York, 1981), 193–223, 271–84, and Faux, *Roe v. Wade,* 263–312. Woodward and Armstrong overemphasize the horse-trading process and quote clerks who decried the decision as social legislation. On the whole, though, the positions they attribute to the justices comport well with the public record.

61. *Roe v. Wade,* 756–62.

62. *Roe v. Wade,* 733–36.

63. *Roe v. Wade,* 755–56.

64. For a critique of the role accorded the medical profession, see Ruth Bader Ginsberg, "Some Thoughts on Autonomy and Equality in Relation to *Roe v. Wade,*" *North Carolina Law Review* 63 (January 1985): 375–86.

65. *Planned Parenthood of Central Missouri v. Danforth* 96 S.Ct. 2831 (1976) and *Colautti v. Franklin* 99 S.Ct. 675 (1979).

66. *Beal v. Doe* 97 S.Ct. 2366 (1977); *Maher v. Roe* 97 S.Ct. 2376 (1977); *Poelker v. Doe; Harris v. McRae* 100 S.Ct. 2671 (1980)

67. For the repeal effort in Britain, see John Keown, *Abortion, Doctors, and the Law: Some Aspects of the Legal Regulation of Abortion in England from 1803 to 1982* (New York, 1988). On these issues generally, see my "Slightly Old-Fashioned Analysis"

JOHN SHARPLESS

World Population Growth, Family Planning, and American Foreign Policy

The U.S. government position on world population growth as it emerged in the early 1960s was a fundamental departure in both content and commitment. We embraced the idea that one of the goals of American foreign policy should be the simultaneous reduction of *both* mortality and fertility across the Third World. It was not simply rhetoric. As the years passed, we committed a growing portion of our foreign aid to that end. The decision to link U.S. foreign-policy objectives with the subsidy of family planning and population control was truly exceptional in that it explicitly aimed at altering the demographic structure of foreign countries through long-term intervention. No nation had ever set in motion a foreign-policy initiative of such magnitude. Its ultimate goal was no less than to alter the basic fertility behavior of the entire Third World! Whether one views this goal as idealistic and naive or as arrogant and self-serving, the project was truly of herculean proportions.

It should not be surprising therefore that U.S. assistance for family planning programs overseas has engendered sharp opposition both at home and abroad. Initially it was fear of foreign domination and the implicit racist implication of such an initiative that brought an angry reaction from overseas. As time passed, hostility toward family planning declined across much of the Third World. As opposition declined overseas, however, the political forces opposing the subsidation of family planning programs in the United States increased. Ironically, domestic opposition forced a major reevaluation of U.S. policy in the Reagan administration at the same time worldwide support for population planning was finding its greatest support. More recently, with the election of Bill Clinton to the presidency, the policy pendulum has swung in the other direction with renewed support for expanded family planning efforts.[1]

In order to understand the shifting currents of controversy over the direction of U.S. population policy, it is necessary to gain a deeper historical perspective on the interrelationship between family planning, global resource utilization, and U.S. foreign policy since 1945. The reactions of policymakers to empirical information on population dynamics must be understood in terms of four historical and contextual dimensions:

1. The deep legacies of various "population ideologies" going back to the nineteenth century and merging, in the twentieth century, to form an uneasy mix of science, morality, and political economy.
2. The overriding constraints of American foreign policy in the postwar era, particularly our ongoing presumptions about the role of Third World nations in America's Cold War ideology.
3. The continuing domestic debate over feminism, birth control, abortion, and what might be called "the politics of the family."
4. And, after the late 1960s, a growing awareness of the global implications of environmental degradation and resource depletion.

Prelude to Policy: Defining the "Population Problem," 1935–1958

The strategic implications of population growth in the balance-of-power equation have seldom gone unacknowledged by diplomats, generals, or politicians. In the late nineteenth and early twentieth centuries, for example, the foreign-policy elites of France, Germany, and Great Britain voiced apprehension over their declining fertility relative to that of their economic and political rivals.[2] The savage consequences of two bloody wars aggravated these concerns.

There is also a deeper, more subtle influence that demographic issues can have on the ongoing processes of foreign-policy decisionmaking. Less formulated, and more a matter of nationalistic ideology, the issue of population growth and national destiny can carry strong components of racial and ethnic bigotry. Although seldom using the technical language of the demographer, advocates of territorial expansion have often appealed vaguely to "internal" population pressures as limiting national growth and welfare. They assert that expansion is both necessary and inevitable. In the absence of expansion, political disorder, starvation, and death will follow. When the "national demographic destiny" is thwarted, racial extinction is the only possible outcome.

Beyond expansionary militarism, the traditional response to perceived "demographic deficits" usually takes the form of domestic programs to stimulate population growth, such as promoting pronatalist, family-oriented legislation, limiting access to birth control and abortion, or placing restrictions on emigration.[3] Less frequently, governments promote immigration schemes to bolster the ranks of soldiers and workers. (The latter option, however, often gave rise to racist claims that the "national blood" was being weakened.) On the other hand, directly affecting the size of the foreign populations was extremely difficult. Short of engaging in a war of attrition (which carries obvious consequences for one's own population), one could only appeal to the gods for plague and famine to befall your adversaries (which, if we believe Greek tragedies, may fail to generate the desired results as well).

Not surprisingly, therefore, "home, hearth, and family" were primary components in the social ideology of nationalist rhetoric. Strong pro-family arguments buttressed support for most health and social services legislation. Moreover, because much of this assistance was aimed at mothers and children, the net effect was to encourage larger families. In Canada, for example, the Mothers' Allowance Act was expanded in 1948 to the Family Allowance Act, which paid a monthly benefit to all families with children under the age of eighteen. Similarly, in the United States, the end of World War II brought a renewed emphasis on the American family. Following the unprecedented recruitment of women into the civilian labor force during the war, both government and industry leaders expended considerable effort encouraging female workers to return to the role of housewife and mother. The media portrayed women as happy homemakers caring for their children in the suburbs while their husbands toiled in factories and offices. It was more than simply domestic propaganda, however, that led Americans back to the family and fertility. The tax code heavily favored families with children, as did the subsidized home-loan programs. While there was clearly more than government policy at work, the "baby boom" of the immediate postwar certainly was aided and abetted by public-policy incentives.[4]

At the same time, the distribution of birth control was illegal throughout most of Europe and America. This had been the case, of course, for decades. And while these laws were infrequently enforced, they did serve to suppress open debate on the issue. Of equal importance, however, was the lack of truly effective means of birth control. Poorly funded and operating under a cloud of suspicion, research to find an effective and safe means of contraception was still years away from success. (At this point, induced abortion was universally illegal.)

Although the birth-control movements in Britain, Canada, and the United States had been active for many years, they had made little progress in convincing politicians that the laws should be changed. Clearly, however, there was a subtle shift in public attitudes on the issue of birth control. The declining fertility rates in the two decades prior to the war suggested that most couples had found ways to control family size. Nonetheless, some uneasiness still surrounded public discussion of the subject.

The origins of the birth-control movement lay deep in the nineteenth century and over the years had attracted a variety of adherents. Malthusians, utopian socialists, activists for women's rights, civil libertarians, and advocates of sexual freedom all rallied to the cause. While they may not have shared a common goal, they could agree that open and free access to contraceptive information would produce positive benefits for both the individual and society. The major obstacle at the time was restrictive legislation that not only barred the distribution of birth-control devices but also restrained individuals from disseminating information about birth control and sexual reproduction. And so, much of the early effort of the birth-control crusaders was limited to litigation and legislative reform.

In the 1930s, however, the birth-control movement underwent major changes in both its ideology and its goals. The crusaders for unrestricted access to contraception such as Margaret Sanger no longer simply argued that laws limiting the distribution of birth control should be repealed (that was to be expected) but went on to advocate the inclusion of contraceptive education in New Deal maternal and child health programs.[5] Indeed, advocates of family planning in the Roosevelt administration succeeded briefly in establishing government-sponsored birth-control programs in Puerto Rico, but opposition quickly forced Ernest Gruening, the chief administrator of Territories and Trusts, to abandon the program.[6] Nonetheless, this subtle shift in the nature of the debate over birth control was to have a decisive impact in the postwar period. Increasingly the discussion was not over the issue of birth control per se, but whether it was appropriate for governments to sponsor its distribution.

At the same time (and perhaps linked to this shift in emphasis) was a growing internationalization of the birth-control movement. Birth-control advocates sought new adherents in India and Asia. Margaret Sanger expanded her itinerary to include India, Japan, and the Far East. While she was not always welcomed by government officials, she did find growing support among reform-minded elites.[7] In 1935 the National Planning Committee of the Indian National Congress, headed by Jawaharlal Nehru, adopted a resolution supporting the idea of state-sponsored birth-control programs.[8] Subsequently the Health Survey and Development Committee established by the Indian government would strongly recommend the free distribution of birth control in its influential 1946 report on the state of health in India.[9] Perhaps not surprisingly, Bombay was the site of the founding of International Planned Parenthood in 1952.

Equally important on the academic side, a small but growing literature on world population problems predicted an "impending population crisis" in India, Japan, and China.[10] In fact, with the consistent decline in fertility levels in Europe and America, it was only in the non-European world that the Malthusians could find support for their antinatalist arguments. Their concerns seemed to be confirmed by colonial officials who increasingly viewed rapid population growth as detrimental to effective colonial policy.[11]

In the immediate postwar political environment, however, open debate on birth control was still considered outside political discourse. Among many conservatives it was still identified with leftist radicalism; among liberals it was associated with the rhetorical excesses of the prewar eugenics movements. But the forces for change were at hand.

The 1940s brought important changes in what might be called the self-image of the birth-control movement as it evolved into the "planned parenthood" campaigns of the 1950s. The changes were not merely in name only among the various advocacy groups or simply a public relations gimmick. There was a slow evolution in ideology, which increasingly separated the image of birth control from its past (apparently so tainted by radicalism and feminism). A more genteel image of family planning was incorporated into a mythology of responsible middle-class family life, divorcing it from its more radical feminist roots.[12]

By the early 1950s, therefore, the issue of access to contraception could be legitimately discussed in two ways. At the aggregate level, it was a mechanism—a technological device—for controlling rapid population growth. The empirical settings for these discussions were usually India, China, Puerto Rico, or Japan. Regardless of whether one agreed or disagreed with the idea that intervention was appropriate or necessary, birth control was discussed in abstract terms, remote from the lives of the women who would be the recipients of such programmatic efforts. Although women's health issues were occasionally mentioned, the primary goal of birth-control advocates in this setting was population stabilization.

Ironically, at the individual level, the discourse shifted to a discussion of the stable, well-ordered suburban American family. In such a setting, the planned parenthood ideology actually served to reinforce the traditional roles of women as homemakers in the patriarchal hierarchy of traditional family life. Contrary to the feminist rhetoric of earlier decades, birth control as "family planning" was not intended to free women to pursue their own destinies. Rather, it would make them more efficient housewives. With fewer children, the homemaker could better attend to the needs of her husband and family. While this position was (perhaps) an important public relations compromise and one that was necessary to legitimize discussions of birth-control use and distribution, it also served to suppress for nearly two decades a confrontation over the role of contraception and abortion in the ongoing debate over the role women in society.

Despite some liberalization of sentiment on the issue of family planning, however, much more would have to happen before policymakers and politicians could embrace the idea of overt intervention to reduce population growth at home or abroad. Such a major shift in public policy required first that population growth be viewed as a problem of major significance. Second, given the priorities of the immediate postwar era, the crisis posed by population growth needed to be linked to national security concerns if massive intervention was to be justified. Third, the experts who advised the policymakers (the demographers, sociologists, and economists) had to be convinced that the problem of rapid population growth was tractable—that intervention had a likely chance of success. And, finally, it had to be determined that the means available to resolve the problem were acceptable and legitimate instruments of public policy.

While public officials were reticent about speaking out on the issue of population control, a growing body of statistical evidence suggested that the world indeed was experiencing unprecedented rates of population growth. The postwar period brought a deluge of demographic data from around the world. Many of the newly emergent nations of Asia attempted the first complete census of their populations. Countries with long-established traditions of census-taking expanded both the breadth of coverage and improved the quality of their enumerations. More advanced methods of statistical analysis improved the quality of population estimates. And perhaps most important, international agencies such as the United Nations published, distributed, and continually updated statistical data on a host of health, economic, and population variables.

As demographic data were collected and analyzed, there could be little doubt that world population was growing rapidly. The accelerated growth of the postcolonial nations combined with the "baby boom" growth surge in developed nations generated unparalleled results. While the fertility surge in the West was generally thought to be a temporary phenomenon, the population growth in Asia, Africa, and Latin America appeared to be a more fundamental problem. According to U.N. data, the annual growth rate of the world's population had remained relatively constant (about 1.0 percent for nearly two decades prior to the war. During that time the "developing regions" had moved slightly ahead of Europe and North America with a growth rate of nearly 1.2 percent. In the 1950s, however, the annual growth rate for the world jumped to 1.8 percent, with the rate for the developing areas exceeding 2.0 percent.

America's preeminent position in world politics and economy at the close of World War II combined with the rising tensions of the Cold War forced strategic planners to confront a variety of military, economic, and political questions, many of which involved some component of population dynamics. There was of course the argument that the war itself was in part driven by population pressures. Both German and Japanese expansionist rhetoric supported this notion. But the facts ran counter to such claims. Germany, Italy, and Imperial Japan had shown signs of a downward movement in their fertility rates, which were only sightly abated by very aggressive pronatalist policies. Nonetheless, the argument did awaken policymakers to the issue and rekindle a discussion on the relationship between population pressures and political violence.[13]

But the population issue emerged elsewhere in postwar policy discussions. For example, there was the problem of limited supplies of strategic materials. By the time the United States became involved in the war, the Axis countries had captured many of the major sources of tin, rubber, and oil or were on the doorstep of controlling the remaining areas. The abundant natural resources of the Americas had made the difference, but the message was clear. The United States had a strategic interest in the utilization of mineral and fuel resources not only at home but *worldwide.* "Conservation"—if you could call it that—became a strategic issue. The growing discord with Russia heightened these concerns because within the vast area of the Soviet Union were found many of the major untapped reserves of fuel and mineral deposits. To balance the resource ledger, policy planners looked to the colonial empires of our European allies.[14]

About the same time, however, another more altruistic argument for the conservation of world resources was being developed outside government circles. In the late 1940s we begin to find some of the seminal ideas that would form the basis of a new environmental movement in the 1960s. Fairfield Osborn's *Our Plundered Planet* and William Vogt's *The Road to Survival* both focused on the problems of overpopulation, resource utilization, carrying capacity, and food production. Osborn was particularly forward looking, predicting many of the detrimental consequences of overdependence on fertilizers and insecticides.[15] He warned that assuming an unending agricultural bounty was both naive and dangerous.

Osborn's critique came in the context of a food/population debate, which had raged since the turn of the century but was rekindled and hotly contested in the years immediately after the war.[16] Many of the leading agriculturalists argued that the introduction of modern farming methods in Asia and the development of high-yield strains would resolve the problem of rising population levels. This argument was a particularly powerful one. Much of our foreign aid (PL-480) in this period (and later) focused on agricultural education and technology assistance supplemented by agricultural commodity transfers. The hope that America could feed the world would briefly allay fears that rapid population growth posed a world crisis. It was presumed that American foreign aid could close the gap while the developing economies of the postcolonial world reached sustained levels of growth.

American Aid, the Developing World, and Population Growth: The Benefactor's Dilemma

In the final analysis, U.S. attempts to assist the economic development of Asia, and subsequently South America and Africa, would bring the issue of population growth to light in all its immediacy. It is not surprising that the issue of population growth emerged so strongly in that period. Donor institutions, both public and private, were forced to confront the possibility that all their aid would be wasted in this rising sea of humanity. Foreign-aid programs expanded into the developing world with Truman's "Point Four" initiative; international agencies increased their support for health and agricultural projects, and a growing number of specialized private relief agencies sought to bring the "gift" of Western technology, knowledge, and expertise to the developing nations of the world. As fast as the international gift-giving grew, however, the needs of developing nations always seemed to outpace the flow of resources.

Outside government circles, the large philanthropic foundations were the first to confront the issue of population growth. Private foundations, such as the Rockefeller, Ford, and Carnegie foundations, sought to redefine their role in this environment of international philanthropic competition.[17] The solutions to problems posed by poverty, deprivation, and political instability appeared less obvious than those confronted by foundations before the war. Addressing population growth in particular posed a much more serious and complicated challenge. In the immediate postwar period, therefore, private foundations quietly sponsored several special missions to Asia and subsidized the occasional pilot projects to test the troubled waters of population control. But the conservative directors of the major foundations remained hesitant to make a full commitment to population assistance despite the recommendations of their staff officers.

Frustrated with this lack of action, a small group of scholars and population-control activists led by John D. Rockefeller III founded the Population Council in 1953. A "special-purpose" foundation, the Population Council subsequently found support from the Ford Foundation and the Rockefeller Brothers Fund. While its official mandate was to support research in both demography and reproductive biology, its unofficial purpose was to promote a consensus among academic, governmental, and cultural elites that population problems were not only pressing but were reaching crisis proportions. Although its directors avoided the inflammatory rhetoric of the birth-control advocacy groups, there was never any doubt about their strong conviction that rapid population growth posed a serious threat to economic and social progress in the developing nations of Asia, Africa, and South America.[18]

The importance of the nonprofit sector in this period cannot be underestimated. Despite their hesitance to sponsor family planning directly, private foundations provided the lion's share of support for demographic research prior to 1960. Perhaps most important for the institutional character of demography were the direct grants to population studies centers established at America's most prestigious universities.[19] This network of centers served to reinforce a tightly bound community of scholars who had worked to legitimize the field in the late 1930s and 1940s.

Indeed what happened in the 1950s was the creation of a worldwide network of "population experts" that had a core body of knowledge and a common mode of discourse. These experts came to share a set of assumptions about how population dynamics worked, how the phenomenon was to be studied, and the terms under which intervention was appropriate. A small but powerful group of scholars forged a consistency in methodology, analysis, and language while at the same time establishing the credibility of demography as a policy science. The power to accomplish this task was based in large part on their relationship with the philanthropic community. Expanded federal funding for population studies after 1962 merely recapitulated and reinforced the agenda established by the foundations, population activists, and academic demographers in the 1950s.

The postwar era therefore brought renewed scholarly interest in population dynamics as sociologists and economists confronted issues of modernization and economic development. There was of course a long tradition of discourse on the economic and societal effects of population growth that dated back at least as far as Thomas Malthus's infamous essay on population. The issue of Third World economic development and political stability brought a new urgency to an old scholarly debate.

The "Transition Model" as Demographic Theory and Public Policy: The Reemergence of the Malthusian Debate

In searching for the intellectual origins of the postwar debate over population issues, one of course arrives at the year 1789 and the publication of Rev. Thomas Malthus's *An Essay on Population.* Malthus's *Essay* combined a "scientific calculus" with moral righteousness and a strident political message. It posed a theory of population growth which argued that human beings were ultimately constrained by limited resources, but it was also an attack on sexual license and a political commentary on the state of the poor in England.[20] Despite his attention to the issues of his own time, Malthus's arguments were sufficiently rich in both their theoretical rigor and political implications that they nourished and sustained a debate that still exists today.

At least for nineteenth-century Europe, however, Thomas Malthus's prognostications appeared to have missed the mark. Technological advances, particularly in agriculture, meant productivity gains more than offset increases in population levels. Improvements in transportation technology and processing reduced the cost of food and increased its availability in remote urban markets. Growing trade with the United States, Canada, and, later, South America and Australia more than met any residual need for foodstuffs. But the United States, Canada, and Australia offered something else for Europe: a home for the many millions of Europeans who found no succor or sustenance in their homelands. The "safety valve" of emigration spared Europe a Malthusian crisis of major proportions. While millions of the indigenous peoples of the world would suffer as a consequence, colonial expansion balanced the "demographic equation" for Europe.

The final factor that was ultimately most important in subsequent discussion about long-term trends in population change, however, was the decline in fertility across Europe, which began in the seventeenth century and continued to the twentieth century. The "demographic transition," as it would subsequently be called, was a "natural readjustment" to the

Malthusian paradox. In fact, the demographic trends in Europe and North America were quite the opposite from those predicted by Malthus and his followers. Beginning in various parts of northern Europe as early as the 1600s and spreading to eastern and southern Europe in the late nineteenth and early twentieth centuries was a process of fertility readjustment so profound that it completely altered the nature of discourse about population. By the end of the nineteenth century and well into the twentieth, the major concern of most governments in Europe was declining population, not growth.

The European experience would figure prominently in U.S. thinking about population growth and distribution in the postwar era. Reflecting on the changes that occurred in Europe over the past three centuries, demographers constructed a vision of population change that became the core component underlying most of modern demographic development theory. The basic idea was that during the course of economic development a set of interactive processes occurs that at first serves to accelerate population growth and, subsequently, promotes its decline. While the degree to which these processes are conditioned by time and place has become a source of constant debate, initially there seemed little doubt that what had occurred in Europe would *eventually* happen in the emerging nations of the Third World. The debatable question, however, was *when* would this process take place and under what *specific* conditions.

Most important for the postwar debate over population change in the Third World, in early modern Europe neither the *initial* decline in mortality nor the subsequent changes in fertility were the result of overt human intervention. Improvements in sanitation systems, the introduction of modern health practices, and the scientific discoveries affecting the control of disease all came later. While these factors served to sustain the continued decline in mortality into the era of high urban concentration, the trend was well established over a long period of time and was deeply embedded in changes in agricultural practices, shifts in dietary mix, and subtle changes in lifestyle. Likewise, the European *fertility transition* occurred in the absence of modern methods of birth control and in an atmosphere of widespread official and religious hostility to limiting births.

Although it was first articulated by demographer Warren Thompson in 1929,[21] the policy implication of transition theory seemed remote. Most population scientists in Europe and North America were primarily concerned with declining populations in their respective countries. While the transition model remained a source of some lively intellectual discussion, it appeared to have little relevance to the issues that most demographers were addressing.

Although there were growing indications in the 1920s and 1930s that population levels in some areas of South Asia and the Far East had grown substantially, only in the postwar era did the consistency and quality of the data become sufficient to reveal these trends with any precision. The conclusion was unavoidable that outside Europe and (Anglo) North America, population growth was reaching levels that were never found in Europe during its "transition" period. Moreover, population growth was occurring without a concomitant rise in industrial development or any apparent shift in attitudes toward a Western belief system. In other words, mortality declines were the result of introducing Western advances in health science without the attendant economic and cultural adjustments that had accompanied the European fertility transition.

While it was possible to develop an adjunct to the theory that accounted for colonial situations, it took some effort to propose a policy solution.[22] Initially most demographers assumed that the process of demographic transition that had marked the economic development of Europe in the eighteenth and nineteenth centuries would occur elsewhere in the world, but *only* when the correlative mix of economic and cultural factors was in place. Calls for intervention to speed up the process were viewed as naive. As time passed, however, the deterministic assumptions underscoring these initial formulations of the transition model were challenged and, by the mid-1950s, many leading American demographers were changing their minds.[23] The modern world, they argued, was a profoundly different place than the world of eighteenth-century Western Europe. Biomedical technology in particular had altered the traditional progression of events associated with population growth and economic development. In a postcolonial world with rapidly declining mortality rates, it appeared that accelerating population growth rates could overwhelm fragile economies on the edge of "takeoff."[24]

Although it took professional demographers nearly a decade to change their minds completely, the influence of their old friends the birth controllers began to show itself. Unrestrained by the necessity to maintain scholarly consistency, birth-control advocates such as Margaret Sanger, William Vogt, and Dr. Clarence Gamble argued that it was merely a matter of education and access. "The people" (both at home and overseas) would embrace family planning if only given a chance. While direct intervention initially appeared inconsistent with the logic of the transition model, it seemed to make sense that we could alter the consequences of this mortality/fertility imbalance once again with Western intervention—this time with the systematic distribution of birth control. In this new intellectual environment, an interventionist population policy was not only within the realm of possibility, it was necessary given the problems facing the newly emergent nations of the Third World. The debate now shifted to means rather than ends.

The key to intervention lay of course not only in the development of safe, effective, and inexpensive forms of birth control but also in the acceptance of family planning as a legitimate and appropriate means for *state-sponsored* population control. It is significant therefore that outside the government a diverse mix of people—businessmen, philanthropists, academicians, feminists, biologists, doctors, and public health officials—formed a loose association of pressure groups that brought the issue of family planning into legitimate public discourse.

Again, the growing respectability of the "family planning movement" in the 1950s seems particularly important. The changing public image of the movement as well as the retirement of some of its more controversial leadership made such groups as Planned Parenthood appear politically safe and therefore more acceptable. The popular mythology of the postwar American family—father, mother, and 2.5 children—obviously required some kind of fertility management. Middle-class responsibility and the "planned family" became linked in the mind of many Americans. In fact, this American vision of the "perfect family" mapped into a complex set of connections between Cold War ideology, the idealization of suburban home life, and the rhetoric of "responsible parenthood." The latter component opened the way for a growing acceptability of birth control and identified it with the virtues of democracy and middle-class capitalism.[25]

World Population Growth as a Public Policy Issue: The Transition Period, 1958–1968

Ultimately, the impress of Cold War politics was central in bringing the population growth issue into the realm of public policy and diplomacy. The presumption on the part of American officials was that communism was an ideology embraced by the wicked, the naive, the desperate, and the weak. The first could be dealt with by force of arms, the second, by propaganda (education?), and the last two, by American generosity, modern technology, and food and health assistance. But it was a race against time. If the Third World continued to be plagued by poverty, disease, and starvation, the success of communism seemed inevitable.

Some demographers, such as Frank Notestein of the Princeton Population Center, and Dudley Kirk, who had been at the State Department's Office of Functional Intelligence before joining the staff at the Population

Council, were reluctant to rephrase their appeals for population-control measures in overt Cold War terms. They were worried that nonaligned nations such as India might view the call for population-control measures as just another propaganda ploy by the "imperialist West" rather than as a sincere expression of concern for the health and welfare of the Third World. Other demographers were not so restrained. Kingsley Davis, who throughout his career was a dominant actor in the field of demography, stated boldly that "the demographic problems of the underdeveloped countries, especially in areas of non-Western culture, make these nations more vulnerable to Communism." He went on to argue that "an appropriate policy would be to control birth rates in addition to such activities as lowering death rates, the provision of technical assistance and economic aid. Such a combination of policies, if carried through effectively, would strengthen the Free World in its constant fight against encroachment."[26]

It was often left to nonprofessional "population activists," however, to translate the guarded academic prose into overtly Cold War rhetoric. The most notable of these figures was Hugh Moore, the president of the Dixie Cup Corporation, who spent most of his sizable fortune on alerting the American public to the potential disaster awaiting the world if the population problem was not addressed immediately. Moore published a pamphlet entitled "The Population Bomb," which had on its cover an exploding atomic bomb hurling people in all directions. The pamphlet was unabashed in making the direct connection between rapid population growth, social and economic disorder, communist aggression, and world war. Moore had two versions: one for domestic consumption, which was unrestrained in its message, and an edited version for international distribution. While the audience for Moore's pamphlet was never intended to be demographic experts, it had considerable influence among Washington's policy elite. It was, for example, assigned reading at the State Department's Foreign Service School.

By the end of the decade, the connection between political disorder, subversion, and population pressures had been made by a number of demographers and population-control advocates. The political environment was ripe for the debate over population growth, family planning, and U.S. foreign policy to come out of the closet.

A major reassessment of U.S. foreign aid would establish the context for the first open discussion of world population growth by public officials. In the late 1950s a series of setbacks in international affairs (for example, the ill-fated Hungarian Revolution, Vice President Richard Nixon's violent reception in Latin America, and the propaganda impact of *Sputnik*) led Congress once again to take a close look at the effectiveness of our foreign-aid program. Responding to congressional calls for action, President Eisenhower appointed a "blue ribbon" committee, under the leadership of retired General William Draper, to examine the purpose and effectiveness of our foreign aid. Although the committee was officially delegated to look at military foreign aid, Draper read the committee's mandate broadly to include an examination of both military and nonmilitary aid. One of the committee's primary interests of course was the fate of the developing countries of Asia, Africa, and Latin America, which Draper viewed as the new battleground for the Cold War.

Breaking with the tradition of official silence on the subject, Draper briefly focused the committee's attention on the problem of rapidly growing populations in Asia and Latin America.[27] With the assistance of Robert Cook of the Population Reference Bureau and Hugh Moore (each of whom had adopted the population-control movement as a personal cause), Draper produced a brief section in the final report in which he argued that rapid population growth could completely erode efforts at development and negate all our foreign-assistance efforts. Moreover, in an environment of rising expectations, sagging economic growth created ripe conditions for communist intrigue and political discord. While not all members of the committee were in agreement with Draper on including this section, the official recommendation was that the United States should provide assistance to developing nations that sought to control their population growth.

The obvious implication—that the United States should offer advice and, perhaps, the means to control fertility—was not lost on the public. Eisenhower, while accepting all other aspects of the report, publicly rejected the idea that the government should have any role in affecting population dynamics. What is interesting, however, is how quickly public policy did indeed change. Less than two years into the Kennedy administration, Richard Gardner, Deputy Assistant Secretary of State for International Organization Affairs, signaled a major policy shift in a speech before the U.N. General Assembly announcing that the United States would support expanded programming in the area of population research with an aim toward linking it with development assistance.[28]

Shortly thereafter, Congress took an active interest in the population problem. In 1965–66, Senator Ernest Gruening (Dem.-Alaska) held a series of congressional hearings to highlight the importance of the population crisis and to pressure the White House for more support of family planning programs in U.S. foreign-aid assistance. A parade of witnesses (from both the United States and the Third World) testified to the serious consequences of unrestricted population growth.[29] Many of the major witnesses came from the foundation and NGO community, which had supported the development of demography and population research in the 1950s. The network-building of the previous decade was now paying off.

A parallel but not unrelated chain of events within the United Nations had finally broken international silence on the issue. Throughout the 1940s and 1950s there was considerable resistance to any effort that might expand the United Nations role in the area of population policy. Some expected that various U.N. statistical agencies should merely monitor global trends and report their findings. Moving beyond this prescribed role was resisted by both Catholic and Communist countries alike. Primarily through the efforts of Sweden and India, the "population issue" was finally placed on the agenda of the General Assembly in 1962.[30] The ensuing discussion opened the way for an expanded U.N. role in the area of population assistance. Finally, official international recognition of family planning as a basic right came in 1968, when the United Nations Conference on Human Rights (Tehran) declared that "parents have a basic human right to determine freely and responsibly the number and spacing of their children."[31]

Toward a Moment of Consensus: Family Planning and Population Control, 1967–1974

The period from 1967 to 1974 might be described as the "era of unrestrained enthusiasm" of government-sponsored family planning. International agencies, scientific societies, and national leadership constantly cited population growth as the most pressing problem of the age. President Lyndon Johnson seldom missed an opportunity to extol the wonders of "the Pill." President Richard Nixon sent the first-ever White House message on population to Congress in 1969. What is most impressive was the level of unanimity on the population issue. Leading Republicans as well as Democrats rallied to the cause. Religious leaders, civic groups, businessmen, and scientists all called for a vigorous commitment of both government and nonprofit funding to avoid a worldwide crisis.

Obviously the development of an effective oral contraceptive and an inexpensive IUD presented government officials with a "technological fix" to a problem that previously had seemed insurmountable. For many of the advocates of family planning it was now "merely a matter of education and logistics." The "demand" was assumed to be well established. Although in the late 1970s some experts would question the validity of this assumption, KAP (Knowledge-Attitude-Practice) surveys offered strong confirmation of this bias.[32] Reflecting a growing sense of urgency, the emphasis in practice was on "stand-alone" family planning services relatively independent of public health programs. In theory, unobstructed by bureaucratic interference, independent family planning operations could get birth-control pills, IUDs, and sterilization procedures to "the masses" as quickly as possible.

The late 1960s, therefore, brought a rapid acceleration of funding for population programs with a singular focus on fertility control. Although many of the major foundations had previously been hesitant to fund contraceptive research, they sought to make up for this deficit with aggressive efforts. The Ford Foundation, for example, pledged more than $54 million between 1960 and 1970 and the Rockefeller Foundation, after a decade of discussing but not acting, had donated more than $15 million by 1968.

As the decade passed, however, government funding played an increasingly important role in sponsoring demographic research and population-control programs. With public and congressional support growing, government appropriations for family planning and contraceptive services had risen to the unprecedented level of $60 million by the end of the decade. Expenditures for distribution of contraceptives and family planning services in Third World countries were to become a major component for USAID's budgetary allocation. Of the $125.6 million allocated for population-related programs within USAID in 1974, for example, nearly 50 percent of the funds were earmarked for birth-control services. By the mid-1970s, family planning and population research fully dominated the USAID health budget.

The infusion of public funding revealed the degree to which national security interests had been fused with the idea of population control in the Third World. There seems little doubt that Cold War imperatives served in large part to justify these expenditures. But a word of caution is necessary. The merger of national security interests with population-growth issues did not occur in a political vacuum, nor was it a sudden transformation. One should not overstate the influence of strategic concerns on the implementation of population policies abroad. As with many areas of foreign-aid assistance, our motives were mixed. Certainly one sees increasing references to health issues as well as environmental issues. At least in this early period, however, the major justification was in terms of promoting economic growth and preserving political stability.

Signaling the growing importance of population control in U.S. foreign-policy efforts, the National Security Council under President Nixon prepared National Security Study Memorandum 200, which outlined the detailed justification for U.S. support for population programming worldwide. The crude Cold War logic of the late 1950s was replaced by a detailed analysis of the political, economic, and environmental consequences of rapid population growth. The issue of political instability was discussed, but, not surprisingly, the OPEC oil crisis brought the issue of strategic materials again to the forefront. It was not simply a military question anymore. The fundamental health of the U.S. economy was at risk if we did not focus greater attention on world population and resource issues. NSSM 200, and the "Action Memorandum" that followed, finally (and officially) merged the issue of population control with national security at the highest level.[33]

The emphasis on resource issues in NSSM 200 reflected a renewed concern for natural-resource issues both inside and outside the government. In fact, the merger of the population-control movement with the growing environmental awareness of the late 1960s and early 1970s not only expanded the base of support but made the crusade for universal family planning all the more pressing.

Books such as Paul Ehrlich's *The Population Bomb,* William and Paul Paddock's *Famine—1975,* Joseph Tydings's *Born to Starve,* and Georg Borgstrom's *The Hungry Planet* presented a picture of impending doom triggered by overpopulation and diminishing resources.[34] The new environmental movement perceived not one but a cluster of interrelated problems involving population growth and limited resources. The world, the environmentalists argued, faced an impending crisis of monumental proportions. Sophisticated computer models and technical jargon offered scientific credibility to the catastrophe argument, which is, at its core, quite simple: human populations have grown so enormously and continue to expand so rapidly that, despite our technological capabilities, we would soon exhaust the planet's capacity to support us. Attendant to this rapid growth in population was also the growing abuse of the natural environment, which will only serve to hasten an impending crisis for all mankind. The logic was simple and deadly. Given this perspective, solutions of only the most drastic sort were worthy of consideration.

The rhetoric of imminent disaster declined over the next decade as the environmental movement became more sophisticated in its analysis of resource issues. Its immediate effect, however, was to encourage further the growing American commitment to population control as part of its foreign-aid program. The crisis mentality combined with a growing concern over degradation of the environment and depletion of the world's resources added to the sense of mission felt by U.S. family planning workers overseas.

Unfortunately, the strident rhetoric of the late 1960s and early 1970s had another, more detrimental effect. With its emphasis on the immediacy of the threat and the necessity for aggressive intervention, the stage was set for a resurgence in the political strength of the opponents of population policy. As the decade passed without a worldwide catastrophe, those who had originally voiced suspicion felt they were vindicated. Some critics went further, however. They argued that it had not been simply a case of exaggeration; the fact that no serious crisis had developed suggested that the claims of impending disaster were without any factual basis whatsoever.

But at the time, it *appeared* that the voices calling for worldwide population reduction were strong, clear, and, most important, unified. For the advocates of family planning assistance abroad, the American mission went far beyond the pragmatic goals of strategic policy. The call for population control, formerly justified either in terms of national security or, less often, as a public health issue, merged with a set of issues involving the world's ecology, ultimately, the preservation of the species. Seldom could American strategic objectives be so easily merged with a humanitarian mission of global importance.

Coming Apart: Growing Dissent on the Population Issue, 1974–1980

Just as the triumphant advocates of population control naively presumed an "international consensus" on the issue of family planning, the opposition, which was briefly muted by the choirs of support for family planning assistance, again reasserted itself. Indeed, any presumption that the world was on its way to consensus on population policies would be shattered at the United Nations International Conference on population held in Bucharest in 1974.

The Bucharest meeting departed from its predecessors in a number of important ways. While previous international meetings on population sponsored by the United Nations had aimed primarily at the presentation of recent scientific research, the 1974 Conference was intended to establish a basic plan for population policies in the decade to come. Each country was represented by an "official delegation" empowered to speak for its government. Unlike earlier world population conferences, NGOs, scientific delegations, and advocacy groups no longer had a place at the "official" gathering, so they held a separate conclave. The deliberations in this latter forum proved to be particularly vociferous.

Much to the surprise of American and European delegations, a coalition of Latin American, African, and Eastern European representatives presented a decidedly different interpretation of the population crisis.[35] The group argued that the primary problem was global inequalities in wealth and income, which were only incidently related to rapid population growth. Ironically, two delegations, which on all other matters had little in common, the Vatican and the People's Republic of China, joined with this group in criticizing the Western industrialized nations for not addressing the "real" development issue—inequality between north and south.

It is important to recognize, however, that not all Third World delegations subscribed to this extreme position. Indeed, many of the "middle of the road" delegations made a consistent effort to strike a balance between calls for expanded family planning efforts and the need for broad-based development programs tailored to the needs of each country. While the voices for compromise would ultimately prevail, the acrimony engendered by the debate in Bucharest would have a decided effect on the policy discourse in the ensuing decade.

The opposition to the proposed World Population Plan of Action was partly a reaction to extremist antinatalist rhetoric emanating from the United States. While most U.S. aid officials were more circumspect in their pronouncements, many of America's leading population-control advocates argued that the voluntary approach might not be sufficient.[36] Calls for coercive measures, while not representative of official policy, tended to reinforce the deepest fears of Asians, Africans, and Latin Americans—that they would be the unwilling target of U.S.-sponsored efforts at population control.

When we look back at the vehement international opposition to U.S.-sponsored birth-control campaigns in the early 1970s, we must keep in mind that as the population-crisis message filtered through the popular press, it often became simplistic and myopic. The tempered, qualified tone of the conference report and scholarly article was stripped away and reduced to pat phrases and simplistic slogans. Most professional demographers continued to caution that population programs should be part of a larger development effort, but the complexity of the problem was too often lost in the rhetoric of worst-case scenarios. It was not just a case of sensationalist journalism, however. All too frequently the public discourse of Washington bureaucrats and politicians was as simplistic as it was monolithic in its conception. In the face of dire messages of gloom and doom, it is not surprising that Americans took refuge in a technological fix. If we could get "the Pill" to the people, the problem would solve itself. It was simply a matter of implementing sound advertizing techniques, operational analysis, and logistics.

Viewed from overseas, there appeared to be little or no concern for intrinsic religious, national, or cultural differences. The presumption was that the "problem" was the same regardless of location and the solution was the same regardless of the people involved. Although American aid officials in the field were seldom so blunt, to the many observers in the Third World the primary message emanating from Washington was as rude as it was racist.

Despite the heated rhetoric of the Bucharest conference, however, the World Population Plan for Action was accepted and over the next decade a quiet transition began to occur. With increasing frequency, Third World governments came to accept the legitimacy of family planning. For countries such as Mexico, where family planning programs had initially been in the hands of private voluntary organizations, government-sponsored nationwide programs became the norm. In many African countries family planning, although remaining in the domain of private donor agencies, was increasingly merged with comprehensive health programs. For a few more conservative regimes in the Third World, it was a more modest gesture—simply allowing private family planning organizations to operate unobstructed. Regardless, the trend over the decade was toward a recognition of the need for family planning in national development schemes.[37]

At the same time, however, in North America the political pendulum was swinging back toward a reevaluation of the role of population program assistance in U.S. foreign policy. Although there had never been a moment of complete unanimity on the family planning issue, as the 1970s passed the opposition movement, diverse in both its politics and its goals, grew in strength. Whether it was on the right or on the left of the American political spectrum, the basic thrust of its critique was that population growth was only marginally related to the serious social and economic problems facing the Third World.

For the leftists, the real problem was to be found in the nature of worldwide capitalist exploitation. The solution was socialist revolution, not family planning. Karen Michaelson, a leftist anthropologist, in a restatement of the traditional Marxist position on population growth, argued that "overpopulation is not a matter of too many people, but of unequal distribution of resources. The fundamental issue is not population control, but control over resources."[38]

For the diehard capitalist, of course, it was the lack of economic incentives that gave rise to both poverty and *moments* of overpopulation. Embracing the free enterprise system without unnecessary government meddling would automatically bring the problems associated with population growth into check. Like Julian Simon, his conservative American counterpart, the Tory economist Peter T. Bauer concluded: "Allegations or apprehensions of adverse or even disastrous results of population growth are unfounded. They rest on seriously defective analysis of the determinants of economic performance [and] they misconceive the conduct of the peoples of LDCs [lesser developed countries]."[39]

For *religious* conservatives who opposed most current methods of birth control, the "problem" was one of unChristian-like behavior and greed. The religious challenge merged the presumption of positive technological advances common among conservative economists with a critique of economic and social inequality similar to that of the socialists. The difference of course was the call to spiritual awakening, which both of the other schools would have found naive. Pope Paul VI summarized this view in his famous declaration: "[We] need to multiply bread so that it suffices for the tables of mankind rather than to rely on measures which diminish the number of guests at the banquet of life."[40]

A final source of criticism came from feminists, who saw U.S.-sponsored family planning programs as heavy-handed and unconcerned with the real needs of women. As one feminist put it, "Improvements in living standards and the position of women, via more equitable social and economic development [would] motivate people to want fewer children."[41] It was not that they opposed contraception per se; rather, they felt that family planning should be part of a comprehensive effort to empower women.

The reaction of feminist groups to U.S.-sponsored family planning programs was perhaps the most disquieting for program administrators who often justified their efforts in terms of women's rights. Over the decade, however, there had been a growing number of reports that in the enthusiasm to bring population growth under control, basic rights for women were frequently abridged.[42] Moreover, family planning practitioners *seemed* more concerned with the efficiency of birth-control programs rather than with their humanity. All too often a male-dominated public health and foreign-aid establishment seemed insensitive to the basic needs of women in the Third World. For feminists it was not merely a question of *access* to birth control but an essential issue of freedom and equality. The historical evidence showed conclusively that, if women's status improved, women would seek out appropriate methods of birth control voluntarily. Coercion was not only inappropriate from a human rights standpoint, but in a properly constructed development program it was quite unnecessary.

The emergence of the feminist critique of population-control programs found its origins in the movement for women's rights, which had gained strength both within the United States and overseas since the mid-1960s. However, given the ways in which the family planning ideology of the 1950s had been embedded in the economic development logic of the period, the "woman perspective" had been slow to emerge. The idea that access to safe and effective contraception was an inalienable right found recognition in various U.N. declarations, but the idea that women should have an overt role in the development process was resisted by many of the administrators at USAID and the United Nations.

The closing years of the 1970s brought choirs of criticism from outside the "population policy establishment."[43] But an erosion of confidence occurred from within as well. There was a growing disagreement among economists and demographers over whether population growth was in fact an important factor in economic development.[44] Perhaps not surprisingly, as the quality of data improved and the techniques of analysis became more sophisticated, the demographic theories that posited a negative relationship between economic development and rapid population growth failed to find consistent validity. (Ironically, the pronouncements that had initially justified the inordinate investment in demographic research were increasingly called into question.)

Despite the ongoing debate among academics, however, within policy circles it was not a question of whether family planning was a legitimate component of U.S. foreign-aid efforts. That debate had been settled for nearly two decades. Rather, the debate was over emphasis, strategy, and means. To what extent should the United States *insist* that population programs be part of a recipient nation's development strategy? For example, should U.S. foreign aid be contingent on a pledge to reduce population growth? Should family planning programs be separate from existing health and social services institutions focusing all their resources on a single goal: the overall reduction of fertility? Or should family planning be seen as simply one part of an effective child and maternal health program? If the result is a reduction in fertility, so be it, but the goal should be healthy women and children and not necessarily maximizing population control. (This was the view of many Third World health officials as well as feminists in Europe and North America.)

While funding for family planning activities continued to increase, administrative tensions within USAID's population program served further to weaken the resolve of the family planning movement internationally.[45] The stage was set for an attempt by conservatives to reverse the tide and return to the passive pronatalism of the 1940s.

The Reagan–Bush Era: "The More People, the Better"

The effectiveness of the opposition groups of foreign-policy decisionmakers of course varied substantially. It was not the left-wing arguments or the feminist critique of American population programs abroad that moved the Reagan administration to alter the U.S. position on family planning. Rather, it was the influence of conservative Christian lobbying groups combined with an influential noninterventionist argument advocated by free-market economists.

Signaling the triumph of the "no crisis scenario," Ambassador James Buckley's official statement to the World Population Conference in Mexico City in 1984 de-emphasized the importance of population growth as a barrier to economic development. Buckley cited poorly conceived development policies and a stifling of free enterprise as the root cause of economic stagnation in the Third World.[46] Thus for Reagan strategists population growth was a "neutral" variable having neither positive nor negative consequences for economic development.

The Mexico City Doctrine, as it would subsequently be called, had another dimension quite independent of the demographic theories it espoused. It had a decidedly moral component as well. Buckley also announced that only those groups and agencies that made no reference to or support of abortion rights would receive U.S. aid. This would be the case even if U.S. funds were segregated to assure that they were not part of the abortion side of the programmatic effort.

Naturally the U.S. position was interpreted as a reversal of America's long-standing position on world population growth. Although many U.S. government agencies would continue to argue that Third World population growth posed a serious strategic challenge, the Reagan White House sought to curtail all population-assistance funding through USAID as well as terminating support of U.N. population activities. Despite congressional resistance to reducing U.S. commitments to family planning programs overseas, the overall effect was to send a message to the world of growing indifference to population problems.[47]

The leadership in many Third World nations greeted this policy reversal with consternation. After all, it had been primarily the United States that led them to believe that fertility reduction was an important component of sound development planning. If they had been attentive to domestic politics in the United States over the previous ten years, they might have anticipated the apparent shift in policy. Domestically, it was not simply the changing statistics of world population growth that served to affect support for population control. Although American public opinion generally supported the integration of family planning assistance with foreign-policy objectives throughout this period, the public continued to be deeply divided on the question of means. Particularly important was (and is) the lack of domestic consensus on the abortion issue.

Despite the passage of the Helms Amendment in 1974 (prohibiting foreign-aid funds for abortion), there was continuing suspicion on the part of the anti-abortion lobby that AID funds were secretly assisting the overseas "abortion industry." Moreover, many of these conservative Christian groups also flatly opposed support for contraception in any form. The growing political power of these constituencies within the Republican party did not bode well for the future of population aid. The election of Ronald Reagan therefore brought a group of anti-interventionists to the White House who sought to end a bipartisan foreign-policy initiative that now spanned nearly two decades.

As a result, for most of the 1980s the U.S. government presented a mixed message on population issues. While the pronatalist rhetoric of the Reagan administration continued over the decade for a variety of reasons, U.S. funding for family planning continued to flow into Third World projects. Administration efforts to delay or block funding continued to meet strong opposition in the Democratically controlled Congress, which had succeeded in increasing family planning allocations by the mid-1980s. Moreover, since career AID and State Department officials remained loyal to the population-control doctrines that had dominated U.S. foreign policy for nearly two decades, the right-wing ideological pronouncements by President Reagan's political appointees would not fundamentally alter the day-to-day decisionmaking of project directors and mission officers. Finally, even in the absence of U.S. funding at the United Nations, many of our allies, who continued to support the idea that rapid population growth was a serious threat, increased their assistance and to some extent offset the deficit.

The tensions over the population issue would remain. With his veto of Congress's first version of the 1989 Foreign Aid Bill, President George Bush continued the policies of the Reagan administration in opposing any financial assistance for the United Nations Fund for Population Activities. Only after Congress was willing to compromise on White House–

imposed restrictions on population aid would the President sign the foreign-aid package into law. In doing so, President Bush (like his predecessor) cited the role of UNFPA in the controversial Chinese birth-control program. His veto also signaled that, despite an increase in the USAID commitment to family planning activities overseas, the United States would not return its unrestrained support for population-control programs that prevailed in the late 1960s and early 1970s.

Conflict or Compromise: Global Population and Resource Issues in the 1990s

At his confirmation hearings in January 1993, Secretary of State Warren M. Christopher cited the heightened importance of environmental issues in the conduct of foreign policy in the 1990s. His statements were of course consistent with the positions taken by the Clinton–Gore team throughout their campaign. In their book, *Putting People First,* they state boldly that "environmental protection is fundamental to America's national security."[48]

Much of the logic that informed these views was drawn from Vice President Gore's book, *Earth in the Balance.*[49] While it should not be read as a policy document for the Clinton administration, the book can be seen as a basis for a new direction in environmental affairs at both the domestic and international levels. While specific policies and programs are currently being delineated, the broad outlines are clear. Departing from the inclinations of the previous twelve years, the Clinton administration is likely to take a more active role at the international level in the areas of environmental regulation, population planning, and natural-resource conservation.

In the opening weeks of the administration, the restrictions mandated by the Reagan–Bush "Mexico City Doctrine" were reversed. Assistance to the United Nations Population Fund was restored ($14.5 million in fiscal 1993 and $40 million projected for 1994). Although the pressures of deficit reduction forced cutbacks in many U.S. foreign-aid programs, the recommended allocation for population was increased by $185 million (FY 1995). Clearly the administration is on record as a strong supporter of increasing population planning assistance.

In preparing for the 1994 United Nations Conference on Population and Development in Cairo, the State Department sought to redefine the population issue in terms that will meet the demands of various constituencies. This has proven to be more difficult than expected. Although the opponents of subsidized family planning no longer hold sway, tensions between population-control advocates among environmentalists and feminists concerned with women's status in the Third World threaten to undermine attempts to build a coalition.

The world has changed radically since the United States first embraced family planning as an important component of its foreign-aid program. The changing power relationship between the United States and the former Soviet Union signaled the death knell for the Cold War logic that initially had justified America's family planning crusade. Rephrased, the national-security argument proceeds much differently now. Regardless of the demise of Soviet communism, American interests are still ill-served by economic and political disorder. In a world torn by ethnic, religious, and national tensions, forced migrations can have explosive consequences. There is bound to be continuing concern over global environmental issues as well. There also seems little doubt that population density and growth are key factors in conditioning not only resource utilization but levels of pollution. Another traditional justification for America's "contraceptive diplomacy" was the widely held presumption that an effective family planning program can hasten the onset of sustained economic growth, or, at the very least, remove one of the major barriers to growth. While demographers and economists are in much less agreement on the viability of this assumption, it is likely to remain an important political justification for population assistance in the future.

A final justification for continuing U.S. population program assistance is on the grounds of improving the health of women and children in the Third World. Although often presented as an afterthought in the early days of the population-control crusade, it is now perhaps the primary justification for many of the advocates of U.S. subsidized family planning. In the final analysis, they may be the most compelling justification.

Unlike most foreign-policy issues, however, international population policies impinge directly on deeply personal concerns. If recent history can be our guide, it appears that the major constraining dimension on how we approach these issues is not only domestic in its origins but almost theological in its manifestations. Whether we like it or not, the ongoing debate over birth control, abortion, and what might be called "the politics of the family" will continue to have profound effects on our continuing discussions of population growth, economic development, and resource utilization. Each of these areas engenders highly charged rhetoric, and when combined, there is an unfortunate tendency for the discourse to be muddled and confused.

Obviously, both the historical and the cultural context determine how population issues are defined. Whether population growth, for example, is viewed as a good thing or a bad thing has changed in recent decades. Given the various perspectives on the population problem itself, it is hardly surprising that tensions arise over both the goals and the mechanisms of population policies. Ideology, theology, and political philosophy help to define *both* the empirical issues as well as the nature of the moralistic debates that so often accompany the implementation of policy.

University of Wisconsin

Notes

1. Research for this essay was funded by grants from the Social Science Research Council, the Rockefeller Archive Center, and the Graduate School of the University of Wisconsin. None of these institutions is responsible for the opinions expressed. I wish to thank Wendy Sundby for her editorial assistance in the final preparation of the manuscript.

2. Michael S. Teitelbaum and J. M. Winters, *Fear of Population Decline* (Orlando, 1985).

3. D. V. Glass, *The Struggle for Population* (Oxford, 1936) and *Population Policies and Movements in Europe* (Oxford, 1940).

4. For a discussion of the pro-family social and political environment in the United States during the 1940s and 1950s, see Steven Mintz and Susan Kellogg, *Domestic Revolutions: A Social History of the American Family* (New York, 1988), 177–94; Landon Jones, *Great Expectations: America and the Baby Boom* (New York, 1980), 11–35. For Canada, see Keith G. Banting, *The Welfare State and Canadian Federalism* (Kingston, Ontario, 1982), passim. For France and comparisons elsewhere, see Alfred Sauvy, *General Theory of Population* (New York, 1969). See also Marcel Leroy, *Population and World Politics: The Interrelationships Between Demographic Factors and International Relations* (Leiden, 1978), 11–17.

5. James Reed, *The Birth Control Movement and American Society: From Private Vice to Public Virtue* (Princeton, 1984), 263–69; David M. Kennedy, *Birth Control in America: The Career of Margaret Sanger* (New Haven, 1970), 259–67.

6. Annett B. Ramirez de Arellano and Conrad Seipp, *Colonialism, Catholicism, and Contraception: A History of Birth Control in Puerto Rico* (Chapel Hill, 1983), 30–56; H. B. Presser, *Sterilization and Fertility Decline in Puerto Rico,* Population Monograph Series, no. 13 (Berkeley and Los Angeles, 1973).

7. Ellen Chesler, *Woman of Valor: Margaret Sanger and the Birth Control Movement in America* (New York, 1993), 355–70; Reed, *The Birth Control Movement and American Society,* chap. 22.

8. S. Chandrasekhar, *Population and Planned Parenthood in India* (London, 1955), 75–78.

9. *Report of the Health Survey and Development Committee* (New Delhi, 1946), 2:486–87.

10. W. R. Crocker, *The Japanese Population Problem: The Coming Crisis* (New York, 1931); Etienne Dennery, *Asia's Teeming Millions, and Its Problems for the West* (London, 1931); A. M. Carr-Saunders, *World Population: Past Growth and Present Trends* (Oxford, 1936, 1937), 260–94, 220–29.

11. David M. Anderson, "Depression, Dust Bowl, Demography, and Drought: The Colonial State and Soil Conservation in East Africa During the 1930s," *African Affairs* 83 (1984): 321–41.

12. Elaine Tyler May, *Homeward Bound: American Families in the Cold War Era* (New

York, 1988), 135–61; Phyllis T. Piotrow, *World Population Crisis: The United States Response* (New York, 1973), 15–17; Chesler, *Woman of Valor*, 371–95.

13. Warren S. Thompson, *Population and Peace in the Pacific* (Chicago, 1946); John U. Nef, *War and Human Progress: An Essay on the Rise of Industrial Civilization* (Cambridge, Mass., 1950); Gaston Bouthoul, *Les Guerrs: Eléments de Polémologie* (Paris, 1951).

14. In the records of the Economic Cooperation Administration (a predecessor of USAID) are files dealing directly with the development of the colonial area held by our European allies. The strategic materials problem is only one of a number of issues that concern U.S. development planners. A complete listing would be impossible here. As an initial entry into this material, see Record Group 469, "Strategic Materials," Box 12 (one of three), Overseas Territories Division, Subject Files (1949–51), Special Representative in Europe (National Archives, Washington, D.C.).

15. William Vogt, *Road to Survival* (New York, 1948); Fairfield Osborn, *Our Plundered Planet* (Boston, 1948). See also Osborn's *The Limits of the Earth* (Boston, 1953).

16. The division between the "agricultural optimist" and the "population growth pessimists" has been a constant in the great population debate since the time of Malthus. Early in the twentieth century the food-crisis argument was posed by Warren S. Thompson, *Population: A Study in Malthusianism* (New York, 1915), and Edward M. East, *Mankind at the Crossroads* (New York, 1924). These works, however, often muddled the food/resource argument with the eugenics issues of race and differential mortality. In the postwar period that debate reemerged, this time more technical in style and much less eugenic in tone. See Theodore W. Schultz, ed., *Food for the World* (Chicago, 1945); London International Assembly Conference Report, *Freedom from Want of Food* (London, 1944); United Nations, *The State of Food and Agriculture* (Rome, 1953).

17. J. B. Sharpless, "The Rockefeller Foundation, the Population Council, and the Groundwork for New Population Policies," *Rockefeller Archive Center Newsletter* (Fall 1993): 1–4; Reed, *The Birth Control Movement and American Society*, 283–89: John E. Harr and Peter J. Johnson, *The Rockefeller Century* (New York, 1988), chap. 23.

18. Population Council, *The Population Council: A Chronicle of the First Twenty-five Years, 1952–1977* (New York, 1978); John Harr and Peter Johnson, *The Rockefeller Conscience* (New York, 1991), chap. 3.

19. John Caldwell and Pat Caldwell, *Limiting Population Growth and the Ford Foundation Contribution* (Dover, N.H., 1986), 59–128, 143–50.

20. Actually two essays form the basis of the "Malthusian tradition": the "first essay," of 1798, entitled *An Essay on the Principle of Population as it Affects the Further Improvement of Society* (Harmondsworth, 1970), and the "second essay," *An Essay on the Principles of Population* (London, 1803).

21. Warren Thompson, "Population," *American Journal of Sociology* 34 (May 1929): 959–75.

22. See, for example, Frank W. Notestein, "Summary of the Demographic Background of Problems of Undeveloped Areas," in *International Approaches to Problems of Underdeveloped Areas* (New York, 1948).

23. Dennis Hodgson, "Demography as Social Science and Policy Science," *Population and Development Review* 9 (March 1983): 1–34.

24. Perhaps the most influential contribution to this controversy was the work of two economists, Ansley Coale and Edgar Hoover, who sought to calibrate the economic consequences of continued population growth in India; see *Population Growth and Economic Development in Low-Income Countries* (Princeton, 1958). The book's influence on the theoretical debate over economic development and population growth cannot be underestimated. It is *the* "first footnote" in nearly all the subsequent academic literature. Its importance to government officials is shown by the fact that the Population Council distributed this book free to policymakers, demographers, and politicians throughout the Third World in the years following its publication.

25. May, *Homeward Bound,* 150–51.

26. Kingsley Davis, "Population and Power in the Free World," in J. Spengler and O. D. Duncan, eds., *Population Theory and Policy* (Chicago, 1956), 356. See also Kingsley Davis, "The Political Impact of New Population Trends," *Foreign Affairs Quarterly* 36 (January 1958): 296, and Philip M. Hauser, ed., Preface, *Population and World Politics* (Glencoe, Ill., 1958), 14–15.

27. William Draper et al., President's Committee to Study the United States Military Assistance Program, *Final Report* (Washington, D.C., 1959), 94–97. For a detailed discussion of the background to the Draper Committee, see Piotrow, *World Population Crisis,* chap. 4.

28. The speech was reprinted as *Population Growth: A World Problem, Statement of U.S. Policy* (U.S. Department of State, January 1963). See also Richard N. Gardner, "The Politics of Population: A Blueprint for International Cooperation," *Department of State Bulletin* (10 June 1963).

29. U.S. Senate, "Population Crisis," *Hearings Before the Subcommittee on Foreign Aid Expenditures of the Committee on Government Operations, 90th Congress, November 2, 1967–February 1, 1968 [Published in Four Parts]* (Washington, D.C., 1967–68). For background on the Gruening Hearings, see Ernest Gruening, *Many Battles: The Autobiography of Ernest Gruening* (New York, 1973), and Piotrow, *World Population Crisis,* chap. 11.

30. Richard Symonds and Michael Carder, *The United Nations and the Population Question, 1945–1970* (London, 1973).

31. United Nations, *Final Act of the International Conference on Human Rights, Tehran, April 22 to May 13, 1968,* U.N. Doc A/Conf. 32/41, para. 16.

32. Donald P. Warwick, *Bitter Pills: Population Policies and Their Implementation in Eight Developing Countries* (Cambridge, 1982).

33. U.S. National Archives, Record Group 237 [Documents and Memoranda of the National Security Council], *NSSM 200,* "Implications of Worldwide Population Growth for U.S. Security and Overseas Interests" (10 December 1974), declassified, 1989.

34. Paul Ehrlich, *The Population Bomb* (New York, rev. ed., 1971); William and Paul Paddock, *Famine 1975* (Boston, 1967); Joseph Tydings, *Born to Starve* (New York, 1970); Georg Borgstrom, *The Hungry Planet* (New York, 1967).

35. Jason L. Finkle and Barbara B. Crane, "The Politics of Bucharest: Population, Development, and the New International Economic Order," *Population and Development Review* 1 (September 1975): 87–113.

36. The argument for coercion is stated boldly in Ehrlich's *Population Bomb,* but the basic logic is detailed in a famous essay by Garrett Hardin, "The Tragedy of the Commons," *Science* 180 (December 1969): 1243–48.

37. For a review of trends in family planning policies, see W. Parker Mauldin and John A. Ross, "Family Planning Programs: Efforts and Results, 1982–89," *Studies in Family Planning* 22 (November–December 1991): 350–67.

38. Karen L. Michaelson, "Population Theory and the Political Economy of Population Processes," in *And the Poor Get Children,* Karen L. Michaelson, ed. (New York, 1981), 19.

39. P[eter] J. Bauer, *Equality, the Third World, and Economic Delusion* (Cambridge, Mass., 1981), 64. See also Julian Simon, *The Ultimate Resource* (Princeton, 1981); J. Simon, *The Economics of Population Growth* (Princeton, 1977).

40. Pope Paul VI, "Address to the General Assembly," *United Nations,* 20th Session, 1965; 1347th Plenary Meeting, 4.

41. Betsy Hartmann, *Reproductive Rights and Wrongs: The Global Politics of Population Control and Contraceptive Choice* (New York, 1987), xiv.

42. Bonnie Mass, *Population Target: The Political Economy of Population Control in Latin America* (Toronto, 1976); Hartmann, *Reproductive Rights and Wrongs,* 217–20, 237–41; Donald Warwick, "The Ethics of Population Control," in Godfrey Roberts, ed., *Population Policy: Contemporary Issues* (New York, 1990), 21–37; Francis Rolt, *Pills, Policies, and Profit* (London, 1985).

43. The idea of an international conspiracy to assure the continuation of neo-Malthusian propaganda is discussed by Julian Simon in "The Population, Corruption, and Reform," in G. Roberts, ed., *Population Policy: Contemporary Issues,* 39–59.

44. For a review of this debate and its relationship to ecological issues, see Nathan Keyfitz, "Population and Development Within the Ecosphere: One View of the Literature," *Population Index* 57 (Spring 1991): 5–22.

45. An enormous amont of bureaucratic energy was expended in the controversy surrounding the ouster of Dr. Rei Ravenholt, who had served as director of the Population Program at USAID since the Johnson years. His controversial style had offended many in the family planning community. His removal in the Carter years corresponded with a reorganization of the Population Program, which gave more power to USAID regional directors. See Peter J. Donaldson, *Nature Against Us: The United States and the World Population Crisis* (Chapel Hill, 1990), 76–92.

46. James L. Buckley, "U.S. Commitment to International Population Planning," a statement presented to the International Conference on Population, Mexico City, 8 August 1984, Current Policy no. 604 (Washington, D.C., 1984). See also Jason L. Finkle and Barbara B. Crane, "Ideology and Politics at Mexico City: The United States at the 1984 International Conference on Population," *Population and Development Review* 11 (March 1985): 1–28; Ian Pool, "From Bucharest to Mexico: The Politics of International Population Conferences," *New Zealond Population Review* 11 (1985): 52–63.

47. Sharon Camp and C. R. Lasher, "International Family Planning Policy: A Chronicle of the Reagan Years," *Working Paper* (DRAFT COPY), Population Crisis Committee (Washington, D.C., 1989).

48. Bill Clinton and Al Gore, *Putting People First: How We Can All Change America* (New York, 1992), 93–99.

49. Al Gore, *Earth in the Balance: Ecology and the Human Spirit* (Boston, 1992), 307–14.

JAMES DAVISON HUNTER
JOSEPH E. DAVIS

Cultural Politics at the Edge of Life

To operate within a strictly political frame of reference, the dispute over abortion—the centerpiece of the controversy over reproduction and population control in America—would seem to be over. With the election of Bill Clinton to the presidency in 1992, many observers declared as much. Charles Krauthammer, for one, argued that "one can reasonably declare a great national debate over when all three independently (s)elected branches of government come to the same position." In 1992 the Supreme Court reaffirmed the central holding of *Roe v. Wade* in the *Casey* decision. Given this and an apparent majority of pro-choice votes in both houses of Congress, the new President-elect vowed to make good on his campaign pledge to pass the "Freedom of Choice Act" (FOCA), the legislative equivalent of *Roe*, as a safeguard against any future challenges. Certainly there seemed to be grounds for such a claim.

But is this in fact the end of the matter? In the aftermath of the Clinton election, one pro-life leader drew encouragement from a parallel in history. He said:

> Antislavery leaders must have shared a similar anxiety in March, 1857. After more than 25 years of unremitting toil, they say—within the space of a week—President James Buchanan sworn into office as a proslavery Democrat and the Supreme Court issued its decision in *Dred Scott*, declaring a constitutional right to own slaves and stripping Congress of any power to limit the spread of slavery. The tri-

Portions of this article are adapted from J. D. Hunter, *Before the Shooting Begins: Searching for Democracy in America's Culture War* (New York, 1994).

umph of slavery seemed complete. But, of course, just three and a half years later, Lincoln was elected President, and, even without the Civil War, change would have come.[1]

The observation gives us pause: all three branches of government *did* share a consensus about slavery in 1857—and in 1920 all three shared a consensus about prohibition, and in 1964 they shared a consensus about racial equality, and in each case consensus among the three branches of government did not bring an end to those great national debates. Far from it. So too with abortion.

The *politics* of abortion will continue in a tangled web at every level. At the national level, several strategies will be pursued among the purported losers. Pro-life organizations have vowed to challenge the constitutionality of FOCA in the courts. They have pledged to engage in offensive litigation and legislation to thwart efforts to expand the funding of abortion through the government and through national health insurance companies. They will challenge every effort to expand abortion referral and practice on military bases and other government institutions. They will challenge the legitimacy of the Freedom of Access to Clinic Entrances Act (affecting protest groups like Operation Rescue). Challenging fetal experimentation and fetal tissue research will also be high on the docket for pro-life advocates. At the state and local level, politicans with pro-life inclinations and commitments will continue to chisel away at the legal edifice surrounding access to abortion. In recent years, pro-life activists have made electoral gains and are poised to enact regulations that the Court still views as constitutional. Battles long waged at the national level, then, will be reenacted around the country in state legislatures. At the grassroots level, pro-life organizations will continue to mobilize their largely middle-class, church-going constituencies toward the restriction of abortion practice. Medical malpractice suits against physicians and clinics performing failed abortions will be relentlessly pursued. Operation Rescue and other "rescue" organizations will also continue to create an environment where the private practice of abortion is stigmatized and actual access to an abortion is even more difficult.

It is the last arena that is perhaps most significant, for at this level the battles will be fought over access and provision of abortion services. In some respects, pro-life initiatives are already making the formal legal and political battles beside the point. As is often cited, 83 percent of the counties in America already do not have a single abortion provider. What is more, the number of obstetrical-gynecological residency programs training physicians to do first-trimester abortions has dwindled dramatically.

In 1985, 25 percent of all such programs offered this training; in 1991, it had dropped to 12 percent.[2] Already it is clear that fewer younger doctors are willing and available to replace older abortion providers as the latter prepare to retire. The stigma is great; the practice is low in prestige and fairly isolated from mainstream medicine; and the personal costs (particularly if the physician has children) make the specialization unattractive to say the least. In the end, pro-choice advocates wonder rightly, What good are the laws protecting a woman's access to abortion if the "service" is not available? All combined, then, it is clear that the politics of abortion will continue well into the future. A consensus of the major branches of government will not bring this conflict to an end.

Some suggest that technology may provide the only long-term resolution to this conflict, for it would allow us to circumvent such politics altogether. The argument is that the medical profession and the new technologies created by it may so "medicalize the womb" that abortion as we now know it will simply become a nonissue.[3] For example, to the degree it is successfully distributed and implanted, relatively new contraceptive technologies like "Norplant" (a five-year contraceptive implanted under the skin) and Depo-Provera (a three-month contraceptive injected into the bloodstream) will dramatically reduce conception and therefore the *need* for abortion. For women who do get pregnant, abortifacients such as RU-486 will largely privatize, and therefore depoliticize, the *process* of abortion.

Technology, however, will probably only alter the specific points of political conflict rather than eliminate the conflict. Every technological "advance" will likely spawn new protest movements and countermovements. The activist themselves anticipate this. Speaking of RU-486, for example, Peg Yorkin of the Feminist Majority Foundation declared that the "genie" is "out of the bottle." To get it to American women, "We are prepared to do whatever we have to do."[4] In response, Keith Tucci of Operation Rescue countered, "When they invent new ways to kill children, we will invent new ways to save them."[5] This response has not been idle. It is the threat of a boycott of Hoechst AG, the German majority owner of the French manufacturer of RU-486, that many believe has kept the drug off the market so far in the United States.

The matter does not end there. There are the issues of reproductive technology (such as *in vitro* fertilization, artificial insemination, and surrogate motherhood), prenatal screening, fetal tissue harvesting, and, not unrelated, physician-assisted suicide and euthanasia as well, and here too political polarization defines the character of the debates. Reproduction and population control, in all its diverse facets, will continue to be a major area of social and political conflict in the years to come even as the specific points of conflict shift and change. As with a perpetual check in the game of chess, positions continue to move in all of these areas of public policy, creating the impression of change but no substantive end to the conflicts.

What, then, accounts for the interminable nature of these political disputes? The answer, in brief, is that politics is only an artifact of a conflict that is much deeper, a conflict between fundamentally different moral visions of human life—individual and collective—embedded within different and antagonistic interpretive communities. To say that politics is an artifact is not to say it is unimportant. Rather, politics is an instrument (a weapon, if you will) used on behalf of deeply rooted moral agendas. Yet it is at this subterranean level that the disputes over abortion, reproduction technology, and other edge-of-life issues remain ostensibly fixed and intransigent. Yet even here, within the competing moral understandings and symbols of this controversy, one can observe both conflict and transformation. This essay explores the nature of these cultural tensions and transformations and the structural factors influencing change at this level.

The Struggle to Define Human Nature

In the range of policy disputes mentioned above, abortion remains unquestionably at the center. "Whether by inherent logic or by historical accident." Richard John Neuhaus has said, the abortion debate is "the magnet to which all the other life-and-death debates are attached."[6] The reason is that it raises core philosophical questions about the nature of human life and human community. The dispute certainly contains within it different understandings of womanhood, and motherhood in particular, as Kristin Luker has argued.[7] Yet perhaps even more fundamentally, philosophically speaking, it symoblizes competing ideas of what constitutes meaningful life and death in our society, and in life what is the nature of human community.

Consider abortion through this symbolic prism. Cultural progressives imply that life has meaning as long as it constitutes a conscious and rational existence; choice is the principal expression and political symbol of life. Because the fetus is neither conscious nor rational, it has no meaningful life and therefore its "death"—if one can use that term—is virtually meaningless. The majority of cultural conservatives, by contrast, contend that only God can give life and if he gives it, it is meaningful by definition since humans at all stages of development or states of existence reflect his image and purpose. Every unborn child, therefore, is to be valued; every abortion means the destruction of providentially ordained life.

It follows from this that abortion implicitly symbolizes different ideas about what moral and social obligations we hold toward others. Progressives insist that our primary obligations are to women, whose rights and needs have for too long been denied or suppressed. Certainly, they will say, our obligation to a living person is greater than our obligation to what is at most a "potential person." On the other hand, since the anti-abortion advocate begins with the assumption that the fetus is a human child, she comes to the conclusion that her pro-choice adversary is self-centered. According to this logic, in matters of life and death, our obligations must extend first to those who are most defenseless. To come down on one side or the other of this issue, therefore, is to make a statement about who is qualified for inclusion in the human community, and thus who is worthy of our care and protection.

The nature of human life and human community are also, mutatis mutandis, the symbolic core of all edge of life disputes. For cultural progressives, cessation of the organismic functions (by say, withholding food and fluids) is something of a technicality for those who are in a "vegetative state," since the person's life, in a meaningful (i.e., rational, deliberate) sense of the term, has already ended. For cultural conservatives, the life of such a person has inherent dignity and worth and to end it through starvation is nothing short of barbaric. So too with the terminally-ill who choose to end their lives with the aid of a physician: for progressives, that choice is inviolable because it is an expression of a person's very humanity; for conservatives, the choice is inherently immoral because it involves the individual and the physician "playing God." The promethean assertion of human will in place of divine prerogative (especially as this prerogative is seized by the state or other powerful institutions) is also the core conservative argument against new birth technologies (especially *in vitro* fertilization) and prenatal genetic screening (not to mention euthanasia). For progressives, such technological advances represent the tools by which compassionate intervention can be made on behalf of the infertile couple, families predisposed to genetically based "abnormalities," and those in serious, long-term pain.

In sum, the controversies over abortion, reproduction technologies, and end-of-life issues carry many layers of meaning, but at root they signify different propositions about what it means to *be* human. As in the case of abortion, it makes no more sense to talk about "murdering" a fetus that is "nothing more than a part of a woman's body" than it does to speak of a "harmless surgical procedure" that terminates the life of a "human being." The ontological status attributed to embryonic life (in the case of abortion) is directly linked to the level of moral outrage or indifference that is evoked. The logic extends to the range of other disputes as well.

Popular Opinion

These moral/philosophical distinctions play out most clearly in the worldviews of activists and special-interest organizations, but they play out as well in the experience of ordinary Americans. According to a Gallup survey conducted in 1990,[8] only a small number of Americans believe that the main attribute distinguishing humans from other forms of life is their membership in a community (1 percent), their capacity to experience a range of emotions (5 percent), or their ability to work and be productive (3 percent). When all is said and done, opinions on the meaning of personhood found in the general public tend to settle on one side or the other of the Enlightenment divide: a large group of Americans (36 percent) believes the most important feature of human life is its creation in God's own image, while an even larger group (49 percent) believes it is the human ability to think and reason. Those who view personhood as a function of an ability to think and reason are varied in their ethical evaluation of abortion, although a plurality (37 percent) see it as "the taking of human life" but stop short of calling it murder, a quarter see it as full-fledged murder, and another quarter see it as nothing more serious than a surgical procedure. A stronger consensus emerges among those with a sacred view of personhood—that it is created in God's image. Among these, more than half see abortion as full-fledged murder, and only a few of whom (7 percent) would cast it as a surgical procedure.

Competing understandings of human nature and human life are also consequential for other edge-of-life issues. Of those who held a rationalist understanding of human distinctiveness, two-thirds approved of "withholding food and water from a terminally ill patient who is in great pain and who requests that he or she be permitted to die" compared to one-fourth of those with a theistic understanding. Likewise, in cases of extreme infant deformity, two-thirds of those with secular rationalist understandings of human nature agreed that "the best thing for everyone concerned may be for doctors and parents to let the newborn infant die" compared to two-thirds of those with theistic understandings who *disagreed* with this position. Although the majority of Americans agreed that the family of a person in a vegetative state (and with no real hope for improvement), in consultation with doctors, should have the right to remove life support, those with theistic assumptions about human life were far less likely to agree with this than those with rationalist assumptions. Finally, more than half of those who had theistic understandings of human nature said that is was "always wrong" for "a depressed person, without the will to live, to take their own life," compared to one-third of those with rationlist understandings who took this position.

It is essential to note that the association between conceptions of human nature and their relations to the ethics of abortion, euthanasia, and the like are not free-floating. Different conceptions of what constitutes human nature are embedded in different religious and moral communities. What this means is that such commitments are not only rooted in larger worldviews but that these worldviews are institutionally grounded within and sustained by *communities of moral conversation.* In fact, when all factors are weighted together, the community of moral conversation to which a person belongs is a much better predictor of their position on the abortion issue (in particular) than that person's education, regional identity, race, gender, or any other background factor.[9] Indeed the special-interest organizations typically take form as extensions of these moral communities.

Language, Power, and Public Policy

As the concept suggests, communities of moral conversation operate with their own relatively distinct moral language from which are constructed different moral visions of human being and social life. Given the significance of these communities in the drama of these disputes, it is not surprising that the "subterranean" conflict is over the language by which we describe and interpret the behavior taking place. In the case of abortion, is the object/subject being aborted a "fetus" or an "unborn baby"? Is abortion "murder" or a "safe surgical practice"? Is one side's rhetoric "obscene," "demeaning," and "manipulative," while the other's is "realistic" or just slightly "colorful"? Are people who blockade abortion clinics practicing "civil disobedience" in the name of protecting life, or are they practicing "terrorism" against women?

This tug-of-war over terminology is not uncommon in such disputes. Debates over public policy, as Peter Berger has observed, are often debates over language.[10] The reason is that language both reflects and shapes social reality, for words themselves frame how we make sense of experience. Over time, the words by which we name things shape our most basic dispositions—about what is real and what isn't; about what is significant and what isn't; about what is worthy of moral outrage and what isn't. Naturally, those who have the power to establish the language of public debate will have a tremendous advantage in determining the debate's outcome. When the terms of debate become established, the categories by which resistance can be put forward are, ipso facto, discredited or even eliminated. And so it is that linguistic victories translate into political victories. Activists on both sides themselves acknowledge this. "Language is everything," as one Planned Parenthood executive put it.[11] The question we now consider is how these dynamics play out in the range of controversies at the edge of life.

The Triumph of "Choice" as a Public Language

Mary Ann Glendon has argued recently that the language of "rights" has come to dominate public discourse over most issues of national consequence. This is true of all of the issues under discussion here. In terms of the abortion controversy, Glendon argues, "Prolife and prochoice advocates alike have overwhelmingly opted for rights talk, a choice that has forced the debate into a seemingly nonnegotiable deadlock between the fetus's 'right to life' and the pregnant woman's 'right to choose.' "[12] The conflict over the status of the embryo in in virto fertilization and genetic screening centers on the embryo's right to life or treatment as a patient and the right of parents to conceive a child and their right to abort if fetal defects are found. Indeed, in "wrongful birth" litigation a claim is made to a right to know if the developing fetus has any defects that can be medically identified prior to birth, and in the occasional "wrongful life" suit, even a claim to a right not to be born in the first place.

Underneath this "seemingly nonnegotiable deadlock" between competing rights, however, is a negotiation over language. On the political surface there is deadlock, but beneath the pro-life movement has increasingly accepted the language of choice employed by their opponents.

One poignant illustration of this came from an effort by pro-life organizations in 1990 to determine which of their arguments were the most compelling to Americans, the ones that would allow them to regain ground in the battle for public opinion. Surveys they commissioned, however, demonstrated even further how pro-life and pro-choice Americans live and operate in different moral universes. According to the Gallup survey, those on the pro-choice side of the debate found little compelling in *any* of the pro-life arguments, contentions such as all human life, including that of the unborn, shoud be protected; every unborn child has a basic right to life; human life begins at conception, therefore, abortion is murder; while abortion is sometimes necessary, it is used too frequently as an easy way out—none of these held much credibility. Those with strong abortion rights commitments did not even find the feminist arguments against abortion—that abortion enables men to take advantage of women; that abortion promotes a disregard for the value of human life; that abortion leaves women with emotional scars, etc.—at all convincing.

But what of those Americans who are ambivalent about the issue? It is their option, after all, that the pro-life movement is most eager to influence. Which arguments do they find most plausible? A 1990 Wirthlin study, commissioned by the United States Catholic Conference, pressed this question furthest and concluded that the pro-life movement could best shore up support among its allies—and best undermine its opposition—by concentrating on a "rights/choice-oriented" message, emphasizing the "rights" of the unborn to live and make all of life's choices; the right of women to receive counseling if they choose; the right of a father to have a choice to be involved in the decision of whether his child is aborted; the rights of parents to have a choice to counsel a teenage daughter who is pregnant; and so on. A central part of this strategy, Wirthlin suggested, would be to *reclaim* the language of choice and by so doing, "rename their opponents with the word they promote—abortion." Thus, pro-life supporters were encouraged to call their opponents "pro-abortion," "abortion supporters," and so on, rather than "pro-choice." The conclusion, in other words, was not to rework the old pro-life message or articulate a new message but to adopt the language used by the opposition, infusing it with new meaning that would ultimately lead people to start thinking about the protection of fetal life. In sum, the Wirthlin study found that it is the combined language of "rights" and "choice" that resonates most broadly in the public arena. The pollster's chief advice to the pro-life movement, therefore, was to recognize this appeal and to promote it as the central apologia for the protection of the fetus *in utero*.

The advice was not ignored. Indeed the largest and most expensive campaign ever waged to alter public opinion to the pro-life perspective began immediately after this survey and was based in part on its findings. The Arthur DeMoss Foundation, a conservative foundation based in St. David's, Pennsylvania, began a multi-million-dollar advertisement campaign in print and television formats, declaring "life" as "a beautiful choice."

For the pro-life movement to embrace the language of choice is ironic, for it will likely have the unintended consequence of neutralizing the animating spirit of the pro-life movement. They will have fought their political battle by conceding the cultural/linguistic war. It would not be a consensus among the three branches of government that would bring about a pro-choice victory, as Charles Krauthammer argued. Rather, the pro-choice side would have achieved victory by their opponents embracing the moral/linguistic framework of the pro-choice movement.

The battle over how abortion is to be framed linguistically has been waged for well over two decades, and for this reason we can observe the direction of the transformation taking place. In other related areas the battle over language is only now taking form.

RU-486

Although hailed by its advocates as "the pill that could end the abortion wars,"[13] the drug Mifepristine (or RU-486) will, as we have argued, change only the particular points of controversy. Most of the political conflict (and public attention) centers on its testing and distribution. Underneath these disputes, however, is a debate over what in fact to call the drug. Advocates have typically called it the "abortion pill" because technically it is an abortifacient—it blocks the effect of progesterone, the hormone needed to sustain the uterine wall during the early stages of pregnancy—though it is being tested as a once-a-month contraceptive. Its opponents, however, have been less generous in their description of the drug. The National Right to Life Committee has dubbed it the "death drug" and a "chemical Dalkon shield" and the evangelical magazine *Christianity Today* has called it a "human pesticide."[14]

Deeper yet is a linguistic dispute over what to call the *effects* of the drug. The word "abortion" does present public relations problems for RU-486 advocates. Perhaps it is for this reason that Etienne-Emile Baulieu, French scientist and one of the principal developers of RU-486, has argued that its effect should not be described as "abortion" at all. He contends that the term abortion should be reserved for surgical methods of pregnancy termination and prefers the word "contragestion" (a contraction of the "contragestation") for those methods that work the middle range, "countering gestation before implantation or in pregnancy's earliest stages."[15] By this definition, all of the medical contraceptive technologies are at least minimally contragestion.

This distinction, which seeks to shift the opprobrium of "abortion" off RU-486, also highlights the overlapping effects of various birth-control methods and problematizes the concept of abortion, which has tended to mean for the layman any procedure after fertilization. This blurring of distinctions challenges the pro-life movement, part of which is against medical contraception (e.g., the Catholic Church and the American Life League), part of which does not take a stand on the issue (e.g., the National Right to Life Committee), and part of which is in favor of contraception (e.g., many Protestant pro-life adherents). In addition, though, this blurring of distinctions would seem also to challenge those who are "personally pro-life," that is, in favor of legalized abortion but personally committed to never have one. When does a method cease to be contragestion and begin to be abortion? Would the taking of RU-486 prior to known pregnancy be an acceptable method of birth control? Redefining RU-486 into language that is more acceptable, then, has the potential of dividing the pro-life movement and its various sources of popular support by capitalizing on the lack of consensus in the pro-life movement as to what constitutes abortion. But it also raises many of the same questions for those in the pro-choice movement who see RU-486 as an "eerie drug" and ask themselves "whether there isn't a critical distinction between a contraceptive and a 'contra-gestive.' "[16]

Norplant

The political difficulty over Norplant has centered on its social objectives. Just two days after FDA approval of Norplant in December 1990, for example, the *Philadelphia Inquirer* published an editorial, "Poverty and Norplant—Can Contraception Reduce the Underclass?" which suggested that welfare mothers be offered incentives to use Norplant: " . . . it's very tough to undo the damage of being born into a dysfunctional family," the *Inquirer* reasoned.[17] Similar proposals were later made by various state legislators and, in some instances, mandatory use was suggested. Judges in various states made mandatory Norplant use a condition of parole in certain cases involving women convicted of child abuse, drug use, and related crimes. Various states have introduced Norplant in their public and school-based clinics. In each of these venues, the use of Norplant has been argued in terms of certain benefits that might accrue to society by the temporary sterilization Norplant offers. The frame of reference has been social costs—underclass growth, expanding welfare rolls, public health, crime, teen pregnancy. Kansas Representative Kerry Patrick (R), for example, proposed legislation in his state that would pay $500 to any mother on welfare who used Norplant. Patrick's view was that the incentives program would save taxpayers "millions of their hard-earned dollars."[18] This emphasis starts from social goals and ties in the need of the individuals involved as not inconsistent with and perhaps even fostered by these goals.

The reaction has centered on questioning the social goals of those who have put forth mandatory or incentive Norplant use and recasting the problem in terms of individual choice. Responses to the *Inquirer* editorial, for example, suggested the plan was racist population control. Vanessa Williams, president of the Philadelphia Association of Black Journalists, told the *New York Times* that the editorial was a "tacit endorsement of slow genocide."[19] Responding to a similar outcry over the introduction of Norplant in public schools, Baltimore Health Commissioner Peter Beilenson insisted that students are "never coerced. . . . The population control bit is a myth."[20] In Virginia, after the General Assembly approved an expansion of funds to health clinics for Norplant distribution, Anne B. Kincaid of the pro-life Family Foundation called the program a "technocratic equivalent of ethnic cleansing." "This is not ethnic cleansing," responded Lieutenant Governor Donald S. Beyer Jr. "This is one of the most compassionate things we can do."[21] Similar controversy has erupted in Michigan, California, Texas, and other states.

What one side sees as an act of compassion, the other sees as racial genocide and ethnic cleansing. What proponents call incentives, others, such as ACLU lawyer Julie Mertus, call a "bribe."[22] What one side sees as a concern for social welfare, the other sees as fashioning "birth control, which represents an expansion of personal power, into a threatening instrument of government control."[23] Much is at stake—the subtle and not so subtle struggle over language will continue. The fate of Norplant itself is likely to hang on the terms that come to predominate.

New Birth Technologies

The new birth technologies raise questions that have been endemic to the abortion debate and are articulated by proponents in the same language of rights, undue burden, and quality of life. When does a developing human life become a "person" and therefore the "possessor of rights"? Does a couple have a right to procreate *and* a right not to procreate? Does the right to procreate include the right to a healthy baby or a baby with certain characteristics of the parents' choosing? What kind of life is worth living?

In vitro fertilization (IVF) has been framed by proponents as a therapeutic procedure for the sake of an infertile couple or a homosexual couple. An ova, either the patient's or a donor's, and sperm, either a husband's or a donor's, are brought together in a petri dish and the resulting embryo implanted in the patient. The medical community has generally been of the view that "In vitro fertilization falls within the realm of traditional medical motivation—to remove a limitation on normal healthy life,"[24] that is, infertility. Proponents focus attention on the plight of the infertile couple and speak of IVF as a compassionate and medically appropriate response to that plight. A couple's desire to bear a child, even the right to procreate, is argued over against what opponents of the procedure consider the fundamental issue with this technique—the status of the embryo. Addressing a National Institutes of Health Human Embryo Research Panel in February 1994, Father Matthew Habiger, O.S.B., argued that the human embryo is "a subject of rights."[25] Only treatments in the best interest of *this* patient are just. With IVF, multiple embryos are typically implanted to increase the chances of at least one successful implantation. If more than one begins to develop, a technique called "selective reducton of pregnancy" is used, a euphemism for an abortion process that can involve injections of potassium chloride into the developing fetus to bring about cardiac arrest. Moreover, extra embryos that were not implanted may be frozen for later attempts or discarded. And genetic screening of preimplantation embryos means further wasting. For opponents of all this the focus is not on infertility but on the fact that the IVF technician "kills defenseless human beings."[26] Proponents, naturally, recognize the problem of treating embryos as patients: "The embryo as patient runs the danger of personalizing the embryo and further confusing the question of the beginning of life. It also sets the stage for elevating the embryo to the status of an entity with rights."[27] With this clearly in mind, one advocate, law professor Alta Charo of the University of Wisconsin, Madison, has suggested that "unnecessary controversies" could be avoided by referring to embryos as "products of conception."[28]

Recently a technique has been developed in England whereby ova can be retrieved from aborted female fetuses for the purposes of being fertilized in vitro and then implanted in infertile or homosexual women. Needless to say, this new twist on IVF has generated controversy. Member of Parliament David Alton, as Liberal democrat, called the treatment "reminiscent of grave robbing." "This consumerist approach to the creation of life," he said, "puts it on a par with an American fast-food outlet." Dr. Stuart Campbell, head of obstetrics at King's College Hospital in London, expressed the characteristic sentiment of IVF proponents in shifting the focus away from the origins of the eggs to the therapeutic motivation: "Nonmedical moralists who sound off don't see the desperation of infertile couples."[29]

Here again, the names we give things reflect what they mean to us. Is

IVF compassion for an infertile couple who has a right to procreate or the "commodification" of the reproductive process, as the Vatican and some feminists have called it?[30] Are embryos simply "products of conception"—"property" that can be discarded, manipulated, or experimented upon at will—or are they "human beings"? Is embryo destruction a "reduction of pregnancy" or the taking of human life? Linguistically, it is one or the other; it cannot be both. As Professor Charo observed, the predominance of a certain vocabulary can spell the end of some controversies. The alternative perspectives are simply defined out of the discussion.

Helping an infertile couple to exercise their choice to have a child is also the rationale for surrogate motherhood, the arrangement by which an embryo, fertilized in vitro (or conceivably in vivo, natural conception followed by flushing the uterus before implantation), is implanted in the uterus of a third-party female, typically a woman who is paid for this service (often in the $10,000 to $12,000 range). In the case of surrogate motherhood, the language of choice and rights takes a stark, contractual focus. In the surrogate contact signed in the famous Baby M case in New Jersey, the surrogate contracted to carry a baby to term but not to "form a parent-child relationship" with it, and to deliver, as far as could be medically ascertained, a healthy child. She agreed upon the request of a specific physician to undergo amniocentesis or similar tests to detect genetic and congenital defects. "In the event that said test reveals that the fetus is genetically or congenitally abnormal, MARY BETH WHITEHEAD, Surrogate, agrees to abort the fetus upon demand of WILLIAM STERN, Natural Father, in which case the fee paid to the Surrogate will be in accordance with paragraph 10."[31]

Those in favor of surrogate motherhood argue the issue in terms of the childless couple: it is the only means by which some infertile couples can have a child genetically linked to (at least one of) them. This is a contract, no different from other contracts that society protects and enforces. The surrogate acts within her constitutional right to privacy. Critics, when focusing on the child, call it "baby-selling." If the focus is on the surrogate, concerns are raised about "breeder women," "bioslavery," and "financial exploitation." Feminist author Katha Pollitt argues: "Surrogacy degrades women by devaluing pregnancy and childbirth; it degrades children by commercializing their creation; it degrades the poor by offering them a devil's bargain at bargain prices."[32] "Degradation," "bioslavery," "baby selling" versus "contractual agreement between consenting parties," an "infertility treatment," "compassion"—two languages; competing realities. The heart of the cultural conflict lies in the competition to define reality.

While the agreement to abort in surrogate motherhood contracts may prove to be unconstitutional, the question of abortion is clearly central to the practice of prenatal screening, either to discover genetic defects or the presence or absence of certain desirable traits. Proponents argue in terms of choice, quality of life, and public benefit. With regard to screening for fetal defects, Nobel Prize-winning biologist David Baltimore framed the issue in these terms: "The real question is to what extent are we going to want to have children born with genetic diseases. Within the next few years we will be able to identify nearly all children who are the potential recipients of deleterious genes *in utero* early enough to abort them." His view is that "it would be cheaper, more effective and cause less pain and suffering to abort most cases of genetic lesions, rather than allow them to come to term, and then try to deal with their disease."[33]

Handicapped persons are offended by this line of thinking. It suggests they are a burden that we would rather do without and that living with a genetic handicap is not a quality life. They observe that reaction to sex-selection abortions tends to hinge on the argument that such selection—often of females—expresses the implicit view that females are worth less than males. With new genetic advances on the horizon that might allow for prenatal screening of a wide range of characteristics—hair color, propensity to obesity, low I.Q., short stature, etc.—how this issue is framed takes on new urgency. Are there limits to "choice"? In light of the often-repeated "every child a wanted child," what does it mean to "want" a child?

Euthanasia

The contest over language not only gets played out at the beginning of life but at the end of life as well. Questions over when death occurs and when can ending life be justified are articulated in the same frame concepts of choice and quality of life.

One of the pressures for "clarification" about when death occurs comes from the need for organs. Brain-dead patients are the major source for organs, including all hearts and livers. New definitions are being put forward that would redefine death in terms of "higher" brain death, sometimes known as cerebral death or neocortical death. This would include those in what is known as a "permanent vegetative state" as well as anencephalic newborns, that is, those born with most of their brain missing. An advocate of the new death definition, Dr. Robert Smith, explained the usefulness of this concept:

> A neocortical death standard could significantly increase availability and access to transplants because patients (including anencephalics) declared dead under a neocortical definition would be biologically maintained for years as opposed to a few hours or days, as in the case of whole brain death. Under the present Uniform Anatomical Gift Act, this raises the possibility that neocortically dead bodies or parts could be donated and maintained for long-term research, as organ banks, or for other purposes such as drug testing or manufacturing biological compounds."[34]

Popularizing this linguistic formulation for the difficult circumstances of the terminally ill is Jack Kevorkian, the Michigan physician who has been actively involved with assisting suicides. Kevorkian frames the matter as "medicide," or a "planned death."[35] In an interview with *Free Inquiry,* for example, Kevorkian suggested that a technological end to life would highlight the "goodness of planned death":

> "If the patient opts for euthanasia, or if someone is to be executed, and at the same time opts to donate organs, he or she can save anywhere from five to ten lives. Now the death becomes definitely, incalculably positive. The patient may opt to undergo experimentation under anesthesia, from which he or she won't awaken. This could affect millions of lives now and in the future."[36]

Complimenting this view is Derek Humphry's description of suicide as "self-deliverance" and "death with dignity."[37] Needless to say, opponents of assisted suicide and euthanasia are content to label the actions as "murder," and view the idea of maintaining a human body to serve as an "organ bank" or drug-testing site as deeply repulsive. These, they say, do not make death meaningful.

Is Kevorkian himself a courageous humanist (the American Humanist Association celebrated him in 1993 as their "humanist of the year") or is he "Dr. Death"? The sobriquet that endures over time will invariably be linked to the fate of his ideas and the linguistic field in which these types of actions are framed.

The Eugenics Movement

Finally, the history of eugenics in the United States contains within it another illustration of the way in which language games are played. The early eugenics movement sought control over the fertility of those considered "unfit" out of concern for social decline brought about by the deterioration of American genetic quality. Between 1907 and 1931, thirty states passed eugenic studies providing for sterilization of the "unfit." In the case of *Buck v. Bell,* Supreme Court Justice Oliver Wendell Holmes Jr. expressed the sentiment that prevailed in progressive circles:

> She may be sexually sterilized without detriment to her general health and that her welfare and that of society will be promoted by her sterilization. We have seen more than once that the public welfare may call upon the best citizens for their lives. It would be strange if it [the state] could not call upon those who already sap the strength of the State for these lesser sacrifices, often not felt to be such by those concerned, in order to prevent our being swamped with incompetence. It is better for all the world, if instead of waiting to execute degenerate offspring for crime, or let them starve for their imbecility, society can prevent those who are manifestly unfit from breeding their kind. . . . Three generations of imbeciles are enough.[38]

The issue was framed in terms of a focus on social well-being; though the individual may need to make some "lesser sacrifice," the good of society required it. The well-being of the individual must be subordinate to that larger good. Up through the war years, talk of eugenics was open and actively promoted by a variety of organizations who spoke of its advantages for trimming welfare assistance, reducing crime, purifying the genetic stock, and so on. What is more, it was legitimated by the still-emerging science of genetics, and attracted some of the most luminous scientists and public figures in American life.

The appropriation of the eugenics movement by Germany under Hitler and developments in genetics discredited terms like "eugenics," the "unfit," "bad stock," and notions of "racial superiority." In the immediate postwar years, many of the old eugenicists shifted their focus to the emerging issue of "population control," based on the more global idea of overpopulation. This transition was accomplished with linguistic bridges that rearticulated goals in new and more acceptable terms. With mandatory fertility control for the sake of social betterment discredited, the focus shifted to voluntary fertility control for the sake of social betterment, with considerable organizational support mobilized to facilitate the choice. The New Jersey League for Human Betterment, for example, was founded by a prominent eugenicist and other New Jerseyites in 1937 with a goal of promoting eugenic sterilization. Over the years the organization has changed names many times, becoming in 1965 the Association for Voluntary Sterilization and in

1987 the Association for Voluntary Surgical Contraception. The association operates a worldwide network of sterilization clinics, many of which are in poor countries. Its various name changes, reflecting the shifting emphasis to voluntariness and "surgical contraception," would seem to be a linguistic effort to downplay the permanent nature of sterilization.

Longtime and ardent birth-control activist Clarence Gamble saw population control as a means to reduce welfare costs. The Pennsylvania Birth Control Federation during his presidency in the 1930s issued pamphlets that asked, given the high expenditures of welfare, whether it was "time that the program of sterilization of the unfit be considered anew."[39] They also sounded themes remarkably like those voiced during the recent Norplant debates: "Birth control prevents destitution and dependency. It gives relief to the overburdened taxpayer by preventing the births of children who can only be cared for at public expense."[40] Gamble started the Pathfinder Fund, which continues his legacy today as a major population-control concern.

Since its founding in 1921, the American Eugenics Society has been perhaps the most important eugenicist organization in the United States. Its longtime secretary, Frederick Osborn, was a founder, trustee from 1952 to 1968, and president from 1957 to 1959 of the Population Council. Established in the early 1950s by John D. Rockefeller III, the council was a major player in gaining legitimacy for the then-emerging notion of "population policies" to control fertility, now a central element of development strategies in both developed and underdeveloped countries. The society shared office space with the council for many years, as well as officers and key staff.[41] In 1972 the society belatedly changed its name to the more neutral sounding Society for the Social Biology but, according to one reporter, "assured its members that its policies hadn't changed."[42] Old ideas, new language. The effort to control fertility for the sake of social goals, even national interest, continues apace.[43]

Clearly, the effort to gain cultural legitimacy for public policy initiatives, on all sides of a dispute, is principally an effort to reframe the issues in terms of those who would benefit and to downplay, disguise, or render nonexistent other dimensions of the issue.

Structural Factors Influencing the Environment of Debate

Needless to say, these cultural dynamics do not exist in a sociological vacuum. There are at least three important structural factors that influence the direction they will take over the longterm.

The first factor is the ongoing secularization of public discourse. How is this problematic? Survey research has shown that support and funding for the conservative positions vis-à-vis abortion, contraception and birth technology, and population management are institutionalized within faith communities. It is the moral logic of religious faith and the language which gives it articulation that makes pro-life arguments on all of these matters credible. To be sure, certain local churches and national denominations will continue long into the future as centers of resistance. They face two problems, however. One problem is that the cultural particularities of these communities, though once dominating American public culture, now have less and less general appeal and credibility. Law and public policy, even when it is conservative, is framed in secular language. It can no longer make anything but banal appeals to sacred symbols. The other problem is that cultural fragmentation proceeds apace within these communities. The 1990 Gallup survey, for example, found within the evangelical Protestant and conservative Catholic churches large numbers who are "conveniently pro-life" (those who are strongly pro-life in their philosophy but pro-choice in personal practice) and "secretly pro-life" (those who, despite their distinctly pro-life moral leanings, tend to think of themselves as "neutral" or even "moderately pro-choice" in the controversy itself because they share very little else with the average pro-life advocate). About one out of five evangelicals and conservative Catholics would be considered "secretly pro-life," while another one out of eight would fall into the "conveniently pro-life" category. What this means is that religious communities that are predisposed to conservative positions on these public policy issues are not only having a difficult time defending their position in public, but they are having a difficult time maintaining consensus within their own ranks. As the secularization of American public culture proceeds, the categories by which resistance can be put forward will be rendered increasingly implausible and perhaps, eventually, altogether useless except in small, isolated pockets of social and policy activism.

A second factor influencing the direction of these disputes is the propensity (and perhaps imperative) within technology toward self-augmentation. This is the tendency toward growth in techniques based in the pursuit of the most efficient means possible to accomplish a given task. In brief, the very existence of a given technology calls for its application. In the case of abortion, the very possibility of safe abortion calls for its utilization. So too with new birth technologies, such as prenatal genetic screening. In the latter case, the very premise of the technology is that fetal abnormalities or genetic predispositions toward certain conditions discovered through such tests will lead to the destruction of these embryos/fetuses. Efforts to reduce the incidence of genetic-related maladies by screening of embryos fail entirely if substantial numbers of parents do not follow through with an abortion. The same can be said for technology concerned with infertility. Reflecting on his own experience of trying to overcome infertility, one scholar wrote, "If the technology exists, the expectation is that it will be used. If surgery might repair the problem, even if the chances are not great, how can I not have surgery? If surgery and artificial insemination have not worked, but IVF might, how can I not try IVF? The very availability of the technology appears to exert a sort of tyrannical pressure to use it."[44] In all of these situations, human choice is, for all practical purposes, eliminated, except of course the choice among the most efficient means to deal with problems. Perhaps the most compelling evidence of the self-augmenting character of technology is the fact that technology is rarely, if ever, reversed.

The strength of the technological propensity toward self-augmentation is measured by the general incapacity of bioethical discussion to inhibit this growth. For example, when a George Washington University researcher announced that he had cloned human embryos, splitting single embryos into twins and triplets, public discussion immediately turned to the "ethical challenges" this technology posed for researchers and for society at large. Arthur Caplan, director of the Center for Bioethics at the University of Pennsylvania, however, acknowledged that while most scientists have scruples about such research, the technology can neither be controlled nor contained.[45] If correct, the "ethical challenge" is not so much to control the research outcomes as to provide ethical justifications for, and guidelines for the humane application of, outcomes that will take place anyway. In this sense, the bioethical conundrum is to create a sense of human control and direction to technological developments over which there is little or no control.

A third factor is the pressure of overpopulation. As with foreign-sponsored population control, domestic control would seem to solve so many problems at once—teen pregnancy, urban underclass, welfare dependency, urban crime. One proponent of population control has argued: "[B]efore we can have crime control, we need to have birth control. As the statistics make clear, illegitimacy is no longer a racial issue. . . . In the truest sense, it's a national security issue."[46] Having drawn the state deeply into the issue of fertility control, it is becoming harder for those who lobby for more individual choice to argue against population control when the economic consequences of those individual choices are passed directly along to the state or when the state sees a social need to limit such choice (e.g., in the case of child- or drug-abuse offenders or poor single mothers with many children) and the technology to do so is ready at hand.

There are also the medical and educational costs associated with the disabled and mentally retarded. In a strictly utilitarian sense, the cost of addressing the great needs of these challenged individuals is far more than testing and abortion. The pressures to abort such individuals are great, particularly if the state hesitates or refuses to share the burden with parents. In a survey of British obstetricians conducted in the late 1970s, 13 percent agreed that "the state should not be expected to pay for the specialized care of a child with a severe handicap in cases where the parents had declined the offer of prenatal diagnosis of the handicap."[47]

Not least, of course, are the burgeoning medical costs of a rapidly growing sector of senior citizens. As it is, the constraints upon Social Security, Medicaid, and Medicare are quite high. These are likely to intensify rather than slacken. Debate in public culture about the "worth" and "quality" of the lives of the aged and infirmed will intensify concomitantly. Under strained economic conditions, various forms of euthanasia and assisted suicide may become more plausible to more and more Americans and to policymakers as well. In all of these areas, what is now framed as "rights" and "choice" may, because of these kinds of pressures, come to mean the "social and moral obligation" of those making the choice.

Because of these factors, the cultural politics of abortion, reproduction technology, and population management is not played out on a level playing field. The edge-of-life debates will undoubtedly rage in the public realm for the foreseeable future, occupying much emotion, energy, and resources. The sociological factors behind these disputes, however, would suggest that in the long term, cultural progressives are not in a culture war of indeterminate outcome, but rather in something of a mopping-up campaign. How the particulars will work out of course remains to be seen, but key structural factors now strongly suggest that the historical momentum leans to the progressivist side of these disputes. If true, it is possible such policy will have unintended (antiliberal) consequences, particularly to the extent that the state becomes involved in ensuring a high quality of life.

Resistance and the "Slippery Slope"

Fear of what the future may bring is often articulated in terms of the "slippery slope" argument—the contention that "if we give ourselves permission to do one thing, we are inescapably inviting the question about permission to do the next thing."[48] In some instances, the effort is simply to define a particular question out of existence because to entertain it puts us precariously on the edge of this slippery slope. The observation made by Andrea Bonnicksen above on the question of the embryo as patient is a contention of this kind. More commonly, such arguments take shape when we cannot find grounds to reach a consensus on rejecting any particular current procedure—so we argue ahead to the loss of control that might follow and that would take us to a ravine we can agree should be avoided. For example, in her response to the idea of sentencing women to use Norplant, Kim Gandy, national secretary of the National Organization of Women, argued: "The issue of causing or preventing pregnancies is not something that should be in the province of the state. Once you prevent women who are addicted to drugs or abusing their children from getting pregnant, what's next? Black women? Jewish women?"[49] Seemingly unable to find a reason why controlling the fertility of certain women with Norplant might be unacceptable, she jumps ahead to a frightening future of massive state control.

There is an irony in the use of slippery-slope arguments. The metaphor itself is an image of one of sitting on the edge *about* to slide into apocalyptic disaster but not yet irrevocably over it. If we just stop here, the metaphor implies, we will not go over the edge; civilization will not careen out of control. The edge, however, keeps moving forward. What earlier generations would have called "chaos" are in later generations acceptable but portents of danger. At no point does anyone say the slide has begun. By allowing the edge to move forward, they help to maintain the very sense of human agency that the argument is meant to cast into doubt. In this way, bioethics and slippery-slope arguments operate in a kind of symbiosis—justifying innovations in human technology by implying they are not yet a sign of disaster, only a sign of danger. The danger points move forward.

Whether or not we are poised on the edge of a "slippery slope" cannot be established. And yet we can observe that change does occur. One thing does very often lead to another and this is the point where slippery slope arguments gain credibility. Indeed, powerful social forces and technological developments are pressing issues forward without waiting for ethical debates to begin or conclude. Meanwhile, the substantive moral questions that so greatly animate these conflicts, questions about what constitutes meaningful human life and the nature of our obligations to others—these remain.

University of Virginia

Notes

1. Clarke Forsythe, "Winning with Our Backs Against the Wall," unpublished paper, 30 November 1992, 1.

2. See Alissa Rubin, "The Abortion Wars Aren't Over," *Washington Post,* 13 December 1992, C2.

3. Jonathan Imber cogently lays out the future of abortion policy in light of medical advances in his article "Abortion Policy and Medical Practice," *Society,* 27 (July–August 1990): 27–34.

4. Quoted in David Van Biema, "But Will It End The Abortion Debate?" *Time,* 14 June 1993, 52.

5. Also quoted in ibid., 49.

6. Richard John Neuhaus, "The Return to Eugenics," *First Things,* March 1990, 35.

7. In Luker's frame of reference, abortion, for pro-choice advocates, symbolizes a woman's control over her reproductive capabilities. This control signals that a woman is no longer on unequal biological footing with a man; that she does not need to interrupt her career if she chooses not to, and thus she can achieve the same level of social and economic autonomy and power as a man. For pro-life advocates, abortion symbolizes an affront to the high and holy calling of motherhood. Since only women can have children, motherhood is viewed as a responsibility dictated by nature for the perpetuation of the human race. To sacrifice the life of an innocent child for the sake of economic and social autonomy is a perversion of the natural order. Accordingly, abortion signals also competing ideas about the source of meaning in life. For a pro-life woman, being a wife and a mother in the private realm of the home is intrinsically meaningful; there she can control the pace and content of her work. Paid labor outside the home is viewed as a world that inverts higher moral values for base, utilitarian values. Pro-choice women of course see it just the opposite way—the traditional division of labor between men and women relegates women to "second-class citizenship." It is through productive labor in the public sphere, a social realm long denied her, that a woman can achieve genuine equality. See Kristin Luker, *Abortion and the Politics of Motherhood* (Berkeley and Los Angeles, 1984).

8. The survey was based on in-person interviews with 2,174 adults, age 18 and older, in more than 360 locations across the nation during the period of 4–20 May 1990. As is standard for the Gallup Organization, the sampling procedure for the survey was designed to produce an approximation of the adult civilian population, 18 years and older, living in the United States, except those in institutions such as prisons or hospitals. This sample base, or "universe," approximates 169 million persons. The data were analyzed by the authors.

9. This analysis is elaborated in chapter 4 of J. D. Hunter, ibid.

10. See Brigitte Berger and Peter Berger, "Goshtalk, Femspeak, and the Battle of Language," in *The War Over the Family* (New York, 1984), chap. 4.

11. The statement is from Douglas Gould, former vice president for communications at Planned Parenthood of America, quoted in David Shaw, "Abortion Bias Seeps into News," *Los Angeles Times,* 1 July 1990.

12. Mary Ann Glendon, *Rights Talk* (New York, 1991), 66.

13. Lawrence Lader, *RU-486: The Pill That Could End the Abortion Wars and Why American Women Don't Have It* (Reading, Mass., 1991), 20.

14. Tamar Lewin, "Plans Stall to Put Abortion Pill in U.S.," *New York Times,* 13 October 1993, A17; Dorothy Wickenden, "Drug of Choice," *The New Republic,* 26 November 1990, 26; David Neff, "The Human Pesticide," *Christianity Today,* 32 (9 December 1988), 16.

15. Etienne-Emile Baulieu (with Mort Rosenblum), *"The Abortion Pill": RU-486, A Woman's Choice* (New York, 1990), 18.

16. Wickendon, "Drug of Choice," 27.

17. Editorial, "Poverty and Norplant: Can Contraception Reduce the Underclass?" *Philadelphia Inquirer,* 12 December 1990, reprinted in *Columbia Journalism Review* 29 (March–April 1991): 53.

18. Tamar Lewin, "A Plan to Pay Welfare Mothers for Birth Control," *New York Times,* 9 February 1991, A9.

19. Alex S. Jones, "An Editorial Stirs a Newsroom Feud," *New York Times,* 21 December 1990, A20.

20. Paul W. Valentine, "In Balance, A Tumultuous Hearing on Norplant," *Washington Post,* 10 February 1993, D5.

21. Peter Baker, "Va. Assembly Approves Norplant Money Despite Critics," *Washington Post,* 12 February 1993, D1.

22. Lewin, "A Plan to Pay Mothers for Birth Control." At least one Planned Parenthood affiliate took a different view of the "choice" question. Tina Proctor of the Planned Parenthood Federation in Aurora, Colorado, told *The New Republic:* "Our agency believes that if a woman chooses to accept extra welfare payments for using Norplant, it's a choice that the woman makes and if she can get something extra for using birth control, that's positive." Matthew Rees, "Shot in the Arm," *The New Republic,* 9 December 1991, 17.

23. Jane M. Johnson, vice-president, Affiliate Development and Education, Planned Parenthood of New York, "Letter—Compelling the Use of Contraceptives," *Washington Post,* 27 January 1993, A18.

24. Clifford Grobstein et al., "External Human Fertilization: An Evaluation of Policy," *Science,* 14 October 1983, 127, quoted in Stephen L. Isaacs and Renee J. Holt, "Redefining Procreation: Facing the Issues," *Population Bulletin* 42 (September 1987): 19.

25. Quoted in Mary Meehan, "The Brave New World of Fetal Research," *National Catholic Register,* 20 February 1994, 7.

26. 1987 Vatican Instruction, quoted in Isaacs and Holt, *Redefining Procreation,* 19.

27. Andrea Bonnicksen, "Genetic Diagnosis of Human Embryos," *Hastings Center Report* 22:4 (1992): S5–S11, quoted in James F. Keenan, "What's Your Worst Moral Argument?" *America,* 2 October 1993, 18.

28. Quoted in Mary Meehan, "Makeup of Fetal Research Panel Spells Nightmare," *National Catholic Register,* 6 March 1994, 8.

29. William Tuohy, "Plan to Use Eggs of Aborted Fetuses Fuels Ethics Debate," *St. Paul Pioneer Press,* 3 January 1994, 6A.

30. See the discussion in Paul Lauritzen, *Pursuing Parenthood: Ethical Issues in Assisted Reproduction* (Bloomington, 1993), 26–67.

31. Quoted in Robin Fox, "Babies for Sale," *The Public Interest,* Spring 1993, 18.

32. Quoted in Susan Edmiston, "Whose Child Is This?" *Glamour,* November 1991, 237.

33. Quoted in Jeff Lyon and Peter Gorner, "Altered Fates: The Promise of Gene Therapy," *Chicago Tribune,* Department of Health and Human Services reprint, 1986, 464.

34. David Lamb, *Organ Transplants and Ethics* (New York, 1990), 44.

35. Jack Kevorkian, *Prescription: Medicide—The Goodness of Planned Death* (Buffalo, 1991).

36. Quoted in Elizabeth W. Markson, "Moral Dilemmas," *Society* 29 (July–August 1992): 5.

37. Derek Humphry, *Final Exit: The Practicalities of Self-Deliverance and Assisted Suicide for the Dying* (Eugene, Ore., 1991).

38. Quoted in Thomas M. Shapiro, *Population Control Politics: Women, Sterilization, and Reproductive Choice* (Philadelphia, 1985), 3. This sentiment was also expressed in successful proposals to control immigration and discriminatory marriage laws. See Marc Lappe, *Genetic Politics: The Limits of Biological Control* (New York, 1979), 18.

39. Cited in ibid., 49.

40. Ibid., 50.

41. Mary Meehan, "Pop Council Spins Its Web," *National Catholic Register,* 9 January 1994.

42. Ibid., 9.

43. In January 1994, for example, the Clinton administration announced that it would request $585 million in spending on population programs in the fiscal 1995 budget, up from $502 million in fiscal 1994. According to Timothy Wirth of the State Department and spokesman on population policy for the administration, "When we think about what factors are going to affect the future of the world, population is absolutely at the top of the list." Moreover, "everything that we would think of doing to further our goals of increasing political stability and living standards around the world can be compromised and destroyed by unchecked population growth." "U.S. Seeks More Spending on Birth Control," *New York Times,* 23 January 1994.

44. Lauritzen, *Pursuing Parenthood,* xv.

45. Gina Kolata, "Scientist Clones Human Embryos, and Creates an Ethical Challenge," *New York Times,* 24 October 1993, sec. A1, 22.

46. Richard Cohen, "Dealing with Illegitimacy," *Washington Post,* 23 November 1993, A21.

47. Cited in Elizabeth Kristol, "Picture Perfect: The Politics of Prenatal Testing," *First Things,* April 1993, 20.

48. Richard John Neuhaus, "The Way They Were, The Way We Are: Bioethics and the Holocaust," *First Things,* March 1990, 36.

49. Quoted in Rees, "Shot in the Arm," 17.

KEITH CASSIDY

The Right to Life Movement: Sources, Development, and Strategies

Social movements play a critical role in the development of public policy in modern America. An extensive literature provides us with valuable insights into their growth and evolution, but in the end it cannot substitute for the history of specific movements, which can be understood only in the particular circumstances of their birth and development.[1] Over the last fifty years few movements have had the long-standing visibility, the mass involvement, and the public impact of the Right to Life movement. While there is still no adequate full-length account of the movement, an outline of some of the major aspects of its history, particularly as it is relevant to the public policy process in the United States, can be provided.[2] Before embarking on that task, I will review and assess current interpretations of the movement, at both the popular and scholarly levels, and suggest a plausible explanation of its social sources and characteristics.

Images and Interpretations

Interpretations of the movement cover a wide range in both sophistication and utility. At the most basic level are the stereotypes and impressions created by the mass media. The Right to Life movement has been the subject of numerous television dramas, documentaries, and news accounts. Television portrayals in particular have created a number of negative images. The movement is seen as violent, irrational, insensitive to women, religiously fundamentalist in character, and extremist.[3] These images tend to foster the impression that the movement is marginal, pathological, and deviant rather than having significant similarities to other social movements. In the context of the extraordinarily contentious nature of the abortion debate, it was perhaps inevitable that media portrayals would have a strongly polemical character. Nonetheless, they are incompatible with a realistic picture of the movement's sources and structures and stand in the way of a more dispassionate understanding of its real characteristics as a social actor. Given the wide currency of these negative images, it is not surprising that while the public remains deeply divided over the issue of abortion, it tends to be much more united in its negative view of the movement to end abortion.[4] That many of these images are not well grounded in reality does not change the fact that they play a powerful role in shaping perceptions of the pro-life movement.[5]

When we turn to more substantial analyses, we find a series of interpretive frameworks: for some, the Right to Life movement can be seen largely as a part of the "New Right";[6] for others it as essentially a movement of moral conservatives, in which abortion is linked with sexual sin.[7] The most frequent and influential approach, however, sees the movement fundamentally as a defense of traditional family structures and gender roles. In its simplest form this interpretation suggests that the pro-life movement is part of a male strategy to defend traditional power and privileges.[8] This line of analysis cannot account for the large number of women, often in leadership positions, in the pro-life movement. Accordingly, it is far less satisfactory than the classic and most widely cited exposition of a gender interpretation of the pro-life movement, Kristin Luker's *Abortion and the Politics of Motherhood.* Luker asserts that the abortion debate has been "so passionate and hard fought because it is a referendum on the place and meaning of motherhood" and "while on the surface it is the embryo's fate that seems to be at stake, the abortion debate is actually about the meaning of *women's* lives." In her discussion of the activists in the organizations on the two sides of the issue, she portrays the debate as essentially one between women who have experienced radically different lives. One group, the pro-choicers, is highly educated, has gone to work outside the home, makes higher than average salaries, and does not see motherhood as a primary and defining characteristic of their lives. The pro-life group, by contrast, is less well educated than the pro-choice activists (although better educated than the public as a whole, a fact not stressed by Luker), far more likely to be full-time housewives with more children than their pro-choice counterparts, and sees motherhood as a central characteristic of their lives.[9]

For Luker, the abortion debate is rooted not only in the different life experiences of these women but in the patterns of thought and values—their worldviews—that have been generated by these experiences. Thus, "pro-life activists believe that men and women are intrinsically different and that this is both a cause and a product of the fact that they have different roles in life."[10]

A number of other studies provides a variation on this theme. Thus Faye Ginsburg writes that for pro-life activists "abortion is thus a condensed symbol for the devaluation of motherhood and the central attribute assigned to it in this culture—the self-sacrificing nurturance of dependents. Abortion represents, in addition, a threat to social guarantees that a woman with children will be supported by the child's father."[11]

The interpretation of the movement, particularly in the formulation advanced by Luker, as essentially a product of concern over gender roles has become influential and is widely cited as an established fact. This interpretation has four elements: (1) The Right to Life movement is fundamentally to be understood as an anti-abortion movement, not as a more general "pro-life" movement. (2) The real source of anti-abortion activism is not concern with abortion as such but with the protection, largely by women, of personal cultural commitments. Some analysts see it largely as a "symbolic crusade," others as a defense of substantive as well as symbolic concerns,[12] but in either case the real issue is not abortion. (3) It is to be understood as the expression of a single set of cultural interests, hence a single explanatory theme will adequately account for the movement. (4) The cultural interest being defended through the movement is the traditional set of gender roles.[13]

The Luker thesis and its variants have considerable merit: they are based on a large number of interviews with movement activists and they do recognize the real differences in their life experiences. Surveys indicate that those who oppose abortion do have more traditional attitudes toward family roles than those who are pro-choice. Growing levels of female participation in the paid workforce clearly did have implications for the abortion debate, and abortion is in fact partly about gender roles. But is that all that it is about, or is that even principally what it is about? Do gender attitudes *determine* abortion attitudes? Have we actually dug out the cultural roots of the pro-life movement with this analysis? Several other studies in the social science literature point to a very different conclusion.

The Social Sources and Context of the Pro-Life Movement

Of considerable significance is the question of diversity within the pro-life movement. Mary Jo Neitz discerns "two different conceptual frameworks within the right to life movement: one is 'pro-life' and ties opposition to abortion to other liberal peace and justice issues . . . the other is 'pro-family' and ties opposition to abortion to beliefs about the sanctity of the traditional family."[14] A far more substantial work than Neitz's article also points to a view of the movement as complex and motivated by something more than a defense of traditional gender roles. Michael Cuneo's classic study of the Right to Life movement in Canada, *Catholics Against the Church: Anti-Abortion Protest in Toronto, 1969–1985*, is without doubt the best single study of the movement, and although it is about Canada, not the United States, its conclusions are suggestive for the American situation.[15] For Cuneo, the Right to Life movement is composed of three types: those for whom abortion is essentially a civil rights question, that is, who regard the denial of equal protection of life before birth as after as a form of unjustifiable discrimination; the "family heritage activists," for whom abortion is tied up with support of the traditional family values; and those he dubs "revivalist Catholics," for whom abortion is a central aspect of the battle over the nature of the Church. Clearly this typology offers only limited support for the Luker thesis, and indeed Cuneo offers some pointed criticism of Luker's views.[16] Along similar lines, a student of the American movement, the sociologist James Kelly, has also suggested that the complexity of the movement and its commitment to a "pro-life" philosophy need to be taken seriously.[17]

The accounts of Neitz, Cuneo, and Kelly, like those of Luker and Ginsburg, are largely based on interviews with movement members. Another source of information about the cultural roots of the movement are the polls, both of the general public and of a large sample of the movement activists taken over the years. A recent account of the opinion of the general public, based on an exhaustive analysis of the annual General Social Survey, is Cook, Jelen, and Wilcox's *Between Two Absolutes: Public Opinion and the Politics of Abortion.*[18] They assume the accuracy of Luker's account of the gender basis of the abortion issue among activists and express surprise that the analysis of public opinion does not show a similar trend:

> Attitudes toward feminism and gender roles are not strongly related to abortion attitudes, once other factors are taken into account. Although pro-life citizens are more likely to oppose gender equality than those who take consistent pro-choice positions, in fact more citizens who oppose gender equality favour legal abortion than oppose it.[19]

Doubt can be cast on the assumption that even activists's opinions corresponded to the Luker thesis: looking at Donald Granberg's analysis of a sample of National Abortion Rights Action League (NARAL) and National Right to Life Committee (NRLC) members, we find that while the NARAL respondents are more open to nontraditional gender roles, the great majority of NRLC members also approve of them.[20] The one test item on which this was apparently not true was with respect to the Equal Rights Amendment (ERA), on which pro-lifers were largely negative. The reason for this anomaly was undoubtedly the belief among pro-lifers that the ERA would mandate public funding of abortions: it was most likely this reason rather than a more general antifeminism that produced the reported result.[21]

If there is little to confirm the thesis that the root of the abortion conflict is a cultural clash over gender roles—although that may be a factor for some—then what is crucial? For one thing, anti-abortion sentiment for many is part of a larger pro-life ideology. Turning again to the work of Cook et al., the strongest relationship they found in a multivariate analysis of several factors was between abortion and euthanasia: "The question concerning euthanasia is strongly related to abortion attitudes across all groups."[22] They argue as well that

> . . . it seems apparent that beliefs about the inviolability of life, as measured by our euthanasia question, are strongly related to abortion attitudes. For many there seems to exist a relationship between scepticism about mercy killing and a commitment to an embryonic "right to life." We are confident that attitudes toward mercy killing and abortion are, at least in part, components of a more general respect for the sanctity of human life.[23]

This suggestion based on poll data can be confirmed by examining some aspects of the movement's actual conduct and concerns over the years. If Luker were correct and the primary focus of the movement was the protection—symbolic and actual—of the status of motherhood, then this should be reflected in the collateral issues the movement addresses. One would expect that topics such as pornography, homosexuality, day care, sex education, and so on would figure prominently. Has this been the case? As we will see, some organizations who have opposed abortion have also taken stands on such so-called family issues.[24] However, many organizations, including the largest and most influential, the NRLC, has never taken stands on such issues and has in consequence been regularly attacked for being a "single-issue" group. More strikingly, the pro-life movement includes at least one organization, Feminists for Life, that combines opposition to abortion with an affirmation of gender equality.[25]

In fact, however, that single issue has not been defined as abortion per se but the defense of "all innocent human life"; that is, it has from its origins opposed infanticide and euthanasia.[26] While the abortion issue acted as the "trigger" for the pro-life movement, it was not *the* issue for the movement but rather the most immediate manifestation of what was perceived as a far deeper threat: that human life no longer had an *absolute* value. Indeed a concern about euthanasia has been a staple theme in movement literature from the beginning. One of the first books by a movement activist, Charles Rice's 1969 *The Vanishing Right to Live,* located abortion and euthanasia as part of the same constellation of threats to life. A 1970 editorial in *California Medicine,* which endorsed abortion as the logical prelude to euthanasia, was widely cited by the Right to Life movement because it made public and explicit what they feared. Even in the immediate aftermath of the 1973 *Roe v. Wade* decision, a concern about euthanasia and infanticide was evident: the first issue of the *National Right to Life News* that year contained three articles on these topics, including the first section of a series by Father Paul Marx on euthanasia. This series led to the publication of a widely circulated pamphlet on the subject.[27] The concern about euthanasia intensified in later years. That the largest pro-life organization should make euthanasia its second major topic, rather than issues related to motherhood, and indeed takes no stand on any issues other than "life issues" makes very improbable the notion that gender issues are the real agenda driving the movement.

If concerns about gender are not at the center of the movement, is another hypothesis more plausible? Turning to a seemingly obvious correlation with abortion attitudes—political liberalism or conservatism—we find that it is more complex than might appear. It is certainly true that those who are pro-life are more likely to identify themselves as conservative than are those who are pro-choice. The polarization is hardly absolute: while more than one-half of liberals take a pro-choice position, one-third of all conservatives do as well.[28] In addition, significant liberal minorities exist among some groups of pro-life supporters: thus while 38 percent of white Catholic pro-lifers describe themselves as "conservative," 21 percent describe themselves as "liberal"; 34 percent of black pro-life supporters say they are liberal, while only 28 percent say they are conservative.[29] Once we move away from ideological self-identification, we find that political cleavages are not that pronounced. In response to questions about increasing government funding, 60 percent of pro-life respondents and 62 percent of pro-choice respondents favored increased spending on child care. On the question of funding for food stamps and support for unwanted children, a larger number of pro-lifers favored increased funding (32 percent versus 23 percent and 77 percent versus 72 percent, respectively).[30] Significantly more white Catholic pro-lifers reported a Democratic party affiliation than Republican (50 percent versus 36 percent).[31] While pro-lifers are more politically conservative than their opponents, their ranks contain a significant minority of liberals and a large number of moderates. On specific issues it is not clear that opposition to abortion is associated with a rigid conservatism: the movement's alliance in the Reagan-Bush years with the Republican party may well have had less to do with ideological predisposition than with the fact that the resolutely pro-choice position of the Democratic party made the Republicans the only game in town. The search for the cultural sources of the Right to Life movement will have to go deeper than political preferences.

Other factors identified by the polling data as powerfully connected to abortion attitudes are beliefs about sexual morality and views on the desirability of children and ideal family size. Among attitudinal variables, sexual morality placed second only to euthanasia attitudes as a predictor of abortion views.[32] As a demographic variable, education was extremely important, a finding reported in numerous other studies: the lower the level of formal education, the higher the disapproval of abortion.[33] The significance of this will be explored shortly.

Of course one factor of enormous importance is religion. Consistently, studies have shown that while formal denominational affiliation does not have a decisive impact on attitudes, degree of religious involvement is a major correlate of abortion views.[34] Along with attitudes toward euthanasia, education, and views on sexual morality, religion is a powerful predictor of views, but only when the *degree* of religious commitment is tested.

The linkage of abortion attitudes to religious commitment, sexual morality, and euthanasia leads to the suggestion that the battle over abortion is part of a larger conflict between fundamentally opposed worldviews. This is the argument advanced by James Davison Hunter. Hunter suggests that the fundamental divisions in modern America are not between "left" and "right" in the conventional sense of the words, but rather that America is experiencing a "culture war" between what he calls the "orthodox" and the "progressive":

> Though there are clearly political manifestations of this dispute, the dispute is more than political. Likewise, while each side betrays certain social characteristics, the cultural controversy is much more

> than a reflection of competing class interests. There is, then, a more vital cultural dynamic involved in generating this cultural realignment. In this sense, the conflict is prepolitical and it precedes class. What ultimately explains the realignment in America's public culture are *allegiances to different formulations and sources of moral authority*. (emphasis in the original)[35]

For the "orthodox" the defining characteristic "*is the commitment on the part of adherents to an external, definable, and transcendant authority*"[36] (emphasis in the original) In another work, Hunter suggests that

> people's perspectives and opinions are directly related to even deeper and more fundamental assumptions about the sources of truth and of goodness, about the ultimate meaning of life, and so on. These perspectives we come to see, are born out of participation in distinct moral and religious communities. What this means, in other words, is that people's attitudes toward abortion are not only rooted in larger worldviews but that these worldviews are institutionally rooted within and sustained by "communities of moral conversation."[37]

Hunter's suggestion about the cultural divisions in America helps make sense of the correlations between abortion attitudes and such variables as education, religious involvement, and attitudes toward sexual morality. Those most likely to resist adopting the pro-choice attitudes that became so prominent in the 1960s were members of institutions that provided an alternative belief system to that offered by a highly secular mass media—namely, those people with strong church connections. As well, since participation in schooling serves not only to educate but also to socialize into new attitudes, those with less exposure to schools, particularly postsecondary institutions, were less likely to be socialized into a pro-choice position.[38] It is of course the same degree of involvement in religious institutions and the limited exposure to the secularizing effects of schooling that account for conservatism in sexual morality.

Hunter's thesis helps make sense of much of the poll data and demonstrates that pro-life attitudes are rooted in beliefs that operate at a much deeper level than just religious denomination or gender attitudes or political affiliation. A belief in the indivisibility of human rights at any stage of development is essentially a philosophical position, a way of perceiving reality and reasoning about moral issues that is prepolitical.[39] Much of the bitterness and mutual incomprehension of the antagonists in the abortion debate is the result of the fact that it frequently takes place between people who differ over the most fundamental of issues and for whom the very meaning of words is an issue.

If the Right to Life movement is indeed based on a deeply rooted consensus about basic beliefs, a profoundly different philosophical conception about how to look at the nature and value of human life than that held by pro-choice supporters, it is also the case that the movement represents a considerable diversity in the expression of those beliefs. The Hunter thesis has real limits, and these are apparent when looking at the pro-life movement. Many who are allies on this issue are foes on issues of defense policy, economics, and gender roles. The movement encompasses (although not in equal numbers) Roman Catholics and fundamentalists, moderate evangelicals, members of mainstream Protestant denominations, Mormons, Orthodox Jews, and some such as Nat Hentoff, who profess no religious beliefs at all. Neither is movement diversity confined to religious denominational differences. Among Roman Catholic pro-lifers, for example, sharp splits between conservatives and liberals in both political and religious terms have a long history. While the idea that the movement represents one side in a "culture war" is useful, it must not be overstated. Indeed, even when all the social variables are taken into account, a large measure of indeterminacy about abortion attitudes still exists.[40] Members of the pro-life movement differ over a wide range of issues, of both substance and style, a fact amply testified to by the organizational diversity apparent from an early date and by the rows over strategy and tactics that have frequently convulsed it. In some ways this diversity has been a source of strength: nearly everyone could find a group agreeable to its own ideology and style.[41] But it has also been an obstacle to achieving agreement about goals and at times has led groups to work at cross-purposes.

In reviewing the social sources of the pro-life movement, another characteristic that has shaped and limited it becomes apparent: its class composition. The lower educational levels of the movement's members reflect and help create a social-class composition notably different from that of the pro-choice movement, with pro-life supporters far more likely than their opponents to come from blue-collar and middle-class backgrounds. It should be noted, however, that while they occupy a lower-class position than their opponents, pro-life activists are better educated than the public as a whole and on several other indicators of social class are above the national average.[42] Nonetheless the class differences of the two groups are real and led Christopher Lasch to suggest that abortion is "first and foremost a class issue."[43] The class dimension of the abortion debate has caught the eye of others: Laurence Tribe notes the "uncomfortable fact that the pro-choice movement draws its support disproportionately from various privileged elites, the 'upper echelons' of American society."[44]

Tribe, himself a prominent pro-choice supporter, goes on to deplore the "hypocrisy" of those who supported abortion with protestations of tolerance and open-mindedness but react with scorn and a sense of class superiority to what they regarded as the "prejudiced, superstitious, backward views of pro-life groups."[45] The truth is that it is indeed the case that the relatively lower-class status of pro-life supporters has been a serious obstacle. Virtually all the powerful institutions of society—universities, the media, the professionals of law and medicine—have been predominantly pro-choice. In consequence, the pro-life movement has had to pursue a strategy of grassroots mobilization and embrace a rhetoric of democratic populism. It has also had to forge alliances where it could. Representing a minority of the population, at least for its full program, and cut off by and large from the powerful elites of America, the movement has labored to overcome enormous obstacles.

While pro-life and pro-choice supporters may have been sharply polarized, the public displayed a more complex pattern of beliefs about abortion. Over the years, survey data have consistently revealed that the public does not agree completely with either side. Rather, it supports a right to abortion in some cases but not in others.[46] Support for abortion in "hard" cases—life/health of the mother, rape, incest, fetal deformity—is significantly higher than for "soft" reasons, such as social and economic difficulty. Moreover, many who believe that abortion is morally wrong, and indeed some of those who describe it as murder, will nonetheless refuse to back legislation prohibiting it because they are reluctant to "impose their morality" on others.[47] This pattern of public belief has created the context within which the pro-life movement has operated, setting the limits of its influence and shaping its strategy. It is not that the public rejected the notion of a fetal "right to life" but rather that it saw other values as sometimes, but not always, more important. This gave the pro-life movement an opportunity if it could appeal to the majority by proposing to restrict some but not all abortions, it could make gains. Conversely, what weakened the pro-choice movement was its insistence on an unrestricted right to abortion: to the degree to which the Right to Life movement could focus public attention on that fact, it could win support. However, since a prominent feature of the pro-life movement was its insistence on the *absolute* character of *fetal* rights, it found the question of compromise painful and divisive—and indeed some of the nastiest internal fights in the movement were over this issue. In this way one of the movement's major characteristics, its assertion of the absolute character of the right to life, became a serious obstacle to its success. This was ironic, for it was precisely its uncompromising devotion to an absolute right that gave the movement the emotional force necessary for the effective organization and mobilization of supporters.

Another feature of public opinion, and one of the deepest aspects of American culture—a pervasive anti-authoritarianism and resentment of undemocratic power—also initially helped the Right to Life movement. Because abortion had come by a Supreme Court decision rather than through legislation, the movement could appeal to democratic values by portraying the decision as a judicial *coup d'état.*[48] This advantage was lost, and indeed reversed, in the wake of the *Webster* decision in 1989, which permitted greater state power to regulate abortion. NARAL, after a careful analysis of public opinion (using focus groups, not just standard opinion polls), decided on a public relations approach based on a theme of "Who decides—you or the politicians?" By emphasizing the antigovernment theme, NARAL reversed the populist appeal so long relied on by the Right to Life movement.[49]

While Luker's thesis is currently popular in both scholarly and journalist circles, it is not the only or the most persuasive explanation of the cultural origins of the abortion dispute and the characteristics of abortion opponents. The following seems to represent a more accurate picture: (1) while some members of the Right to Life movement are primarily antiabortion, for many others, indeed for a majority, opposition to abortion is part of a larger commitment to a "pro-life" philosophy. (2) While gender is certainly an interpretive theme, others, such as class, are at least as significant; the cultural roots of the conflict are complex and tangled. (3) The most important cultural root of the conflict is religion, if that word is understood to mean not specific denominational allegiance but the deeper question of a belief in transcendant and immutable truth. (4) Movement supporters and activists display considerable diversity, and no account that overlooks that fact can be considered valid. (5) Even after all factors are taken into account—race, gender attitudes, educational level, religious practices and beliefs, region of birth, etc.—a large amount of the variance in attitude remains unexplained. Even the most sophisticated set of cultural explanations must recognize the profoundly individual nature of belief. (6) The diverse social backgrounds and cultural styles of movement members often created serious problems in agreeing on organizational and tactical questions, and this proved a source of weakness in winning political power. (7) Because both the pro-choice and Right to Life movements represented minorities of the population, it was crucial to frame issues in a way that drew into each side elements of the middle.

This was particularly important for the pro-life movement because it had little elite support and could flourish only if it had mass appeal. However, any move to meet the public desire to outlaw some but not all abortions could be seen as a "compromise" and thus draw the ire of those pro-lifers who saw the issue as uncompromisable and not subject to a strategy of incrementalism.

One of these themes, the diversity of groups within the Right to Life movement, will become more apparent from a review of the movement's institutional development.

Institutional Origins and Development

The phrase "right to life" applied to groups opposing abortion seems to have been used as early as 1963.[50] The first permanent local group in what was later to be called the "pro-life" movement came from the efforts of Edward Golden of Troy, New York, who first became concerned about attempts to liberalize the state abortion laws in 1965. Within a year he had formed a small group to work against the proposed changes. The first permanent state group was founded in Virginia in 1967.[51] The story of this group was typical of many others formed in the mid- to late 1960s: characteristically they began when an individual read about or heard of an attempt to reform or repeal a state's abortion laws and undertook to campaign against the proposed change, with a letter to the editor of a local paper or by some other public statement. Other pro-lifers joined them, recruited either through secing the letter or statement or through the first pro-lifer's existing network of friends or church contacts. Groups were usually small and lacked ready access to existing power structures, since their members were generally new to politics. In some cases the organization initiative came from the Catholic church.

Groups began in reaction to abortion reform efforts, and it is not surprising that some of the earliest and most vigorous groups formed in states with active pro-choice lobbies. Besides New York and Virginia, groups were found in Minnesota, California, Florida, Colorado, Michigan, Illinois, Ohio, and Pennsylvania. With some exceptions the most active states were those with large urban populations and a significant number of Catholics. This is not to say that only Catholics belonged to these groups, though Catholics were clearly a majority of active pro-lifers. A number of the prominent early leaders were Protestants, such as Dr. Mildred Jefferson in Massachusetts, Dr. Carolyn Gerster in Arizona, Judy Fink in Pennsylvania, and Marjory Mecklenburg in Minnesota. In general the South was a weak area for the pro-life movement and remained so until the later mobilization of large numbers of evangelicals. Perhaps the most interesting and important state organization was Minnesota Citizens Concerned for Life (MCCL), formed in 1968. An astonishing number of later national figures in the pro-life movement came out of this state, but even during the pre-*Roe v. Wade* years Minnesota had clearly become a national leader, sending out teams to help organize neighboring states. Because of the relatively small and scattered nature of pro-life groups in the years before 1973 and the fact that they tended to form spontaneously, it is difficult to compose an exhaustive inventory of them. Clearly they had become a significant force in some states. New York pro-lifers were able to secure a legislative repeal of the liberal 1970 abortion law in 1972. This victory was obviated, however, by Governor Nelson Rockefeller's veto of the repeal. Groups in Michigan and North Dakota won victories in referendum campaigns in 1972 in their states, and there is evidence that these groups were slowing the tide of abortion law liberalization.[52]

Meanwhile, a national pro-life organization had begun to appear. In 1966 the National Conference of Catholic Bishops had asked the head of its Family Life Bureau, Monsignor James McHugh, to begin monitoring abortion law reform efforts across the United States. Within a year he had formed an advisory committee, which became the National Right to Life Committee (NRLC). It acted as a clearinghouse for information, started the process of creating links among the Right to Life groups springing up across the country, and began in 1970 to hold annual conferences. The NRLC came under attack on two fronts within the pro-life movement. Conservative Catholics who believed that the NCCB was too liberal in its theology and politics felt that the fight against abortion was being prosecuted with insufficient zeal.[53] This line of criticism was to become a constant theme in the history of the movement, as some Catholics insisted that the bishops were more wedded to a social-justice agenda with a heavy emphasis on economic policies than they were to the Right to Life cause. Cardinal Bernardin's call in 1983 for a "seamless garment" approach to life issues, insisting on a linkage not only of abortion and euthanasia but to social justice and peace issues as well, seemed to some simply a ploy to de-emphasize abortion and thus make it easier for Catholics to vote for pro-choice Democrats.[54]

Others were also upset by the NRLC as established by McHugh: Protestants and Catholics who feared the appearance of clerical control wanted a secular organization, without institutional ties to any church, and based on mass membership rather than controlled by a small executive committee. In the years before *Roe v. Wade* the organization of the NRLC became a more pressing issue: one group chartered a competing national group, the American Right to Life Association (ARTLA), in a bid to pressure changes in the structure of the NRLC. Ultimately it was successful and ARTLA, though chartered, was never activated. Change in the NRLC would most likely have occurred even had *Roe v. Wade* not been handed down, but the decision increased pressure to move to a new structure. Significantly, in the same week that the NRLC was given a federal charter, a rival national group was also chartered, by some of the same people who had incorporated the NRLC. Their intention was to prepare an alternative in case the battles among the executives of the NRLC produced unsatisfactory results. The new organization, American Citizens Concerned for Life (ACCL), remained dormant until 1974, when two prominent Protestants in the NRLC moved to activate it. For many years it was an alternative national organization to the NRLC, although far smaller, and pursued a different approach to the abortion issue. It wanted more emphasis on programs to aid pregnant women in order to reduce the pressure to abort and in general pursued a policy of coalition building on specific issues, such as the workplace rights of pregnant women, event if the coalition partners were pro-choice.[55] It wound up its Washington lobbying efforts in the mid-1980s but continued thereafter as a Minnesota-based provider of educational material.

The NRLC went through a difficult period in the 1970s with frequent battles over policies and administrative issues. Nonetheless, it began a process of remarkable institutional development and maturation, which accelerated in the 1980s as it grew in both size and sophistication. By 1992 the program for the annual meeting contained a staff list, most of them in the Washington office, of nearly fifty people. Even more striking than the change in size was the appearance of a substantial group of professional administrators, most of whom had come to the movement through volunteer activity in local groups. This professionalization occurred as well at the state level, as more and more states set up permanent offices with executive directors. A similar professionalization occurred in the other organizations that grew up alongside the NRLC. The implications of this process for the movement are not clear-cut: while a permanent and knowledgeable staff was essential for effective operations in the legal, legislative, and media worlds, the effect on grassroots participation was potentially negative.[56]

With the withdrawal of the NRLC from the purview of the Catholic bishops, the bishops in 1974 created an organization under their influence, the National Committee for a Human Life Amendment (NCHLA). The bishops also operated an educational project directly out of the NCCB, the

Respect Life Program, directed by the Committee for Pro-Life Activities. Its annual *Respect Life,* a glossy magazine-style publication designed for use in parish educational campaigns, is a clear expression of a "seamless garment" approach to abortion and euthanasia, with articles on the rights of the disabled, racial justice, peace, and social justice. Nor did this exhaust the list of organizations operating at the national level. Americans United for Life, created in 1971, was orginally an educational organization located in Washington. By 1972 it had moved to Chicago and by the end of the 1970s had become a pro-life public-interest law firm that played a crucial role in court cases involving abortion.[57] In addition, the National Youth Pro-Life Coalition (NYPLC) had been formed in 1971 and indeed was one of the first pro-life organization to have an office in Washington. It called for an ethic of "consistency" and linked the abortion issue to questions of social justice.[58]

Several organizations that appeared in the post-1973 period displayed even more vividly the diversity of people attracted to the movement: Pro-Lifers for Survival was begun as a pro-life and anti-nuclear group, which attracted the Left. A similar appeal was made by Feminists for Life. Much longer was the Christian Action Council (CAC), founded in 1975 at the urging of the Reverend Billy Graham, which became a Protestant center of pro-life work. One of the most significant new groups was the American Life Lobby (ALL), founded in 1979 by Paul and Judie Brown. Mrs. Brown had been an employee at NRLC and was increasingly at odds with some of the others there. ALL was formed in close association with the New Right and from the start merged pro-life with a generally conservative political stance: its motto, "For God, For Life, For the Family, For the Nation," accurately captures its thrust. Appealing to a conservative and largely Catholic group, ALL blended discussion of abortion with attacks on contraception and sex education, and was a prime example of the attempt in the 1980s to present the pro-life message as part of a "pro-family" agenda. A similar appeal was evident in Human Life International, founded by Father Paul Marx in 1981.[59] Finally, a very different kind of pro-life work was carried on by groups that ran pregnancy counseling and support centers. The first and best known of these was Birthright (founded in 1968 by a Canadian, Louise Summerhill), which grew rapidly. Other pro-life counseling centers appeared later, under the aegis of such groups as the Christian Action Council, Alternative to Abortion International, and the Pearson Foundation.

There were numerous other groups, often denominationally based, such as Presbyterians for Life and Lutherans for Life, or else committed to a function, such as the March for Life, which each year, beginning in 1974, organized a mass demonstration on the anniversary of the *Roe v. Wade* decision. Some were essentially the expression of a small group or individual but had a national audience; thus the Ad Hoc Committee in Defense of Life published "Lifeletter," a newsletter that focused on political developments in Washington, D.C., from 1974 to the late 1980s. None was as large or had the visibility of the leading national groups, especially the NRLC. It is apparent that the movement spanned a wide range, from the conservatism of the ALL and HLI to the mainstream Protestantism of the CAC, to the nondenominational single-issue focus of the NRLC to the liberalism of ACCL and the Catholic bishops, to the leftish Pro-Lifers for Survival. There was a home for virtually every temperament and political or religious persuasion; but would this diverse assemblage be able to agree on a common strategy and set of tactics?

The Search for a Strategy: I

At one level there was no disagreement about strategy. The movement recognized that success could come only if the pubic could be brought around to the pro-life view, and this involved an extensive and ongoing educational campaign. The persuasive materials available to the early pro-lifers were limited, but by the time of *Roe v. Wade* an increasing number of print and film materials had become available. Most widely used was the *Handbook on Abortion*, a paperback book using a question-and-answer format, written by Ohio pro-lifer and NRLC board member Dr. Jack Willke, in collaboration with his wife, and a slide-tape presentation he developed. The use of photographs showing prenatal development and aborted fetuses was a contentious aspect of these materials. Pro-life materials of this sort were always controversial because they sought to remove the abortion debate from the realm of abstraction and make it dramatically real. Later, controversy would flare over the 1984 film *The Silent Scream*, which used ultrasound pictures of a fetus.[60] While the use of dramatic images became a hallmark of pro-life literature and one characteristic of a wide range of the movement, a close examination of movement literature reveals some intriguing differences between groups. Groups and authors with a Catholic background tended to use a "natural-law" approach, assuming that the evil of abortion could be demonstrated by an essentially secular line of argument.[61] Later, as large numbers of evangelical Protestants entered the fray, materials emphasizing Scripture became common.[62]

While an intensification of the existing educational campaign seemed natural, the movement had to confront a new political situation, which called for a dramatic reexamination of its political strategy. Prior to *Roe v. Wade* the movement's orientation had been defenseive, except in states like New York, where a liberal law was on the books and the intent was to reverse it. After 22 January 1973 everything changed. With little exaggeration it can be said that more than any church the Supreme Court, by its decision in *Roe,* helped shape the Right to Life movement. Not only was there new pressure for restructuring the NRLC, but a new strategy focusing on the national level seemed called for. All state laws were invalid, and no state legislature could undertake any radical challenge to the new dispensation. What political strategies were now appropriate? With remarkably little debate, the movement agreed that a constitutional amendment was the only route to take. This was affirmed on 8 December 1973 by the NRLC board, which saw the "first program priority" as being "the development and implementation of a political campaign to effect passage of a Human Life constitutional Amendment."[63] The group that founded ACCL was less enthusiastic about this strategy and preferred a more incremental approach, but in general the HLA was accepted as a goal without reservation.[64]

A constitutional amendment, then, was the strategic objective, but what type of amendment? It had to meet several incompatible goals. First, it should be capable of garnering overwhelming support in Congress and in the state legislatures required for passage. This fact pointed to an amendment with limited objectives. Second, it had to be sufficiently sweeping in scope to inspire pro-life supporters to engage in the struggle—something a less ambitious amendment would not do. In addition, it had to represent an intellectually consistent and defensible philosophy respecting the sanctity of life, acceptable to the majority of pro-life members. Finally, it had to be crafted to withstand the interpretive skills of its opponents, who could be counted on to discover and use every ambiguity. Given these requirements, it is hardly surprising that in the decade following the *Roe* decision the movement was racked by endless controversy over an amendment strategy. Some favored a states-rights approach, which essentially negated *Roe v. Wade* and returned jurisdiction to the states. This approach had long been anathema to the majority in the movement. Again, if there was to be a Human Life Amendment forbidding abortion, what about an exception for the protection of the life of the mother? Over this and similar questions, debate went on furiously for years.

All this debate was academic until the 1980 election produced a Congress at least conceivably open to some sort of action on abortion and a president publicly committed to helping in the task. Suddenly it was critical that the movement agree on what it sought from Congress. This never happened. Bitter controversy continued and indeed intensified as two approaches came to dominate the agenda: the Hatch Amendment, which sought to give both the state and federal government concurrent power to regulate abortion, and the Helms Human Life Bill, which sought to take jurisdiction from the Supreme Court in abortion cases. Eventually the Hatch Amendment mutated into a straight states-rights bill, which in its final form as the Hatch-Eagleton Amendment simply declared: "A right to abortion is not secured by this Constitution." Even in this most limited form, it failed to win approval of a majority of the Senate, failing 49 to 50, with Senator Jesse Helms abstaining. His own Human Life Bill also underwent modification, but it too failed. By 1983 the strategy of seeking to reverse *Roe v. Wade* by constitutional change had clearly failed and a chapter had closed in the movement's history.

The battle over the HLA revealed enormous tensions within the movement, in which the lines of division were often surprising. Thus the Catholic bishops and their supporters favored a states-rights approach, but so did the evangelicals and fundamentalists of the Christian Right. Opposition derived not only from the Protestant CAC but also from the conservative Catholics allied with the ALL, who favored an amendment that provided federal protection of fetal life. The NRLC was itself badly split and suffered severe internal disruption.[65] The diversity of the movement was such that, even during a period of maximum opportunity, it could not agree on a common approach.

It is clear that the HLA never had a chance of passage. Was it therefore a mistake for the movement to pursue it? It can be suggested that the decision to make an HLA the strategic goal of the movement, though it created problems over wording and method and ultimately led to bitter internal rows, provided the movement with a goal that on balance was unifying, kept a national focus, and by raising the stakes in the abortion battle served to legitimize and make more accetable such lesser measures as the Hyde Amendment restrictions on abortion funding. Further, by raising as its standard an absolute, or nearly absolute ban on abortion, the movement sought to arrest—and to a striking degree did arrest—the drift toward public the acceptance of the legitimacy of an unqualified pro-choice position.[66] Any measure less radical than the HLA would have involved, or been perceived as involving, the acceptance of some degree of the legitimacy of abortion. It was vital for the movement to state the issue in stark, clear, uncompromising terms. Finally, it gave a central purpose to a national organization, provided a focus for educational work, and carried it through the days when there was no hope on the horizon. In so doing it helped to create and sustain pro-life as a mass movement with a strong *esprit de corps* and increasingly sophisticated organizations. The problem came when there appeared to be a real prospect of legislative success. While in the political wilderness the HLA was a shared ideal, regardless of the differences over it, once it appeared that something could be achieved, if not everything, the pro-life movement came face to face with the classic conundrum all movements for social change face: to hold out for the whole loaf or to compromise. With the death of the dream of an HLA, the movement had to consider other approaches.

The Search for a Strategy: II

By 1983 the movement had come to see that the HLA was impossible. One alternative was to continue the process begun years earlier of attacking abortion through funding restrictions and other forms of legislation at the state and local level as well as in Congress.[67] These incremental restrictions would not be the victory sought, but they could prepare the way for it and in the meantime keep the movement alive by showing its supporters that victories were possible. The list of legislation connected to the pro-life movement was considerable. Conscience clauses for doctors and hospitals opposed to abortion had been passed early in the abortion struggle, as had prohibitions on the use of foreign-aid funds for abortions. As well, the movement worked against the authorization of experiments on fetal-tissue transplants and RU-486. The most significant movement victories were the regular passage of "Hyde Amendment" restrictions on abortion funding. Legislative activity was not restricted to abortion but included concern about infanticide as well. The "Baby Doe" case in 1982 led to demands for greater protection for infants born with disabilities who were in danger of being denied medical treatment. The 1984 amendments to the Child Abuse Prevention and Treatment Act were secured by an alliance of Right to Life forces with disabilities-rights activists. While the HLA did not pass, the movement did have a real impact on Congress and could point to real political impact in a number of areas.

In the end, however, legislation would not prove feasible if the courts were hostile to pro-life initiatives; neither could it provide the sort of victory sought, namely, the abrogation of *Roe v. Wade* and at least the return to the previous status quo. Accordingly, the focus of the movement increasingly shifted to the judiciary and the quest for pro-life judicial appointments, first from the Reagan and then the Bush administrations. The ultimate goal was to reverse *Roe v. Wade* through the courts, a subject to which AUL devoted an entire conference and a subsequent volume of essays.[68] Some of the most spectacular political battles of the 1980s and 1990s in Congress did indeed revolve around Supreme Court nominations, and in each case the question of the candidate's attitude toward abortion was central. Of course concern about Supreme Court nominations was apparent even before the demise of the HLA, as the nomination of Sandra Day O'Connor to the Court made apparent in 1981, but after 1983 it was clearly the Court that held the key to a pro-life victory.

This being the case, it was more vital than ever that the White House be occupied by a president sympathetic to the cause, and that the Senate not be dominated by pro-choice supporters able to block the nomination of a pro-life justice. Since the Democratic party was apparently adamantly committed to a pro-choice position, this meant support for Republican presidential nominees and for pro-life members of Congress of either party. Of course the movement had been active in elections since the early days, when its focus was on the state level. The tactic of single-issue voting attracted criticism as early as 1970, when the *New York Times* launched an editorial attack on the attempt "to seek a special revenge at the polls."[69] Abortion entered the national political arena in 1972, when Richard Nixon attempted to pick up pro-life votes through his endorsement of efforts to repeal New York's liberal abortion law.[70]

After 1973 the focus on national politics by the Right to Life movement became inescapable. The abortion issue played a role in the 1976 campaign, which saw Ellen McCormack of New York run for the Democratic party nomination on a Right to Life platform. Although she attracted few votes, they were enough votes to obtain federal matching campaign funds and to win twenty-two convention delegates. Nonetheless, in that year the Democratic party adopted a platform that explicitly rejected any attempt to reverse *Roe v. Wade.* Meanwhile the Republicans became more clearly identified with the pro-life cause, and while Gerald Ford's support of a states-rights position was not all that the movement wanted, it was clearly preferable to Jimmy Carter's position, in which he made clear his personal dislike of abortion but refused to support any constitutional amendment to reverse it. Of more significance for the future was the Republican party's adoption of a cautiously worded but nonetheless clear plank on abortion, which expressed support for "the efforts of those who seek enactment of a constitutional amendment to restore protection of the right to life for unborn children."[71] Moreover, the party's nomination of the pro-life Robert Dole for the vice-presidency and Ronald Reagan's explicit support for the pro-life cause during his campaign for the 1976 nomination suggested that the Republicans were the most realistic hope for the movement in mainstream politics.

While the abortion issue played little role in the outcome of the 1976 election, it was a watershed year for the pro-life movement nonetheless.[72] Politicians could not ignore the issue, if only because of the flood of mail and relentless picketing. In addition, the movement had received the respectful attention of a major party. One reason for the growing power of the movement was the central role the Catholic bishops now played in the debate. With the removal of the NRLC from the institutional orbit of the church in 1973, the bishops, as noted above, had moved to create their own organizations and strategies. One was the NCHLA in 1974; another was the publication in November 1975 of the Pastoral Plan for Pro-Life Activities, which called for the creation "in each congressional district of an identifiable tightly knit and well-organized pro-life unit."[73] The NCHLA was to provide support for these groups, and a subsequent NCHLA flyer declared that "over the last eight years, NCHLA flyer has organized and developed grass roots pro-life groups in almost 1/2 of the 435 U.S. Congressional Districts."[74]

The impact of the bishops' actions is difficult to measure. Clearly they made the issue more visible and legitimized for many an active pro-life political role. On the other hand, the fact that after eight years there were not even paper organizations in half of the nation's congressional districts says volumes about the variability of support to be expected from local church officials. It also seems likely that the best-organized areas were those already committed to an activist role on the issue. In general, pro-life activity was the result of grassroots initiative, not the product of top-down organizing by the hierarchy.

In the years after 1976 the political success of the Right to Life movement rested not only on the efforts of the bishops to organize Catholics on the issue but on three other factors as well. One was the emergence of a "New Christian Right," which mobilized large numbers of fundamentalists and evangelicals for the pro-life cause. Such groups, however, were not single-issue organizations and had other items on their agendas besides abortion. Moreover, religious differences between Catholics and fundamentalists prevented full participation by Catholics in organizations such as the Moral Majority.[75] As well, these groups lacked political sophistication and sometimes caused problems for their pro-life allies,[76] and the poor public image of the Christian Right may have created problems among other potential supporters.[77]

The pro-life movement gained politically from the rise of the New Right, which, while more secular in orientation than the Christian Right, also regarded abortion as a crucial issue. The tactical alliance of many Right to Life groups and individuals with the New Right led to the claim that the latter had essentially absorbed or co-opted the other, and certainly for groups like ALL the relationship was very close. Many Right-to-Lifers, however, were wary of too close an embrace, in part because, as in the case of the Catholic bishops, they did not share the economic and foreign-policy agenda of the New Right.[78] Also the NRLC never wanted to become solely identified with the Republican party, but it was always eager to support liberal Republicans and Democrats committed to a pro-life position.[79] Still, the success of the New Right in the 1980 elections gave the pro-life movement a unique window of opportunity. The association of the movement in the minds of many with the Right created problems in attracting liberal support to the cause.

Finally, the pro-life movement developed an increasingly sophisticated and effective political apparatus of its own, independent of the Christian Right and the New Right, in programs designed to mobilize pro-life voters and in the creation of single-issue political action committees. The Voter Identification Program had originated in New York but was taken up and elaborated by an Illinois pro-lifer. Begun at the local level in 1975, in 1977 it was made an official project of the NRLC. Its goal was a vast telephone poll of the U.S. electorate to identify all pro-life supporters in order to permit more efficient targeting of voters during elections. Although it has never lived up to its full promise, in some areas it has had an impact.[80]

The first pro-life PAC, the Life Amendment Political Action Committee (LAPAC), was created in 1977 and announced a policy of targeting vulnerable pro-choice politicians, using single-issue voting to defeat them. Although legally independent of the NRLC, it had close ties to it. Ultimately a fight erupted between LAPAC and NRLC, part of a complex battle within the NRLC, which saw the departure of Judie Brown and the creation of ALL. In the wake of this, NRLC created its own organization, NRLCPAC, an internal PAC, which became the largest pro-life PAC.[81]

For some pro-lifers the approach of stressing coalition building, PACS, and educational campaigns was ultimately unsatisfactory. For them a direct confrontation with abortion, through demonstrations and through blocking access to abortion facilities, was required. Direct action had existed during the 1970s and early 1980s, but it achieved much greater prominence with the rise of Operation Rescue in 1988.[82] The actions of these groups were enormously energizing for many, but their impact on public policy is less clear. Not only did they not stop abortions from beging performed, but they may have helped fix in the mind of the public the impression that the movement as a whole was involved, and that it was in some fashion linked to violence against abortion facilities and providers. The NRLC adopted a policy in the 1980s of not only not supporting direct-action campaigns that involved illegal activity, but it even refused to report on them in the *National Right to Life News.*

The Post-Webster World

On 3 July 1989 the United States Supreme Court by a 5 to 4 vote in the case of *Webster v. Reproductive Health Services* held that the state of Missouri's regulations on abortion were constitutional. The Court did not overthrow *Roe v. Wade,* but it did signal a significant change: the road appeared to be open to substantial state regulation and hence restriction of abortion. This was a triumph for the movement, but far from being the sign of impending victory it signaled a period of profound internal and external challenge.

Internally it revived the battle of purity versus pragmatism, which had laid dormant since the collapse of the movement for the HLA in 1983. States could restrict abortion but not ban it, and the NRLC moved swiftly to prepare such legislative proposals. One wing of the movement, however, objected strenuously to any steps that would, in their eyes, acquiesce in abortion by settling for anything other than a complete end to the practice.[83] Several state organizations were split by this struggle.

More menacingly for the movement, the *Webster* decision began to alter the political landscape. One pro-life leader later declared that from the day the decision was announced, the movement suffered a steady decline in support.[84] A revitalized pro-choice movement experienced a surge of support, as NARAL memberships doubled from 1989 to 1990.[85] Even before the decision, a massive pro-choice demonstration in Washington, D.C., in April 1989 had impressed politicians. While the possibility of banning abortion had been remote, there were few political risks associated with opposing it; now a number of politicians announced a conversion to a pro-choice stand. This was not necessarily to their benefit, as the public frequently saw them as unprincipled opportunists and defeated them anyway. More ominously for the pro-life movement was the growing pressure within the Republican party for a "big tent" strategy, of dropping its call for a constitutional amendment and thereby appeal to pro-choice voters.

The movement had fallen victim to the structure of public opinion on abortion: while the majority wanted some restrictions on abortion, it wanted others to be freely available. If forced to choose between a complete ban and completely free access, it would choose unrestricted access, at least within the first three months of pregnancy. The pro-choice movement was able to portray the *Webster* decision as inevitably leading to a complete ban rather than being a limited opening to some state restriction. Accordingly, when some pro-life candidates suffered defeats in electoral contests after the decision, it was natural to adduce the abortion issue as a cause, although the degree to which other factors contributed was not clear. Indeed, there is evidence that the abortion issue helped rather than hurt George Bush in the 1992 election. Nonetheless, several pro-life commentators stressed that the movement had to create a strategy that recognized the reality of public opinion and therefore proceeded in an incremental and piecemeal fashion.[86]

While the movement was able to keep a pro-life plank in the Republican platform in 1992, the defeat of George Bush seemed to spell disaster. The first years of the Clinton administration, however, would demonstrate continued strength for the movement in Congress as it blocked the Freedom of Choice Act and was able to continue Hyde Amendment restrictions on abortion funding.

The movement seems destined to remain a factor in American politics for the foreseeable future not only because of the continued salience of the abortion issue (for example, in any discussion of a national health care plan) but also because the issue of euthanasia appears likely to become more prominent. James Kelly has suggested that the movement will neither succeed nor disappear but will remain "in a permanent state of nascence," continuing to insist on a "sanctity of life" ethic in a society whose elites often hold different values.[87] Indeed in the thirty years since its emergence, the movement has demonstrated surprising vitality and impact. While accorded scant respect by America's elites, the movement clearly expresses the sentiments of a substantial minority and is able to speak to some of the concerns of an even larger number. Because the issues it raises are fundamental, it will almost certainly persist, although not necessarily in the same institutional forms.

University of Guelph

Notes

1. For some of the literature on social movements, see Suzanne Staggenborg, *The Pro-Choice Movement: Organization and Activism in the Abortion Conflict* (New York, 1991), 3–8. See also James Kelly's "Seeking a Sociologically Correct Name for Abortion Opponents," in Ted G. Jelen and Marthe A. Chandler, eds., *Abortion Politics in the United States and Canada* (Westport, Conn., 1994), 14–40.

2. Two older histories of the movement are Andrew H. Merton, *Enemies of Choice: The Right to Life Movement and Its Threat to Abortion* (Boston, 1981), and Connie Paige, *The Right to Lifers: Who They Are, How They Operate, Where They Get Their Money* (New York, 1983). Both contain useful information, but the Paige book is more extensive. Both are essentially journalistic accounts, hostile in tone and lacking balance. Some of the writings of the sociologist James Kelly are helpful in understanding the movement. His critique of *Enemies of Choice* is significant. He compares Merton's conclusions with the actual contents of one of the interviews Merton taped and says: "It was as though he had not listened to his own taped interviews when he sat down to write his book"; "Turning Liberals into Fascists: A Case Study of the Distortion of the Right-To-Life Movement," *Fidelity* 6 (July–August 1987): 17–22. See also Kelly's "Beyond the Stereotypes: Interviews with Right-To-Life Pioneers," *Commonweal*, 20 November, 1981, 654–59; "Toward Complexity: The Right to Life Movement," *Research in the Social Scientific Study of Religion* 1 (1989): 83–107; "Learning and Teaching Consistency: Catholics and the Right-To-Life Movement," in Timothy A. Byrnes and Mary C. Segers, eds., *The Catholic Church and the Politics of Abortion: A View from the States* (Boulder, Colo., 1992), 152–67; and "Seeking a Sociologically Correct Name for Abortion Opponents." Robert J. Spitzer's *The Right to Life Movement and Third-Party Politics* (Westport, Conn., 1987) deals with New York but contains information relevant to an understanding of the larger movement.

3. While pro-lifers tend to be viewed negatively, abortion itself is given a more complex treatment. Celeste Condit Railsback notes: "Even in the strongest cases, therefore, the mass cultural medium of television admitted abortion only as an ambiguous and constrained practice"; *Decoding Abortion Rhetoric: Communicating Social Change* (Urbana, 1990), 139. On television's treatment of abortion, she summarizes a number of shows in which pro-lifers appear and it is striking how frequently they appear as violent picketers or as arsonists and bombers. Pro-lifers have frequently lamented what they perceive as negatively biased treatment: see, for example, Dave Andrusko, "Zealots, Zanies, and Assorted Kooks: How the Major Media Interprets the Pro-Life Movement," in Dave Andrusko, ed., *To Rescue the Future: The Pro-Life Movement in the 1980's* (Toronto, 1983), 183–200. Support for the view that the media present a biased view of the movement can be found in a series of articles by David Shaw in the *Los Angeles Times*, 1–4 July, 1990, and in Marvin Olasky, *The Press and Abortion, 1838–1988* (Hillsdale, N.J., 1988). There is a lengthy discussion of media bias in the treatment both of the abortion issue and of the pro-life movement in James Davison Hunter, *Before the Shooting Begins: Searching for Democracy in America's Culture War* (New York, 1994), 154–67. In this connection it is significant that S. Robert Lichter, Stanley Rothman, and Linda S. Lichter report in *The Media Elite: America's New Powerbrokers* (Bethesda, Md., 1986) 29, that 90 percent of news officials interviewed took a pro-choice position.

4. In a review of public opinion polls dealing with abortion, the sociologist James Davison Hunter notes: "Outside the rank and file of the anti-abortion movement, the average American—even when numbered among the closest allies of the anti-abortion movement . . .—tends to view the anti-abortion movement the same negative way that the pro-choice coalitions do. The average American is much more likely to view the anti-abortion movement as unconcerned about women and the poor, and marked by judgementalism, extremism and intolerance"; "What Americans Really Think About Abortion," *First Things* 24 (June–July 1992): 20. A similar discussion by Carl Bowman, "The

Anatomy of Ambivalence: What Americans Really Believe About Abortion," is found in Hunter's *Before the Shooting Begins*, 85–119.

5. Hunter, in ibid. (20), notes: "The success of the activists of the abortion rights movement in demonizing the anti-abortion movement is all the more surprising when one compares image to reality. When asked in the surveys to express their personal concerns on a wide range of issues, individuals who identified themselves as being 'pro-life' were, with but a few exceptions, as 'liberal' as, and in most cases even more 'liberal' than, the so-called socially progressive abortion rights group."

6. This is a central theme in Paige's *The Right to Lifers*. Rosalind Pollack Petchesky stresses the connection of the New Right to the anti-abortion movement in *Abortion and Women's Choice: The State, Sexuality, and Reproductive Freedom* (New York, 1984). Nonetheless, she notes that "the organized antiabortion movement, however, in its political and ideological roots is distinct from the New Right and should not be confused with it" (254).

7. For an expression of this view, see Donald Granberg, "Pro-Life or Reflection of Conservative Ideology? An Analysis of Opposition to Legalized Abortion," *Sociology and Social Research: An International Journal* 62 (April 1978): 414–29.

8. Thus Susan Faludi in her book *Backlash: The Undeclared War Against American Women* (New York, 1991) declared that "the patriarch's eclipsed ability to make the family decisions figured as a bitter subtext, the unspoken but pressing agenda of the anti-abortion campaign" (403). A similar theme can be found in Marian Faux, *Crusaders: Voices from the Abortion Front* (New York, 1990).

9. Kristin Luker, *Abortion and the Politics of Motherhood* (Berkeley and Los Angeles, 1984), 193, 194. The comparison of the two groups is made on 194–97.

10. Ibid., 159.

11. Faye Ginsburg, *Contested Lives: The Abortion Debate in an American Community* (Berkeley and Los Angeles, 1989), 7. Pamela Johnston Conover and Virginia Gray, *Feminism and the New Right: Conflict Over the American Family* (New York, 1983), suggest that the abortion issue "does appear to be a life-style conflict rooted in basic values central to how people view the American family" (127).

12. For discussions of the "symbolic crusade" thesis, see Stephen L. Markson, "The Roots of Contemporary Anti-Abortion Activism," in Paul Sachdev, ed., *Perspectives on Abortion*, (Metuchen, N.J., 1985), 33–43; Peter J. Leahy, David A. Snow, and Steven K. Worden, "The Antiabortion Movement and Symbolic Crusades: Reappraisal of a Popular Theory, "*Alternative Lifestyles* 6 (Fall 1983): 27–47; and Amy Fried, "Abortion Politics as Symbolic Politics: An Investigation into Belief Sytems," *Social Science Quarterly* 69:1 (1988): 137–54.

13. Ginsburg in *Contested Lives* argues: "Viewed from an anthropological perspective, one can see in the abortion controversy the most recent manifestation of an ongoing process in which struggles over the material, political, and symbolic definitions of gender are intertwined, dramatized, coded and continualy transformed. As the abortion debate has come increasingly to stand for opposing views of gender, the possibility of mutual recognition seems to decrease as each side claims to speak a truth regarding contemporary as well as past and future generations of women" (220).

14. Mary Jo Neitz, "Family, State, and God: Ideologies of the Right-to-Life Movement," *Sociological Analysis* 42:3 (1981): 277.

15. Michael Cuneo, *Catholics Against the Church: Anti-Abortion Protest in Toronto, 1969–1985* (Toronto, 1989).

16. Cuneo states: "As evidence by their different social backgrounds, value commitments, and aspirations, it is clear that not all activists inhabit the same cognitive and cultural world. . . . In addition to its Procrustean bent, Luker's thesis suffers from an implicit monocausality: the impugned status of housewives in the face of the exodus of women from homemaking into the public workplace is adduced as the primary if not

exclusive impetus behind anti-abortionism. This explanation perhaps conceals an ideological bias. In locating the roots of anti-abortionism in the sociocultural circumstances of activists it seems to imply that the question of abortion itself cannot or should not carry sufficient moral weight to arouse people to activism. Rather than taking seriously the claims of anti-abortionists regarding the inherent value of fetal life, these claims are dismissed *tout court* as a facade for what is essentially an alarmist reaction to the realignment of gender roles in contemporary society"; *Catholic,* 82.

17. Kelly, "Toward Complexity," 83–107.

18. Elizabeth Adell Cook, Ted G. Jelen, and Clyde Wilcox, *Between Two Absolutes: Public Opinion and the Politics of Abortion* (Boulder, Colo., 1992).

19. Ibid., 192. Cook, Jelen, and Wilcox note (80) that opponents of abortion are indeed more likely to be supporters of traditional gender roles. However, multivariate analysis makes it clear that these attitudes are not the *cause* of abortion beliefs. Thus they also note that "for all denominational families, feminism is *not* strongly related to abortion attitudes, once other attitudes have been taken into consideration" (125).

20. Donald Granberg, "The Abortion Activists," *Family Planning Perspectives* 3 (July–August 1981): 162.

21. The belief that the ERA would result in the mandating of abortion funding was based in part on the experience of several states with state ERAs. See Lincoln C. Oliphant, "ERA and the Abortion Connection," *Human Life Review* 7 (Spring 1981): 42–60; Henry J. Hyde, "The ERA-Abortion Connection," *Human Life Review* 9 (Summer 1983): 81–86; and John T. Noonan, "The ERA and Abortion," *Human Life Review* 10 (Spring 1984): 29–46. The NRLC took the position that the ERA was unacceptable unless it was rendered "abortion neutral" by the insertion of clarifying language. The same position was taken by the National Conference of Catholic Bishops; for the latter, see *National Right to Life News,* 3 May 1984, 1.

22. Cook, Jelen, and Wilcox, *Between,* 123 (Table 4.7). The Beta for the correlation with euthanasia attitudes was − .27; for sexual morality it was − .20; 125. See also Barbara Finlay, "Right to Life vs. the Right to Die: Some Correlates of Euthanasia Attitudes," *Sociology and Social Research* 69 (July 1985): 548–60.

23. Cook, Jelen, and Wilcox, *Between,* 76. A finding consistent with this is reported in Hunter's *Before the Shooting Begins,* 103–6. Donald Granberg in "Pro-Life or Reflection of Conservative Ideology?" disputes the notion that opposition to abortion "is part of a more generalized pro-life stance" (421). However, his test of such consistency is open to question because he believes that pro-lifers should be "disproportionately opposed to capital punishment, have less confidence in the military, and to favor increased spending to improve and protect the health of people while favoring a decrease in expenditures on the military and armaments" (421). Clearly this is one view of what a pro-life philosophy ought to entail, but it is hardly the only one possible. Cook, Jelen, and Wilcox, *Between* (74), point out the problems with the sort of consistency test used by Granberg. Interestingly, Granberg's survey of abortion activists revealed that NARAL and NRLC members were similar in their opposition to capital punishment (60 percent and 56 percent, respectively) and far more likely to oppose it than the general public (28 percent); Donald Granberg and Donald Denney, "The Coathanger and the Rose," *Society* (May–June 1982): 40.

24. While this is not proof that the status of motherhood is indeed the fundamental concern, since all of these issues may be driven by a deeper set of ideological, philosophical, or religious concerns, it does at least leave open the possibility.

25. For an expression of their views, see Gail Grenier Sweet, ed., *Pro-Life Feminism: Different Voices* (Toronto and Lewiston, N.Y., 1985).

26. For a clear statement of this view, see "Why Is N.R.L.C. a Single-Issue Organization?" by Douglas Johnson, the NRLC legislative director. This statement has frequently been inserted in the program for the NRLC's annual meeting and clearly is an official statement. It says in part the NRLC "has defended the principle that every innocent human

being has a right to life" and "socially sanctioned abortion, infanticide and euthanasia all violate that principle" (quoted from the 1990 program [108–9]).

27. The pamphlet was entitled "Death Without Dignity: Killing for Mercy" (Minneapolis, 1975). A later version was entitled "And Now Euthanasia" (Washington, D.C., 1985). Other pamphlets produced by the movement on this subject inlcude Denyse Handler, "Mercy Killing: How, Why, and Where" (Lewiston, N.Y. 1977). Books include Dennis J. Horan and David Mall, eds., *Death, Dying, and Euthanasia* (Washington, D.C., 1977), and Germain Grisez and Joseph M. Boyle, *Life and Death with Liberty and Justice for All: A Contribution to the Euthanasia Debate* (Notre Dame, Ind., 1979). A number of films used by the movement also deal with infanticide and euthanasia, including *The Slippery Slope* (1982) and *Death in the Nursery* (1984).

28. Cook, Jelen, and Wilcox, *Between,* 72. Donald Granberg and Beth Wellman Granberg reported an even weaker linkage: "We conclude that although abortion attitudes are not completely independent of political ideology, the two are not closely related"; "Abortion Attitudes, 1965–1980: Trends and Determinants," *Family Planning Perspectives* 12 (September–October 1980): 250–61.

29. Cook, Jelen, and Wilcox, *Between,* 141.

30. Ibid., 138. Ross K. Baker, Laurily K. Epstein, and Rodney D. Forth, "Matters of Life and Death: Social, Political, and Religious Correlates of Attitudes on Abortion," *American Politics Quarterly* 9 (January 1981): 89–102, report that "we found no relationship between the abortion *scale* and questions which tapped attitudes on the government's role as a guarantor of employment and its role in aiding minorities" (97; emphasis in the original).

31. Cook, Jelen, and Wilcox, *Between,* 141.

32. Ibid., 87. The pattern of opposition to abortion they note is complex: opposition to euthanasia is the best predictor of opposition to abortion for "traumatic" reasons, this is, for rape, incest, and fetal deformity; attitudes toward sexual morality are the best predictors of attitudes toward "elective" abortion (the terms are those of Cook et al.).

33. Ibid., 48: "Of all the social characteristics that help us understand abortion attitudes, education is the best predictor." Granberg and Granberg, "Abortion Attitudes, 1965–80," also reported that of five indicators of social status (prestige, formal education, income, informal education, and social class), "the level of formal education is more strongly related to abortion attitudes than the other four indicators" (253).

34. Baker, Epstein, and Forth, "Matters of Life and Death"; A. Lewis Rhodes, "Religion and Opposition to Abortion Reconsidered," *Review of Religious Research* 27 (December 1985): 158–68; Jerome S. Legge, "The Determinants of Attitudes Toward Abortion in the American Electorate," *Western Political Quarterly* 36:3 (1983): 479–90; Judith Blake and Jorge H. del Pinal, "Predicting Polar Attitudes Toward Abortion in the United States," James Tunstead Burtchaell, ed., *Abortion Parley* (Kansas City, Mo., 1980), 29–56.

35. James Davison Hunter, *Culture Wars: The Struggle to Define America* (New York, 1991), 118. Along similar lines Robert Wuthnow argues that among the most important changes in the role of religion in public life in America "has been the deepening polarization between religious liberals and religious conservatives"; *Christianity in the Twenty-First Century: Reflections on the Challenges Ahead* (New York, 1993), 140.

36. Hunter, *Culture Wars,* 44.

37. Hunter, "What Americans Really Think About Abortion," 18.

38. Cook, Jelen, and Wilcox, *Between,* state that "an important part of the relationship between high levels of education and liberal attitudes toward legal abortion is clearly due to the socializing experience of education" (52).

39. Along these lines Randall A. Lake has argued that "pro-choice forces, I suggest, confront more than adamant beliefs about abortion; they also confront a powerful set of beliefs about the very nature of morality and the process of ethical judgement"; "The Metaethical Framework of Anti-abortion Rhetoric," *Signs* 11:3 (1986). Lake further asserts that "anti-abortionists view humans as at best weak, selfish, and callous, and at worst

maliciously immoral." The warrant for this remark is dubious and attributes to members of the movement a homogeneity of view that simply does not exist.

40. Legge, "Determinants of Attitudes" (488): "It would appear that the overall structure of abortion attitudes among the American public is relatively weak with few consistent predictors."

41. Kelly makes this point as well in "Toward Complexity", 91–92. Ronald G. Walters made a similar suggestion with respect to the diversity of organizations among the abolitionists: "The very diversity of antislavery after 1840 probably encouraged the maximum number of people to enlist in the cause"; *The Antislavery Appeal: American Abolitionism After 1830* (New York, 1978), 5.

42. Luker discusses the social-class differences between pro-choice and pro-life activists in *Abortion,* 194–97. The argument that abortion is a class issue was first advanced by Peter Skerry in "The Class Conflict over Abortion," *The Public Interest* 53 (Summer 1978): 69–84. The educational attainments of the two groups, and their standing relative to the general population, have been compared by Professor Raymond J. Adamek of the Sociology Department of Kent State University in an unpublished work, "Socio-Demographic Characteristics of Pro-Life and Pro-Choice Activists as Reported in Four Studies, Compared to the U.S. Adult Population (In Percent)." Professor Adamek draws upon the work of Kristin Luker, Marilyn Falik, and Donald Granberg. Luker's California data are found in *Abortion and the Meaning of Motherhood* and also in "Abortion and the Meaning of Life" in Sidney and Daniel Callahan, eds., *Abortion: Understanding Differences* (New York, 1984), 25–45. Falik's data are in *Ideology and Abortion Policy Politics* (New York, 1983). The relevant work by Granberg is cited above in notes 20 and 23; Adamek also uses his "Comparison of Pro- and Anti-Abortion Organizations in Missouri," *Social Biology* 28 (Fall–Winter): 239–52.

43. Christopher Lasch, *The True and Only Heaven: Progress and its Critics* (New York, 1991), 491. In his view an upper class fully committed to the mystique of progress believes that the future is and ought to be controllable and it therefore supports abortion as a necessary means of achieving that goal. In his judgment, "The debate about abortion illustrates the difference between the enlightened ethic of competitive achievement and the petit-bourgeois or working class ethic of limits" (489). While he overstates the degree to which abortion is a class issue, he reinforces Hunter's point that what is involved is the collision of competing worldviews. Lasch bases his observations on his reading of Luker's work but gives it a distinctive turn: Luker recognizes class differences between abortion activists but does not assign to class the centrality ascribed by Lasch.

44. Laurence Tribe, *Abortion: The Clash of Absolutes* (New York, 1990), 238.

45. Ibid., 239.

46. This point was made forcefully by Judith Blake in "Negativism, Equivocation, and Wobbly Assent: Public 'Support' for the Prochoice Platform on Abortion," *Demography* 18 (August 1981): 309–20. It is reinforced in Cook, Jelen, and Wilcox, *Between,* who declare that "the majority of Americans hold positions that do not fall neatly in either camp—they support legal abortions in some but not all circumstances" (37).

47. This disjunction of morality and legality was discussed in Stanley K. Henshaw and Greg Martire, "Morality and Legality," *Family Planning Perspectives* 14 (March–April 1982): 53–62. It has been observed in other polling data, for example, the Wirthlin survey commissioned by the NCCB in 1990. In his discussion of this survey James Kelly observes: "In the N.C.C.B. survey, the 'pro-life' advantage recorded on answers about the *moral* dimension of abortion shrank on the explicitly *legal* questions, from about a three-quarter predominance to about half, and sometimes less"; "Abortion: What Americans *Really* Think and the Catholic Challange," *America,* (2 November 1991), 310–16, 314.

48. That the Supreme Court decision had run ahead of public opinion was also the opinion of Karen Mulhauser of NARAL, who said: "The country wasn't with us at that point. Had we made more gains through the legislatures and referendum process, and taken

a little longer at it, the public would have moved with us." The quote is from Roger Williams, "The Power of Fetal Politics," *Saturday Review,* 9 June, 1979, 12.

49. This is discussed in Staggenborg, *The Pro-Choice Movement,* 139, and in Tribe, *Abortion,* 174–75.

50. Kelly, "Toward Complexity," 87.

51. Interview with Edward Golden, Troy, New York, 1 June, 1989. Interview with Mrs. Geline Williams, Houston, Texas. 2 July, 1994.

52. Raymond Tatalovich and Byron W. Daynes, *The Politics of Abortion: A Study of Community Conflict in Public Policy Making* (New York, 1981) 62–63.

53. For an early instance of tension between a group of conservative Catholics and Monsignor McHugh, see "A Catholic Abortion," which reprints the communications between them over a proposed national pro-life initiative, in the conservative Catholic magazine *Triumph,* April 1971, 7–12.

54. The addresses setting out the "seamless garment" philosophy are found in Thomas G. Fuechtmann, ed., *Consistent Ethic of Life* (Kansas City, Mo., 1988), along with a number of essays discussing them. See also Patricia Beattie Jung and Thomas A. Shannon, eds., *Abortion and Catholocism: The American Debate* (New York, 1988). For a criticism by a conservative Catholic, see James Hitchcock, "The Bishops Seek Peace on Abortion," *Human Life Review* 10 (Winter 1984): 27–35.

55. Interview with William Hunt, 1 July, 1989; interview with Joe Lampe, July 1989. The ACCL approach is also apparent in Judith Fink and Marjory Mecklenburg, "Developing Alternatives to Abortion," in *Facing the Future* (Waco, Texas, 1976), 123–36.

56. Staggenborg has discussed this issue in relation to the pro-choice movement and suggests that professionalization did not hinder but rather may have facilitiated grassroots mobilization; *The Pro-Choice Movement,* 109. Certainly the pro-life movement tried to stimulate the organization of new members through the efforts of professional staff, although the degree of success remains uncertain.

57. Interview with David Mall, 9 July, 1983. Mall was AUL's second executive director, taking over in 1972 and overseeing the move to Chicago.

58. Interview with Burke Balch, 16 July, 1982.

59. For a discussion of the origins and work of HLI, see Fr. Paul Marx, *Confessions of a Prolife Missionary: The Journeys of Fr. Paul Marx, OSB* (Gaithersburg, Md., 1988).

60. For some discussion of these materials, see Condit, *Decoding Abortion Rhetoric.* For more studies on the rhetoric of the abortion controversy, see David J. Mall, ed., *When Life and Choice Collide: Essays on Rhetoric and Abortion, Vol. 1, To Set the Dawn Free* (Libertyville, Ill., 1994). *The Eclipse of Reason,* in response to criticism of *The Silent Scream,* another film, was produced.

61. One of the first pro-life books, Charles Rice's *The Vanishing Right to Live: An Appeal for a Renewed Reverence for Life* (New York, 1969) manifests this clearly. Not a single biblical text was cited and the essential argument was "the compelling secular and constitutional reasons against abortion" (28). Again Jack and Barbara Willke's *How to Teach the Pro-Life Story* (Cincinnati, 1973) suggested that arguments were to be secular: "Perhaps it is best then to take the whole package of theologic judgement of this question, give it the honor it is due, and place it on the pedestal where it belongs" (18–19).

62. It is instructive that the Christian Action Council's *Abortion Debater's Handbook* (Falls Church, Va., 1984) devoted the first fourteen pages to "Biblical and Theological Material."

63. Quoted by Carolyn Gerster in *National Right to Life News,* 12 January, 1981 "What Is the Best HLA Wording?" 1.

64. Interview with Joseph Lampe, 1 July, 1989, Minneapolis.

65. This episode is discussed in Michele McKeegan, *Abortion Politics: Mutiny in the Ranks of the Right* (New York, 1992), 43–44; Matthew C. Moen, *The Christian Right and Congress* (Tuscaloosa, Ala., 1989), 103–6. The somewhat belated Protestant support for

the Hatch Amendment was reported in *National Right to Life News* 9.8 (22 April, 1982): 1. Representatives of the National Association of Evangelicals, the Southern Baptist Convention, the Moral Majority, Pro-Life Ministries, and Lutherans for Life, along with James Robison, "came down firmly on the side of pro-life unity, and endorsed the Hatch amendment, apparently in response to president Reagan's calls for a united front by pro-lifers."

66. See Judith Blake, "The Abortion Decisions: Judicial Review and Public Opinion," in *Abortion: New Directions for Policy Studies* Edward Manier, William Liu, and David Solomon, eds., (Notre Dame, Ind., 1977). Helen Rose Fuchs Ebaugh and C. Allen Haney, "Shifts in Abortion Attitudes: 1972–1978," *Journal of Marriage and the Family* (August 1980): 491–99, see a sharp jump in approval of abortion after the 1973 decision and a subsequent stabilization or decline in levels of support. They attribute the decline in support in the 1975 figures to "the influence of the Pro-Life movement" (493).

67. An early expression of this view in the wake of the 1983 defeat was Lynn D. Wardle, "Restricting Abortion Through Legislation," in Andrusko, ed., *To Rescue the Future,* 101–17.

68. The conference, entitled "Reversing *Roe* v. *Wade* Through the Courts," was held in Chicago on 31 March, 1984. For a report on it, see *National Right to Life News,* 3 May 1994, 12. Its proceedings appeared as *Abortion and the Constitution: Reversing Roe v. Wade Through the Courts,* ed. Dennis J. Horan, Edward R. Grant, and Paige C. Cunningham (Washington, D.C., 1987).

69. *New York Times,* 26 June, 1970, 40.

70. William Safire, *Before the Fall: An Inside View of the Pre-Watergate White House* (New York, 1975), 556–58.

71. Tatalovich and Daynes, *Politics,* 198.

72. For the argument that abortion was not a major factor, see Maris Vinovskis, "Abortion and the Presidential Election of 1976: A Multivariate Analysis of Voting Behaviour," in Carl E. Schneider and Maris Vinovskis, eds., *The Law and Politics of Abortion* (Lexington, Mass., 1980), 184–205.

73. National Conference of Catholic Bishops, *Pastoral Plan for Pro-Life Activities* (Washington, D.C., 1975), 11–12.

74. NCHLA, one-page flyer (Washington, D.C., n.d.).

75. Clyde Wilcox and Leopoldo Gomez, "The Christian Right and the Pro-Life Movement: An Analysis of the Sources of Political Support," *Review of Religious Research* 31 (June 1990): 380–89.

76 Moen, *The Christian Right in Congress,* 153–56.

77. For the poor image of the New Christian Right as early as 1980, see McKeegan, *Abortion Politics,* 27; for its later problems, see Moen, *Christian Right,* 151–53.

78 McKeegan, *Abortion Politics,* 25–26.

79. Paige, *The Right to Lifers,* 223.

80. The founder and director of the program is Felicia Goeken, who indentified the states with the best VIP organizations as Michigan, Wisconsin, Illinois, and Ohio; interview, 11 July, 1989.

81. Useful information about this subject can be found in Clyde Wilcox, "Political Action Committees and Abortion: A Longitudinal Analysis," *Women & Politics* 9:1 (1989): 1–19.

82. Joan Andrews with John Cavanaugh-O'Keefe, *I Will Never Forget You: The Rescue Movement in the Life of Joan Andrews* (San Francisco, 1989), and Randall A. Terry, *Operation Rescue* (Springdale, Pa., 1988).

83. For an expression of this view, see Charles Rice, *No Exceptions: A Pro-Life Imperative* (Notre Dame, Ind., 1990).

84. The unnamed leader is quoted by Hadley Arkes in "The Strategy of 'The Modest First Step,' " *Crisis* 12 (February 1994): 17.

85. Staggenborg, *The Pro-Choice Movement,* 138.

86. See Arkes, "The Strategy of 'The Modest First Step' "; see also William McGurn, "Abortion and the GOP," *National Review,* 15 March, 1993. The 1992 exit poll conducted by Voter Research and Surveys, an association of leading news organizations, revealed that while 55 percent of Bush voters saw abortion as an important issue, only 37 percent of Clinton and 8 percent of Perot supporters did so as well. *Newsweek,* November/December 1992, 10.

87. Kelly, "Toward Complexity," 103–4.

SUZANNE STAGGENBORG

The Survival of the Pro-Choice Movement

The battle over abortion in America is seemingly endless. The long-standing nature of the conflict is due in part to the ability of both the "pro-choice" or abortion rights movement and the "pro-life" or anti-abortion countermovement to continue to organize support for many years. The pro-choice movement is particularly remarkable in that it has not only survived for more than twenty-five years, but it has grown stronger since achieving its greatest victory, legalization of abortion in 1973.

In this article I want to explain the longevity of the pro-choice movement by looking at both internal organizational changes in the movement and external changes in the political environment of the movement. I begin with a general discussion of these theoretical factors in the growth and maintenance of social movements. I then describe the history of the pro-choice movement in the United States, showing how these elements come into play. I conclude with a discussion of the lessons of this history for theories of social movements.[1]

The Growth and Maintenance of Social Movements

The Political Opportunity Structure

One explanation as to why particular social movements emerge and flourish at certain times and not others is that the political climate is more or less receptive at different times. A number of theorists argue that movements are most likely to arise when the "political-opportunity structure" is favorable.[2] For example, when government authorities and other elites are receptive to movement demands, when allies are present, when elites are divided among themselves, or when shifts in electoral alignments create openings for movement influence, aggrieved groups are likely to take advantage of the situation and organize a movement.[3]

In some situations, political opportunities are generalized, rather than specific to a particular issue, and widespread collective action occurs. A "cycle of protest" is a period in which numerous groups organize to take advantage of perceived opportunities for making gains through collective action.[4] When the political opportunity structure becomes less favorable, many movements decline and there is less visible collective action. A period of widespread protest in the 1960s, for example, was followed by the comparatively quiescent 1970s and 1980s.

As many theorists note, the structure of political opportunties changes over the course of a protest cycle.[5] Movements that come early in a protest cycle may facilitate the growth of subsequent movements by providing tactical models and generating activism among various groups. Movements may also generate countermovements, which oppose the goals of the original movement.[6] In competing with movements, countermovements change the nature of the political opportunity structure. The activities of both movement and countermovement also produce outcomes that create changes in the political climate during subsequent "rounds" of collective action.[7]

Organizational Characteristics

Aspects of the internal organization of movements, as well as the external political climate, influence the growth and maintenance of social movements. Two characteristics of movement organization that are particularly important are *professionalization* and *formalization.* Professionalization is the trend toward leadership of social movements by paid leaders who make a career out of movement activism.[8] Formalization (or bureaucratization) of movement organizations involves the creation of a clear-cut division of labor, established procedures for decision making, explicit membership criteria, rules governing subunits, and so forth.[9]

There is some debate among theorists as to the benefits of building large, formalized movement organizations led by professional leaders. In their important work on poor people's movements, Frances Fox Piven and Richard Cloward argue that grassroots protest declines when large bureaucratic organizations are formed.[10] This work has led to a great deal of debate over the issue of whether or not "organization" furthers or hinders protest.[11] Pamela Oliver and Mark Furman have tried to reframe this debate by pointing out that there are different forms of organizational strength.[12] They suggest that national organizational strength may not be compatible with active local mobilization because links to national organizations increase the burden of organizational maintenance activities for local organizations. For example, local chapters may have to engage in a variety of activities that take time away from local organizing, such as communicating national concerns to their members, filing reports, and paying national dues.

The History of the Pro-Choice Movement

The history of the pro-choice movement reveals an interesting mix of organizational strength and environmental support that explains its survival. The blend of internal and external strength changed over time in response to critical outcomes in the abortion struggle. To highlight these outcomes and their effects, I have divided the history of the movement into periods marked by critical events: (1) pre-1973—the Supreme Court's *Roe v. Wade* decision legalizing abortion; (2) 1973–76—the Hyde Amendment; (3) 1977–83—pro-choice victories in Congress and the Supreme Court; (4) 1983–89—the Supreme Court's *Webster* decision; and (5) 1989–92—the Supreme Court's *Casey* decision.

Pre-1973

In the 1960s there were no large formal organizations behind the movement to legalize abortion. Established organizations such as Planned Parenthood and the American Civil Liberties Union (ACLU) did not become heavily involved in the abortion conflict until *after* legalization in 1973. Interest-group organizations such as the American Medical Association (AMA) were very conservative in supporting limited reform of the abortion laws rather than their complete repeal from the criminal codes. Some movement organizations were involved before 1973. The National Organization for Women (NOW) endorsed abortion law repeal in 1967, as well as the National Association for Repeal of Abortion Laws (NARAL), formed in 1969. However, these were not mass-membership organizations at that time. In short, the movement at this early stage was not strong on formal organization.

The protest cycle of the 1960s was important in compensating for the organizational deficits of the "abortion movement," as it was then called.

The civil rights movement provided tactical models and stimulated activism among groups such as Protestant and Jewish clergy members who formed the Clergy Consultation Services on Abortion prior to legalization.[13] Activists from the women's liberation movement and the population movement provided a base of support for the movement.

Before legalization in 1973, abortion was a radical cause that fired people up. The movement to legalize abortion was a grassroots movement and the people who were part of it had a real grievance in that abortion was illegal in most states. At the same time, the movement was not a complete "outsider" to the political system. There were people in the abortion movement who had long years of experience in voluntary organizations, including family planning organizations, who had connections to political leaders and established interest groups, and who had skills and experience in conventional methods of political influence. The movement employed a mix of direct-action tactics and conventional lobbying and litigation tactics that ultimately resulted in legalization. In 1973 the Supreme Court struck down all the state laws prohibiting abortion with its *Roe v. Wade* ruling.

1973–1976

After legalization the movement was faced with the problem of maintaining itself. The objective of legalization had been achieved and there was no longer an immediately felt grievance to motivate supporters. Pro-choice groups might have adopted new goals, but by the mid-1970s the protest cycle of the 1960s had declined. This was an important loss because other protest groups provide support to a movement. How can one particular movement survive when the general period of protest that nourished it comes to an end?

I argue that in the case of the pro-choice movement, the development of more formalized organizational structures compensated for the decline of the protest cycle of the 1960s. Ironically, the anti-abortion countermovement pushed the movement to develop such structures and helped keep the pro-choice movement alive. The countermovement got a huge boost from *Roe v. Wade* and shifted the arena of the abortion conflict from the states to Congress, where anti-abortionists immediately began trying to pass a constitutional amendment banning abortion. The need to respond to these countermovement initiatives forced pro-choice movement organizations to begin developing more formal organizational structures that allowed them to participate in congressional lobbying tactics. Thus, the impetus for formalization can come from outside a movement organzation. Once the formalized structure is in place, however, it tends to be self-perpetuating.

Established organizations like Planned Parenthood and the ACLU also helped out by lending strong support to the cause after legalization. This support, together with the changes in movement organizations, helped maintain the pro-choice movement. Contrary to popular belief, the pro-choice movement did not demobilize after legalization and remobilize later in the decade; although it was not a period of highly visible grassroots protest, there was an ongoing movement in the years following 1973. NARAL gradually began to rely on paid staff rather than on volunteer leaders, beginning with a part-time lobbyist, and began to formalize its organizational structure by recruiting individual members, strengthening ties to state organizations, and establishing decision-making procedures. These changes put the movement in a stable organizational state and set the stage for its expansion in the late 1970s.

1976–1983

The anti-abortion movement had its first major triumph in 1976, when Congress passed the Hyde Amendment to the Medicaid appropriations bill, banning federal funding of abortions for the first time. Paradoxically, it was after the countermovement scored this first victory that the movement expanded greatly. The anti-abortion movement, to be sure, benefited from its encouraging success and further expanded, but so did the pro-choice movement. The organizational dilemma for both movement and countermovement is that, while victories are necessary to keep supporters from losing faith, they also mobilize opponents.

Passage of the Hyde Amendment and other developments, including the visibility of the New Right in the late 1970s, aroused pro-choice passions once again. Consequently there was a resurgence of grassroots activism in the late 1970s, which increased even more in the early 1980s after the election of Ronald Reagan to the presidency. Thus, countermovement threats played an important role in the growth of the pro-choice movement after 1976, illustrating the importance of external events in mobilizing movements.

Internal organizational developments, however, are also critical. In the pro-choice movement, grassroots activism increased among feminists, who organized themselves in informal reproductive rights organizations. It also increased among participants in single-issue pro-choice organizations such as NARAL, which became more formalized in its structure and professional in its leadership in the post-Hyde period. The importance of organizational structure in movement maintenance becomes apparent when informally organized grassroots feminist groups are compared to more formally organized single-issue pro-choice groups. Here I compare the history of feminist reproductive rights groups with NARAL and one of its local affiliates.

Reproductive rights groups. Many local reproductive rights groups formed in the late 1970s, some as part of a national organization called the Reproductive Rights National Network (known as R2N2), which was formed in 1978 and dissolved in 1984. These feminist groups were reacting to new threats to abortion rights, particularly the rise of the New Right, which they saw as attacking the women's movement in general as well as abortion rights in particular. They were also reacting to what they saw as shortcomings of the pro-choce movement itself. Rather than focusing solely on abortion, reproductive rights groups wanted to promote all the conditions beyond legal abortion that would make having a child a real choice, such as access to health care, child care, and employment. With regard to abortion itself, reproductive rights groups emphasized such access issues as poor women's rights to government funding.

For a while, these groups were quite successful in rallying supporters to engage in demonstrations and other tactics like collecting signatures on petitions against the Hyde Amendment, the Human Life Amendment, and so on. When supporters were enraged by threats to abortion rights, as they were in the late 1970s and early 1980s, it was relatively easy to mobilize them. Of course, movements are not generated by outrage alone; there also needs to be an organizational basis for the mobilization. The reproductive rights movement built on the organizational foundations of the earlier women's movement, including alternative institutions such as women's health clinics, which created an organizational continuity after social-movement organizations of the women's liberation movement declined in the early to mid-1970s.

The problem was that many reproductive rights groups could not maintain themselves as the threats seemed to subside. An important reason for this was that they had not created the kinds of structures that facilitate organizational maintenance. R2N2 members wanted to avoid creating a bureaucratic structure in an attempt to promote equal participation in the organization. Initially, all decisions were made at biannual membership conventions, but this proved to be an unwieldy way to get things done, so a steering committee made up of regionally elected representatives was later created to implement decisions made at an annual convention. Unfortunately the organization had to rely on the motivations of its steering committee members to expend the energy to coordinate programs. Resolutions were passed at annual meetings, but in order for a program to get off the ground, someone had to organize it, and this simply did not happen on a regular basis. There was a lot of turnover on the steering committee and it often did not include the kind of highly energetic individuals needed to make the organization run. There was one national staff person (funded by grants from local New York foundations), but she was unable to do everything herself. The result was uneven leadership and lack of attention to organizational maintenance tasks such as fundraising. In 1984, R2N2 dissolved, largely because of financial problems. Reproductive rights groups could survive on enthusiasm when the abortion issue was "hot" as it was in the late 1970s and early 1980s, but they had a difficult time remaining active after the threats that helped them to mobilize subsided.

NARAL and NARAL of Illinois. Movement organizations with more formal divisions of labor are better able to sustain themselves because tasks necessary to maintenance are routinely performed. But what effect does attention to organizational maintenance have on a movement? Does goal displacement occur? Does the movement lose its ability to mobilize grassroots participation? In the case of NARAL and its Illinois affiliate, professional leaders and formalized structures led to organizational maintenance *and* an ability to engage in externally targeted tactics such as lobbying and political campaign work. Thus, collective-action goals were not displaced by an exclusive focus on organizational maintenance.

NARAL was able to capitalize on concerns about threats to abortion rights in the late 1970s through direct mail, which increased its resources tremendously. The organization could then hire more staff and use the staff to generate grassroots participation. NARAL did this in the late 1970s and early 1980s in its grassroots organizing program "Impact '80," which was intended to create a pro-choice political force to match the political force that was being created by anti-abortion forces.

The development and successful implementation of this program were made possible by NARAL's organizational structure. One feature of this structure was that strong connections to state affiliates had been created and affiliates were providing board members to the national organization. NARAL's Massachusetts affiliate pioneered the use of a "house meetings" organizing technique, which became an important component of NARAL's grassroots organizing strategy. The affiliate brought the strategy to the national organization, which then tested it in other settings before introducing it to the rest of its affiliates. To implement the strategy nationwide, the national organization provided training and financial aid to its affiliates, including money to hire organizers for the programs. By the early 1980s, the relationship between affiliates and national NARAL was quite formalized; the affiliates were signing contracts with the national organization to implement the program.

The grassroots organizing program, which included the house meetings and also political-skills training sessions, was highly successful in expanding the organization and in channeling pro-choice volunteers into political campaigns. NARAL of Illinois, for example, held 121 house meetings in 1981, built its membership up to 4,000, and trained 185 campaign workers who worked for candidates in 18 state legislative races in November 1982. The organizing was successful because the countermovement was creating visible threats to abortion rights, including some highly publicized defeats of pro-choice candidates. The Reagan administration, moreover, was also supporting anti-abortion measures so that pro-choice forces felt very much under siege. Thus it was a combination of external events and internal organizational arrangements that led to the expansion of the pro-choice movement, with the result that many women were brought into participation in the political arena for the first time.

1983–1989

Following these years of expansion, it became more difficult for the pro-choice movement to survive in the period between 1983 and 1989. There were some key victories for the movement in 1983, including the defeat of anti-abortion legislation in Congress and a Supreme Court ruling that reaffirmed *Roe v. Wade*. Victories such as these can present opportunities for movements in that they provide legitimacy and a chance to take the offensive. However, they may also lead to a decline in interest among supporters and therefore decreased resources for the movement.

The pro-choice movement was showing some signs of decline after 1983, as evidence by a dropoff in membership in organizations like NARAL and a decrease in the activities of local groups. Two factors contributed to the survival of the movement. First, the countermovement, and the Reagan administration, continued to create threats that alarmed pro-choice supporters and provided tactical opportunities for the movement. For example, the anti-abortion film *The Silent Scream*, which used ultrasound to show the fetus during abortion, was released in December 1984 at a time when the pro-choice movement was in a real slump. The film received a great deal of media attention and, to counter this, pro-choice groups busied themselves with various responses, including "speak-outs" to refocus the debate over abortion on the problems of women.[15] The local Chicago affiliate of R2N2, a group called Women

Organized for Reproductive Choice (WORC), was almost defunct when the film aroused supporters to participate in speak-outs and tell women's side of the abortion story.

Second, the movement survived because it included formal groups like NARAL that are able to maintain themselves during "cold" periods. Through the use of direct mail and systematic attention to organizational maintenance by paid staff, such groups can hang on, even if they do suffer membership losses, when interest among supporters lags. Then when the issue gets hot again, they are ready to expand. More informal groups that lack professional leaders have a hard time doing this, particularly when they cannot produce victories.

Movements must produce victories to keep going because eventually supporters will give up when they do not see any progress. WORC, for example, continued to try to address issues related to access to abortion by all women, such as Medicaid funding and the closing of the Cook County abortion clinic, which served poor women.[16] The group finally died out in 1989 after existing in name only for a number of years. As a leader of WORC noted in an interview, "The problem has been how to keep going when we're not winning any victories, when nobody is doing anything. People after a certain point felt like there was not a lot more we could do." In the absence of formalized structures, the movement could not keep *itself* going—it had to rely on countermovement initiatives to get supporters riled up and to provide tactical opportunities.

In the late 1980s Operation Rescue became important in stimulating grassroots activism among pro-choice supporters. In Chicago, after WORC died, the Emergency Clinic Defense Coalition (ECDC) was formed in response to Operation Rescue. For a while ECDC was successful in mobilizing protests against Operation Rescue, but when the Operation Rescue threat subsided in Chicago, the group began to decline, even though its leaders wanted to continue to fight for goals such as the restoration of Medicaid funding.

1989–1992

The 1989 Supreme Court decision in the *Webster v. Reproductive Health Services* case revitalized the pro-choice movement once again. In this ruling, the Court permitted important restrictions on abortion services, such as a ban on the use of public facilities for abortion counseling, and seemed to invite further challenges to *Roe v. Wade.* As a result, anti-abortion forces eagerly worked to get state anti-abortion laws passed in order to generate a court case that might reverse the 1973 decision.

Abortion rights supporters were duly alarmed and flocked to pro-choice groups in response.

At this point it was important that there were existing organizations for pro-choice constituents to join. NARAL survived the 1980s and in fact had started to expand in 1987 with the fight over the nomination of Robert Bork to the Supreme Court.[17] As a result, the movement was prepared to capitalize on concerns about the *Webster* decision, which represented a significant challenge to abortion rights.

The pattern of movement expansion in the post-*Webster* period was similar to that following passage of the Hyde Amendment, but organizations now grew much larger and wealthier. By 1983 NARAL had a membership of about 150,000; by 1990 it had reached 400,000 after having declined to about 90,000 in the mid-1980s. This increase in resources allowed NARAL to pump money into its state affiliates, which again led to an increase in grassroots activism. Professional organizers were able to channel volunteers, who were once again aroused by threats to abortion rights, into state legislative campaigns. Again, the trend toward professionalization facilitates, rather than inhibits, grassroots mobilization.

In 1992 the abortion conflict reached another major turning point, when the Supreme Court ruled in *Planned Parenthood of Southeastern Pennsylvania v. Casey*. Contrary to the hopes of anti-abortionists, the Court did not overturn *Roe v. Wade* with this ruling. The Court did, however, allow key restrictions in the Pennsylvania law, including a required twenty-four-hour waiting period for abortion, a required lecture on alternatives to abortion, and parental consent for teenagers. Such restrictions would be allowed, the Court ruled, unless they were shown to create an "undue burden" on the right to abortion.

Interestingly, both sides in the abortion battle eagerly declared themselves the losers in the *Casey* decision, understanding, no doubt, the value of a good threat for mobilizing supporters. Abortion rights forces emphasized the burdens on women allowed by the law and the need to fight attempts by the states to impose further restrictions on abortion. The decision certainly did create new battles at the state level, as well as a real opportunity for anti-abortion forces to impose new restrictions on abortion. Despite the new opportunities to restrict access to abortion, however, the *Casey* ruling was a great victory for pro-choice forces in that the Supreme Court refused to reverse *Roe v. Wade* and prohibit abortion outright. Moreover, the restrictions allowed by the Court, although significant, are subject to review if "undue burden" can be shown. In a 1993 ruling, the Supreme Court upheld a twenty-four-hour waiting period in a Fargo, North Dakota, case, but Justices Sandra Day O'Connor and David

Souter indicated that they wanted to consider evidence of the practical impact of such laws. It is not clear at this point how many restrictions the Court will disallow as undue burdens on women.[18] Nevertheless, the remarkable fact is that, despite all of the Reagan and Bush appointees to the Supreme Court, pro-choice forces are faring better than anti-abortion forces in this arena. The Court may continue to allow restrictions on abortion rights, but it will not overturn *Roe v. Wade.*

The other important event in 1992 was the election of Bill Clinton, a pro-choice supporter, to the presidency. After taking office, Clinton quickly reversed a number of anti-abortion policies of the Bush administration, including a ban on the abortion-inducing drug RU-486 and a regulation know as the "gag rule," which prevented clinics receiving federal funds from counseling patients as to the availability of legal abortion. Moreover, Clinton's appointees to the Supreme Court, beginning with Ruth Bader Ginsburg in 1993, would be supporters, rather than opponents, of legal abortion. In short, the political climate had shifted dramatically in favor of pro-choice interests.

Can the Pro-Choice Movement Survive Victory?

Favorable outcomes do not necessarily aid movement mobilization. In 1983, after anti-abortion forces were stymied in Congress and after the Supreme Court narrowly reaffirmed *Roe v. Wade,* pro-choice organizations suffered a drop in membership as the threats that had mobilized supporters in the late 1970s and early 1980s seemed to dissipate. Since 1992, similarly, the pro-choice movement has declined in terms of donations to organizations such as NOW, NARAL, and Planned Parenthood.[19] Can the pro-choice movement survive a favorable political opportunity structure?

There are certainly important battles left to fight in the abortion war. Perhaps most central is the street-level battle surrounding abortion providers. Increasingly, abortion clinics and doctors have become the targets of both legal and illegal tatics by abortion foes. Groups such as Operation Rescue blockade clinics and picket the homes of doctors who perform abortions. Clinics are also the targets of bombings, damaging chemicals, and other costly forms of harrassment. Doctors have been featured on "wanted" posters and have endured threats to themselves and members of their families. In the spring of 1993, Dr. David Gunn, who performed abortions at a Florida clinic, was murdered by an anti-abortionist, and in 1994 another Florida doctor, John Britton, and his volunteer escort were killed outside an abortion clinic. Not surprisingly, many abortion clinics are having difficulty finding doctors to perform abortions.

Attempts by anti-abortion groups to limit access to abortion through direct action have created major difficulties for abortion providers. They have also, however, generated outrage and spirited responses from abortion rights supporters. Pro-choice activists, including many students and other young people, have organized clinic escorts and defenses in response to demonstrations by Operation Rescue and other groups. Because the street-level battle is so emotional and immediate, it has greatly strengthened the grassroots pro-choice movement.

The battle over RU-486 and other abortifacient drugs that eliminate the need for surgical abortion is critical because it could reduce the importance of abortion clinics as visible targets for anti-abortion protests.[20] With a sympathetic Clinton administration in power, RU-486, and perhaps other drugs, may soon be made available in the United States. Anti-abortion groups do have strategies for dealing with this eventuality, such as a boycott of manufacturers. Some claim that they would also send women to find out which doctors prescribe RU-486 and target those doctors for harassment.[21] Nonetheless, safe and effective abortion-inducing drugs would make abortion providers much less visible as targets and might eventually hinder protests. Of course this would also reduce the need for responses on the part of abortion rights forces, thereby demobilizing part of the movement.

The state legislatures are another major battlefront in the current abortion conflict. In allowing restrictions that do not place an "undue burden" on women seeking abortions, the Supreme Court opened the way for anti-abortion groups to limit abortion by imposing waiting periods, parental-consent laws, and other preconditions. Abortion rights groups generally concede that anti-abortion forces are better organized at the state level, providing the countermovement with a real opportunity. Pro-choice groups may have a difficult time convincing grassroots supporters of the importance of fighting state-level restrictions, given that there is no longer the possibility of overturning *Roe v. Wade* with new state laws. However, there are abortion rights organizations with professional leaders that keep track of state-level developments and that can help to mobilize action when necessary. Moreover, staff members of groups such as the Center for Reproductive Law and Policy collect information needed to document the burdens imposed by state laws and eventually take their cases to the courts.

In Congress, some pro-choice groups have pushed for a Freedom of Choice Act that would codify *Roe v. Wade* into law. Before the *Casey* decision, this strategy seemed necessary in order to circumvent the Supreme Court, which was expected to overturn *Roe.* After Clinton was elected, the strategy was pursued even though the Court did not make abortion illegal because there was an opportunity for its passage; unlike his predecessor, President Clinton supported the bill and would sign it into law. However, anti-abortion forces in Congress succeeded in adding amendments to the act to permit states to ban abortion funding and impose parental notification or consent requirements on minors. As a result, pro-choice groups split over whether to support the bill. Pro-choice groups had also hoped to pass a Reproductive Health Equity Act, which would repeal the Hyde Amendment and require federal funding of abortions, but this legislation has also languished in Congress. In 1993 both houses of Congress did pass the Freedom of Access to Clinic Entrances Act (FACE), which prohibits violence and blockades against clinics and threats of violence against doctors and nurses who perform abortions.

A large part of the current struggle over abortion is a battle over the framing of the abortion issue. FACE passed the Senate by a wide margin in part because it was presented as a "law and order" measure, which was acceptable even to some opponents of abortion.[22] Abortion rights forces have also been successful in attracting support with their "Who decides?" theme of keeping the government out of such personal decisions as abortion. This approach, which was generated by focus-group research, is calculated to appeal to mainstream Americans. Anti-abortionists have also had success when they appear to be moderate voices and support specific laws on the grounds that they are "reasonable" or oppose others on the grounds that they are "extreme."[23] Indeed, some research suggests that the anti-abortion movement could score some successes by focusing on "reasonable restrictions" to abortion that have public support, such as parental-consent laws.[24]

The ability of each side to frame the abortion debate in such a way as to attract mainstream public support may, however, depend on intramovement dynamics. In the case of the anti-abortion movement, moderate groups working to pass "reasonable" restrictive laws will have to compete with more extremist groups such as Operation Rescue that advocate direct action against clinics and doctors. Media attention is likely to focus on the more dramatic tactics of extremists, making it difficult for other anti-abortionists to cultivate a moderate image. Thus there may be a negative "radical-flank effect" operating within the anti-abortion movement.[25]

Within the pro-choice movement, there are also conflicts over strategy. Some groups want to court "mainstream" Americans, while others want to push hard for the rights of poor women and young women at a time when there is finally a pro-choice president in office.[26] Some disagreements over strategy may exist between professional leaders and grassroots activists. Although the trend toward professionalization has facilitiated, rather than inhibited, grassroots mobilization in the pro-choice movement, there is an interesting new development in the professionalization of movement organizations. Increasingly, professionalization seems to involve not only paid leaders but also the latest political technologies. NARAL, for example, has used polls, focus groups, and paid political consultants for advice in running its media and political campaigns. Although the expertise gained at the national level is shared with state affiliates, conflicts may occur with grassroots activists created by this new trend in professionalization.

Whereas focus groups and polls conducted for NARAL suggest the need to tone down abortion rights rhetoric in appeals to the middle-of-the-road public, grassroots activists might be more inclined toward feminist rhetoric about women's right to control their bodies.[27] Moreover, given the favorable political opportunity structure, many might prefer to push more radical demands rather than appeal to the mainstream. In addition, the use of new political technologies may make it difficult for grassroots activists to influence the strategies of national organizations (as occurred with NARAL's Impact '80 campaign) because expertise may increasingly come from the top down rather than from the grassroots up.

For both movement and countermovement, the abortion conflict has clearly reached a critical juncture. The long battle over abortion fought in the courts is all but concluded and future battlegrounds are now being staked out. Some groups on both sides will contend for the "middle ground" of public opinion,[28] while others will fight in the streets over access to abortion. The pro-choice movement is likely to survive its current difficulties for two reasons: First, countermovement threats will continue to provoke movement support. Second, despite potential disagreements over strategy, formal organizations with professional leaders will keep tabs on developments and alert supporters to new issues. If countermovement threats cease and there are no new issues, the pro-choice movement need not survive, but few would predict the end of the abortion conflict in the near future.

Changes in the political climate are an important factor in the ability of the pro-choice movement to grow and survive. However, theories of social movements need to look beyond the receptiveness of authorities to the impact of political developments on movement organizations and mobilization in assessing the nature of the political opportunity structure. When authorities are favorable toward movement initiatives, movements may have difficulty remaining mobilized in order to take advantage of the opportunities. Countermovements, as well as authorities, clearly play an important role in the mobilization and tactics of movements and ought to be considered part of the political opportunity structure.

The history of the pro-choice movement also suggests the value of large, formalized organizations in keeping movements alive. Although movements often arise during cycles of protest when grassroots activism is widespread, they may survive by developing professional leaders and formal organizations. The experience of the pro-choice movement shows that these developments are not necessarily incompatible with grassroots protest. While informally organized grassroots protest often emerges in response to external events, formalized movement organizations are generally more effective than informal organizations in sustaining movement activity through "slow" periods.

Although formalized organizations led by professional leaders have played a positive role in the maintenance of the pro-choice movement, potential conflicts may arise between national organizations and their local affiliates. In some cases, national organizations may press "mainstream" strategies on their affiliates as a result of their use of political technologies. In others, some local groups may be more conservative than national organizations in response to local conditions.[29] Research is needed to specify the conditions under which different types of national-local tensions exist within organizations.[30] There is also a need for further clarification of concepts such as "professionalization" and "formalization" because movement organizations within these categories differ greatly. For example, NOW's national leadership is elected by its membership, whereas other groups such as NARAL hire executive directors. This kind of difference among formalized organizations with professional leaders has implications for the amount of grassroots input available to an organization.

The strength of the pro-choice movement lies in the fact that it has enjoyed both professional leadership *and* grassroots participation. Organizations like NARAL help the movement to survive through hot and cold periods of the abortion conflict. And there have been many hot periods over the years because abortion is an immediate kind of issue that arouses intense passions. For local pro-choice activists, the battle for safe, legal, and accessible abortion is worth fighting for again and again because it affects women's lives. The abortion issue continues to bring more participants into the political process, extending indefinitely the legacy of protest begun in the 1960s.

McGill University

Notes

1. See Suzanne Staggenborg, *The Pro-Choice Movement: Organization and Activism in the Abortion Conflict* (New York, 1991), for a fuller account of the history of the movement up to 1990.

2. See Peter K. Eisinger, "The Conditions of Protest Behavior in American Cities," *American Political Science Review* 67 (March 1973): 11–28; Doug McAdam, *Political Process and the Development of Black Insurgency, 1930–1970* (Chicago, 1982); Sidney Tarrow, *Struggle, Politics, and Reform: Collective Action, Social Movements, and Cycles of Protest* (Ithaca, N.Y., 1989).

3. Tarrow, *Struggle, Politics, and Reform*, 34.

4. Ibid.

5. See Sidney Tarrow, *Democracy and Disorder: Protest and Politics in Italy, 1965–1975* (Oxford, 1989).

6. See John D. McCarthy and Mayer N. Zald, "Resource Mobilization and Social Movements: A Partial Theory," *American Journal of Sociology* 82 (May 1977): 1212–41.

7. See David Snyder and William R. Kelly, "Strategies for Investigating Violence and Social Change," in Mayer N. Zald and John D. McCarthy, eds., *The Dynamics of Social Movements* (Cambridge, Mass., 1979), 212–37.

8. See John D. McCarthy and Mayer N. Zald, *The Trend of Social Movements in America: Professionalization and Resource Mobilization* (Morristown, N.J., 1973).

9. See William A. Gamson, *The Strategy of Social Protest* (Homewood, Ill., 1975); Suzanne Staggenborg, "The Consequences of Professionalization and Formalization in the Pro-Choice Movement," *American Sociological Review* 53 (August 1988): 585–605.

10. Frances Fox Piven and Richard A. Cloward, *Poor People's Movements: Why They Succeed, How They Fail* (New York, 1977).

11. See, for example, William A. Gamson and Emilie Schmeidler, "Organizing the Poor," *Theory and Society* 13 (July 1984): 567–85, and Richard A. Cloward and Frances Fox Piven, "Disruption and Organization: A Rejoinder," *Theory and Society* 13 (July 1984): 587–99.

12. Pamela Oliver and Mark Furman, "Contradictions Between National and Local Organizational Strength: The Case of the John Birch Society," *International Social Movements Research* 2 (1989): 155–77.

13. See Arlene Carmen and Howard Moody, *Abortion Counseling and Social Change* (Valley Forge, Pa., 1973).

14. In both 1982 and 1983 the Senate tabled anti-abortion bills, in large part because of infighting among anti-abortion supporters in Congress as to strategy. And, in a 5–4 ruling, the Court struck down most of the restrictions on abortion rights that had been passed by state and local governments. See Eva R. Rubin, *Abortion, Politics, and the Courts: Roe v. Wade and Its Aftermath, Revised* (Westport, Conn., 1987), 140–43.

15. Speak-outs were originated in the late 1960s by women's liberation activists who believed that women should speak out publicly about their experiences with abortion and other issues rather than letting doctors or other "experts" define the debate.

16. In 1980 the president of the Cook County Board of Commissioners ordered the hospital abortion clinic closed, resulting in a long battle to reopen the clinic. In 1993 a new board president issued an executive order to the hospital to resume operation of the clinic. See Patricia Donovan, "The Restoration of Abortion Services at Cook County Hospital," *Family Planning Perspectives* 25 (September–October 1993): 227–31.

17. Judge Bork, who was President Reagan's first choice to fill a vacancy on the Supreme Court, was on record as opposing *Roe v. Wade.* His nomination was defeated through pressure from a coalition of groups opposed to his judicial philosophy, including civil rights as well as pro-choice organizations.

18. The Court did strike down a requirement that a married woman inform her husband of her intention to have an abortion as an undue burden in its *Casey* decision.

19. See Eliza Newlin Carney, "Those Winds of Change Are Tricky," *National Journal* 25 (May 1993): 1176–77; Judith Warner, "Mixed Messages," *Ms.*, November–December 1993, 21–25.

20. RU-486 is the French-made "abortion pill" available in Europe that was banned by the U.S. Food and Drug Administration during the Bush administration.

21. Jill Smolowe, "New, Improved, and Ready for Battle," *Time,* 14 June 1993.

22. Adam Clymer, "Senate Passes Abortion-Clinic Crime Bill," *New York Times,* 17 November 1993.

23. Eliza Newlin Carney, "Abortion-Rights Test," *National Journal* 24 (October 1992): 2304–7.

24. Debra L. Dodson, "Abortion Politics in State Elections: Comparisons Across States" (New Brunswick, N.J., 1991).

25. A "radical-flank effect" is the impact of more radical groups within a movement on more moderate groups. As Herbert Haines shows in *Black Radicals and the Civil Rights Mainstream, 1954–1970* (Knoxville, 1988), this effect can be either negative or positive. In the case of the civil rights movement, Haines found a positive radical-flank effect when black power groups came into the movement. As a result of their presence, the resources of moderate civil rights organizations increased as contributions came in from those who preferred the moderate goals of integration and civil rights to the radical goals of separatism and black power. In this instance, however, the moderate groups had already established the legitimacy of their cause and had gained widespread public sympathy prior to the emergence of the black power movement. Anti-abortion groups, however, have always had to battle with abortion rights groups for the moral upper hand (and there have always been some more radical groups within the anti-abortion movement). Consequently, moderate groups were not able to establish themselves as the proponents of an undeniably just cause like civil rights before a highly visible radical flank entered their movement.

26. See Warner, "Mixed Messages."

27. Ibid.

28. Polls show that the majority of Americans fall between the extremes of the "pro-choice" and "pro-life" views on abortion. Most favor legal abortion, but only under certain circumstances, whereas the anti-abortion movement opposes all abortions and the pro-choice movement wants to keep abortion legal regardless of the circumstances for it. See Victoria A. Sackett, "Between Pro-Life and Pro-Choice," *Public Opinion* 8 (April–May 1985): 53–55.

29. Warner, "Mixed Messages," discusses this problem in Planned Parenthood.

30. See Oliver and Furman, "Contradictions Between National and Local Organizational Strength."

DONALD T. CRITCHLOW
CHRISTINA SANDERS

Selected Bibliography

General

Randy Alcorn, *Pro-Life Answers to Pro-Choice Arguments* (1992); John Ankerberg and John Weldon, *When Does Life Begin?* (1989); Don Baker, *Beyond Choice: The Abortion Story No One Is Telling* (1985); Francis J. Beckwith and Norman L. Geisler, *Matters of Life and Death: Calm Answers to Tough Questions About Abortion and Euthanasia* (1991); James Tunstead Burtchall, C.S.C., *Abortion Parley* (1982); Mary S. Calderone, ed., *Abortion in the United States* (1958); Daniel and Sidney Callahan, *Abortion: Understanding Differences* (1984); Marie Costa, *Abortion: A Reference Handbook* (1991); Charles P. Cozic and Stacey L. Tipp, eds., *Abortion: Opposing Viewpoints* (1991); Thomas A. Glessner, *Achieving an Abortion-Free American by 2001* (1990); Germain Grisez, *Abortion: The Myths, the Realities, and the Arguments* (1970); Ben Graber, M.D., F.A.C.O.G., with Eileen K. W. Cudney, *Abortion: A Citizens' Guide to the Issues* (1990); Robert E. Hall, ed., *Abortion in a Changing World*, 2 vols. (1970); Elizabeth Mensch and Alan Freeman, *The Politics of Virtue: Is Abortion Debatable?* (1993); Maureen Muldoon, *The Abortion Debate in the United States and Canada: A Source Book* (1991); Hyman Rodman et al. *The Abortion Question* (1987); Betty Sarvis and Hyman Rodman, *The Abortion Controversy* (1973); Suzanne Staggenborg, *The Pro-Choice Movement: Organization and Activism in the Abortion Conflict* (1991); Gilbert Y. Steiner, ed., *The Abortion Dispute and the American System* (1983); Laurence H. Tribe, *Abortion: The Clash of Absolutes* (1990); Robert N. Wennberg, *Life In the Balance: Exploring the Abortion Controversy* (1985); Peter Wentz, *Abortion Rights as Religious Freedom* (1992); Dr. and Mrs. John C. Willke, *Abortion: Questions and Answers* (1990).

Historical

Dave Andrusko, *To Rescue the Future: The Pro-Life Movement in the 1980s* (1983); Janet Farrell Brodie, *Contraception and Abortion in Nineteenth-Century America* (1994); Ellen Chesler, *Woman of Valor: Margaret Sanger and the Birth Control Movement in America* (1992); John Connery, *The Development of the Roman Catholic Perspective* (1977); Nanette J. Davis, *From Crime to Choice: The Transformation of Abortion in America* (1985); David J. Garrow, *Liberty and Sexuality: The Right to Privacy and the Making of Roe v. Wade* (1994); Linda Gordon, *Woman's Body, Woman's Right* (1974); David M. Kennedy, *Birth Control in America: The Career of Margaret Sanger* (1970); Lawrence Lader, *Abortion* (1966), *Abortion II: Making the Revolution* (1973), and *The Margaret Sanger Story* (1955); Thomas B. Littlewood, *The Politics of Population Control* (1977); Loretta McLaughlin, *The Pill, John Rock, and the Church: The Biography of a Revolution* (1982); James C. Mohr, *Abortion in America: The Origins and Evolution of National Policy, 1800–1900* (1978); Gloria Moore and Ronald Moore, *Margaret Sanger and the Birth Control Movement: A Bibliography, 1911–1984* (1986); Marian J. Morton, *And Sin No More: Social Policy and Unwed Mothers in Cleveland, 1855–1990* (1994); John T. Noonan, *Contraception: A History of Its Treatment by the Catholic Theologians and Canonists* (1965); Noonan, ed., *The Morality of Abortion: Legal and Historical Perspectives* (1970); Noonan, *A Private Choice: Abortion in America in the Seventies* (1979); Marvin Olasky, *Abortion Rites: A Social History of Abortion in America* (1992); Phyllis T. Piotrow, *World Population Crisis: The United States Response* (1974); James Reed, *The Birth Control Movement and American Society: From Private Vice to Public Virtue* (rev. ed., 1983); John M. Riddle, *Contraception and Abortion from the Ancient World to the Renaissance* (1992); Victor Robinson, *Pioneers of Birth Control in England and America* (1919); Roger Rosenblatt, *Life Itself: Abortion in the American Mind* (1992); Paul Sachdev, ed., *Perspectives on Abortion* (1985); Rickie Solinger, *Wake Up Little Susie: Single Pregnancy and Race Before Roe v. Wade* (1992); Catherine Whitney, *Whose Life? A Balanced, Comprehensive View of Abortion from Its Historical Context to the Current Debate* (1991); John C. Willke, M.D., *Abortion and Slavery: History Repeats* (1984).

Politics and Policy

Dallas C. Blanchard, *The Anti-Abortion Movement and the Rise of the Religious Right* (1994); Dorothy D. Bromley, *Catholics and Birth Control* (1965); Timothy A. Byrnes and Mary C. Segers, *The Catholic Church and the Politics of Abortion* (1992); Barbara Hinkson Craig and Barbara Hinkson O'Brien, *Abortion and American Politics* (1993); Marilyn Falik, *Ideology and Abortion Policy Politics* (1983); Marlene Gerber Fried, ed., *From Abortion to Reproductive Freedom* (1990); Frederick S. Jaffe et al., *Abortion Policy: Private Morality and Public Policy* (1991); Sagar C. Jain and Steven W. Sinding, *California Abortion Act 1967: A Study in Legislative Process* (1969); F. M. Kamm, *Creation and Abortion* (1992); Jerome S. Legge Jr., *Abortion Policy: An Evaluation of the Consequences for Maternal and Infant Health* (1985); T. J. Lowi, ed., *Private Life and Public Order: The Context of Modern Public Policy* (1968); Kristen Luker, *Abortion and the Politics of Motherhood* (1984); Edward Manier et al., eds., *Abortion: New Directions for Policy Studies* (1977); Michelle McKeegan, *Abortion Politics: Mutiny in the Ranks of the Right* (1992); Andrew H. Merton, *Enemies of Choice: The Right-to-Life Movement and Its Threat to Abortion* (1981); Milton Silverman and Philip R. Lee, *Pills, Profits, and Politics* (1974); Russell B. Shaw, *Abortion and Public Policy* (1966); Raymond Tatalovich and Byron W. Daynes, *The Politics of Abortion: A Study of Community Conflict in Public Policymaking* (1981).

Legal

J. Douglas Butler and David F. Walbert, eds., *Abortion, Medicine, and the Law* (1992); Daniel Callahan, *Abortion: Law, Choice, and Morality* (1970); C. Thomas Dienes, *Law, Politics, and Birth Control* (1972); Dan Drucker, *Abortion Decisions of the Supreme Court* (1990); Marian Faux, *Roe v. Wade: The Untold Story of the Landmark Supreme Court Decision That Made Abortion Legal* (1988); Leon Friedman, ed., *The Supreme Court Confronts Abortion: The Briefs, Argument, and Decision in Planned Parenthood v. Casey* (1993); Fred M. Frohock, *Abortion: A Case Study in Law and Morals* (1983); Jay L. Garfield and Patricia Hennessey, eds., *Abortion: Moral and Legal Perspectives* (1984); Mary Ann Glendon, *Abortion and Divorce in Western Law* (1987); Robert D. Goldstein, *Mother-Love And Abortion: A Legal Interpretation* (1988); Randal J. Hekman, *Justice for the Unborn: Why We Have Legal Abortion, How We Can Stop It* (1984); Dennis J. Horan et al., eds., *Abortion and the Constitution: Reversing Roe v. Wade Through the Courts* (1987); Roger J. Huser, *The Crime of Abortion in Canon Law* (1942); William J. Robinson, *The Law Against Abortion* (1933); Eva R. Rubin, *Abortion, Politics, and the Courts: Roe v. Wade and Its Aftermath* (1987); Irving J. Sloan, *The Law Governing Sterilization* (1988); Lynn Wardle, *The Abortion Privacy Doctrine* (1981); Sarah Weddington, *A Question of Choice* (1992).

Personal Stories and Social Impact

Angela Bonavoglia, ed., *The Choices We Made: Twenty-five Women and Men Speak Out About Abortion* (1988); James Tunstead Burtchall, C.S.C., *Rachel Weeping: The Case Against Abortion* (1982); Marian Faux, *Crusaders: Voices from the Abortion Front* (1990); Faye D. Ginsburg, *Contested Lives: The Abortion Debate in an American Community* (1988); Sue Hertz, *Caught in the Crossfire: A Year on Abortion's Front Line* (1991); Ellen Messer and Kathryn E. May, Psy.D., *Back Rooms: Voices from the Illegal Abortion Era* (1988); Patricia G. Miller, *The Worst of Times* (1993); Bernard N. Nathanson with Richard N. Ostling, *Aborting America* (1979); David Reardon, *Aborted Women: Silent No More* (1987); Susan Neiburg Terkel, *Abortion: Facing the Issues* (1988).

Contraceptives and Sterilization

Etienne-Emile Baulieu with Mort Rosenblum, *The "Abortion Pill": RU-486. A Woman's Choice* (1990); Rodolfo A. Bulatao et al., eds., *Choosing a Contraceptive: Method Choice in Asia and the United States* (1989); Michael J. K. Harper, *Birth Control Technologies: Prospects by the Year 2000* (1983); Betsy Hartmann, *Reproductive Rights and Wrongs: The Global Politics of Population Control and Contraceptive Choice* (1983); Elise F. Jones et al., *Pregnancy, Contraception, and Family Planning Services in Industrial Countries: A Study by the Alan Guttmacher Institute* (1989); Joseph F. Fletcher, *Morals and Medicine; The Moral Problems of: The Patient's Right to Know the Truth About Contraception, Artificial Insemination, Euthanasia* (1960); Lawrence Lader, *RU-486: The Pill That Could End the Abortion Wars and Why American Women Don't Have It* (1991); Philip R. Reilly, *The Surgical Solution: A History of Involuntary Sterilization in the United States* (1991); Godfrey Roberts, ed., *Population Policy: Contemporary Issues* (1990); Thomas M. Shapiro, *Population Control Politics: Women and Reproductive Choice* (1985); Irving J. Sloan, *The Law Governing Abortion, Contraception, and Sterilization* (1988); Norman St. John-Stevas, *Sterilization and Public Policy* (1965); Horatio Curtis Woo Jr., *Sex Without Babies: A Comprehensive Review of Voluntary Sterilization as a Method of Birth Control* (1967); Evan McLeod Wylie, *A Guide to Voluntary Birth Control* (1972).

Saint Louis University

Contributors

DONALD T. CRITCHLOW, Professor of History at Saint Louis University, is the author of *The Brookings Institution, 1916–1952: Expertise and the Public Interest in a Democratic Society,* as well as the editor of five other books. He recently completed a book-length study, *Studebaker: Tradition, Historical Memory, and Corporate Regimes.* He is currently working on the history of family planning policy in the postwar years.

JAMES W. REED, Professor of History at Rutgers, The State University of New Jersey, is the author of *The Birth Control Movement and American Society: From Private Vice to Public Virtue* (Princeton, 1993). From 1985 to 1994 he served as Dean of Rutgers College. He is currently at work on a history of biomedical sex research in the United States to 1965.

IAN MYLCHREEST is a Lecturer in History and Director of American Studies at Monash University. He has taught at Wells College and the University of Nevada, Las Vegas. He is currently writing a comparative history of "victimless crimes" in the English-speaking world.

JOHN SHARPLESS is Associate Professor in History and Demography at the University of Wisconsin. He is currently writing a book on U.S. foreign policy and population issues, 1945–1995.

JAMES DAVISON HUNTER is the William R. Kennan Professor of Sociology at the University of Virginia and the author of *Culture Wars: The Struggle to Define America* (1991).

JOSEPH E. DAVIS is a graduate student in the Department of Sociology at the University of Virginia.

KEITH CASSIDY is a member of the Department of History at the University of Guelph in Canada. His first area of research and publication was the Progressive Era. In recent years he has been engaged in the preparation of a full-length study of the Right-to-Life movement in the United States.

SUZANNE STAGGENBORG is Associate Professor of Sociology at McGill University. Her work includes *The Pro-Choice Movement: Organization and Activism in the Abortion Conflict* (Oxford University Press, 1991) and a number of articles about abortion politics and social movements.